Twenty-Four Ways
of Looking at Mary McCarthy

TWENTY-FOUR WAYS OF LOOKING AT MARY MCCARTHY

The Writer and Her Work

EDITED BY

Eve Stwertka and Margo Viscusi

Contributions to the Study of World Literature, Number 70

GREENWOOD PRESS

Westport, Connecticut • London

Library of Congress Cataloging-in-Publication Data

Twenty-four ways of looking at Mary McCarthy : the writer and her work
   / edited by Eve Stwertka and Margo Viscusi.
        p.   cm.—(Contributions to the study of world literature,
ISSN 0738–9345 ; 70).
     Based on papers originally presented at a conference on Mary
McCarthy held at Bard College in 1993.
     Includes bibliographical references and index.
     ISBN 0–313–29776–2 (alk. paper)
     1. McCarthy, Mary, 1912– —Criticism and interpretation—
Congresses.   2. Women and literature—United States—History—20th
century—Congresses.   I. Stwertka, Eve.   II. Viscusi, Margo.
III. Series.
PS3535.A1435Z88   1996
818′.5209—dc20   96–5801

British Library Cataloguing in Publication Data is available.

Library of Congress Catalog Card Number: 96–5801
ISBN: 0–313–29776–2
ISSN: 0738–9345

First published in 1996

Greenwood Press, 88 Post Road West, Westport, CT 06881
An imprint of Greenwood Publishing Group, Inc.

Printed in the United States of America

The paper used in this book complies with the
Permanent Paper Standard issued by the National
Information Standards Organization (Z39.48–1984).

10 9 8 7 6 5 4 3 2 1

Contents

Part II   Questions of Politics and Religion

Part III   Mind and Body

Part IV   Facts in Fiction

A Note to Readers

In the fall of 1993 a conference on Mary McCarthy held at Bard College brought together a miscellany of writers and scholars, young academics and old friends. It was the first meeting of this kind since the author's death, in 1989, at the age of seventy-seven. As it turned out, the theme of the conference, "Truth Telling and Its Cost: Mary McCarthy, Writing, and Intellectual Politics," served the conferees mainly as a point of departure for many different topics and approaches. The result was not a cohesive academic study but an array of glimpses into Mary McCarthy's work as seen by both people who had studied her long and thoroughly and others for whom she was a fresh discovery.

Most of the conference talks, revised by their authors, are published for the first time in this book. The collection is diverse but makes no attempt to cover the entire scope of Mary McCarthy's writing. Indeed the range of her subjects and genres may help to explain why, until now, books about her remarkable life have outnumbered studies of her equally remarkable work. The kind of complexity that attracts biographers may well have deterred literary scholars. After all, Mary McCarthy was a novelist, short story writer, essayist, and reporter. She was a formidable theater critic. Her books on Venice and Florence are prized by travelers. In her works on Vietnam and Watergate she became a political gadfly. And, while she is often cited for ferocious satire, she has a large following of readers who grow tender over her memoirs and letters. In short, no category will quite accommodate her.

We know the rich striations that formed Mary McCarthy's character: the Irish/Catholic/Protestant/Jewish influences, the Dickensian deprivations and patrician pleasures, the teachings of the convent and of Vassar, the brush with revolutionary movements and literary bohemia. Later, her friendships with Hannah Arendt and Nicola Chiaromonte and the years she spent in Europe added further overtones to her intellectual life.

Finally, what makes it hard to corral her work and person into a niche is her stance toward the feminist movement. Certainly she transcended the conventional limits placed on women of her time in matters of career, pleasure, fame, and sexual activity. But acts of liberty, acts of valor, would have seemed to her options for anyone, and not subject to gender. In any case, she had no eye for feminism as a political imperative and was tone-deaf to its language.

This phenomenon, like much else about Mary McCarthy's life and work, needs more study and we intend this volume as an incentive to further scholarship. Needless to say, we don't endorse the tone or content of every essay printed here, but we do endorse in concept the variety and diversity of approaches. Chiefly, though, we hope this collection will help new readers to enjoy her ideas, wit, style, and erudition, and to be struck by the sheer fun of her palpable presence.

We thank Leon Botstein and Bard College for organizing and hosting the first Mary McCarthy conference, and Deirdre d'Albertis and Peter Gadsby of Bard for their work in making it a success. We very much appreciate the additional support for the conference provided by Deborah Pease, Joanna Rose, Anthony Viscusi, and Harcourt Brace. Harcourt graciously permitted the writers collected here to quote liberally from Mary McCarthy's works. We are grateful to Mary Ann Caws for consenting, on very short notice, to give the Bard conference keynote address, which appears in these pages. Finally, we thank our many well-wishers, both professional and private, for the encouragement that helped us in this project.

Eve Stwertka and Margo Viscusi

I

Of Intellect and Culture

1

Living and Reading

Thomas Flanagan

The company that manufactures T-shirts and sweatshirts with pictures of famous writers—Jane Austen, Ernest Hemingway, Virginia Woolf—also has one with a quotation rather than a face, from Logan Pearsall Smith: "People say that life is the thing, but I prefer reading." I suspect that many writers, like myself, have wanted to send away for one, but have lacked the courage. It is shameful to admit how fully and how deeply one's reading has encroached upon one's living.

I was reminded of the T-shirt by a sentence in Carol Gelderman's biography of Mary McCarthy: "It was her reading, precocious for a fourteen-year-old, and her sexual experiments that really set her apart" (40). There seems at first something a bit off about that sentence, as though the adjective "precocious" were modifying the wrong noun. But then one remembers passages in *Memories of a Catholic Girlhood* which place reading and living, living as sexual experiment, in curious juxtaposition.

The fourteen-year-old has been motoring through Yellowstone with girl-friends and with Bob Berdan, twenty-five and married, whose unexciting kisses have led only to more kisses. Then, in Great Falls, after another tepid night in a hotel, "I found a book store and while the others waited in the car I hurried in to make a purchase: the latest volume, in a boxed de luxe edition, of James Branch Cabell" (186). It is a disappointment: as it turns out, she has "outgrown" Cabell. (This was a common disappointment among bookish teenagers of her generation and my own. Cabell was a shameless tease: you took him home from the library, but he never really put out.)

Her excitement as she buys the book is real upon the page:

I was tremendously excited by this act. It was the first expensive book I had ever bought with my own money. The whole trip to Montana for a moment seemed worthwhile, as I stood in the wide dull main street with the book, wrapped, in my hands. I was in love with Cabell and had written him many letters that I had not the courage to mail. Why, it would change my grandmother's whole life, I would tell her, if she would only let herself read a few pages of Cabell or listen to me recite them. Now, as the owner of a limited edition, I felt proudly close to him, far closer than to Bob Berdan or to the girls, who were already honking the horn for me to get in and join the party (186–87).

Poor Bob Berdan, with his drugstore gin and unexciting kisses. But after making allowance for the affectionate self-mockery of reminiscence, there is a striking difference of tone as the prose moves from Bob to the deluxe edition. And in that avowal of belief that reading a book will somehow change one's life, every writer will guiltily, fondly, recognize one of his own former selves.

In McCarthy's explicit memoirs of education, *Memories of a Catholic Girlhood* and *How I Grew*, two intertwined subjects confront one another, each mocking yet affirming the other. They are the histories of two educations, an education into living and an education into reading. The contrasts provide dramatic and often comic differences of tonality.

This is largely a rhetorical strategy, a matter of decorum. The account of sexual education is offered in a manner deliberately dry, clinical, wryly self-observant, and deflationary. Here, as in the stories and novels, from the front seat of Forrest Crosby's Marmon to the Pullman sleeper in *The Company She Keeps* to Dolly and her diaphragm in *The Group*, sex is forever skidding on the banana peels of physiology and rubber goods.

But the account of the other education is written with an affection that is both romantic and nostalgic, as of entrance into a vocation. It is not simply an education into language. Language is for every writer an instrument of liberation, and she was to become one of the finest of American prose stylists. It is an education into books, of printed pages opening up an alternative existence, and she evokes their looks and weight, the smell of their bindings. And, especially, she commemorates the looks and bearings of the teachers who conducted that education, a series of women sternly or sweetly or primly dedicated to their task, beginning with "the tiny old whiskered nun" who read aloud to the girls from *Emma* or *A Tale of Two Cities*: " 'Charles Evremonde, called Darnay!' —the red-rimmed old black eye levelled and raked us all, summarily, with the grapeshot of the Terror" (103). The scene, she tells us, is generic, occurring, for such was the universal and sweetly archaic rule of the Ladies of the Sacred Heart, at four each afternoon not only in Seattle but in Roscrea, Ireland, and Roehampton, England, a nun reading while the girls, heads bent, stitched French seams of embroidered bureau scarves with wreaths of flowers.

Nostalgia, no doubt, leads McCarthy herself to embroider this account, which joins reading with an aristocratic and obsolete regimen, but it is an instructive nostalgia. She was fresh from a parochial school, where little reading was done and where "grievous" was pronounced as "grievious" (103). (My own upward progress was rather like hers, and I well remember that parochial school solecism—"through my fault, through my fault, through my most grievious fault.") By a giddy feat of the historical imagination, she (not the girl, but rather the woman looking back upon girlhood) employs the rituals and traditions of her Seattle convent school to affiliate herself with France of the Restoration, "embalmed in the Sacred Heart atmosphere, like a period room in a museum with a silken cord drawn across it. The quarrels of the *philosophes* still echoed in the classrooms: the tumbrils had just ceased to creak" (104). Byron's great star had arisen, and America beckoned in the romances of Chateaubriand and Fenimore Cooper. In the study hall, Madame MacIllvra adjured the pupils against doubt, the sin of fine intellects, reminding them of the awful fate of Shelley, who came of good family, but had contracted atheism at Oxford.

They were indomitably bookish, these nuns, or at least so she makes them in retrospect. "Madame MacIllvra, while she would have held it in bad taste to bow down, like Father Zossima, before the murder in Dimitri Karamazov's heart, would certainly have had him in for a series of long, interesting talks in her office." And, "like all truly intellectual women, these were in spirit romantic desperadoes. . . . The great atheists and sinners were the heroes of the costume picture they taught as a subject called history" (93).

This soft-hued, romantically bookish retrospect is not corrected in those italicized afterpieces to *Memories of a Catholic Girlhood* in which she scrutinizes her memories for truthfulness, what her nuns would have called an examination of conscience. What she remembers is the power of books and their ability to make experience, to make life comely, powerful, and seductive. " 'You're just like Lord Byron,' " Madame Barclay the French mistress tells her, " 'brilliant but unsound' " (94):

The reproof was a declaration of love as plain as the sentence on the blackboard, which shimmered slightly before my eyes. My happiness was a confused exaltation in which the fact that I was Lord Byron and the fact that I was loved by Madame Barclay, the most puzzling nun in the convent, blended in a Don Juanesque triumph (95).

So was it also to be, with appropriate changes of tonality and decor, at Annie Wright, the Episcopalian seminary at Tacoma, with mentors different in background, but equally bookish, equally genteel: Black-haired, Scottish Miss Gowrie, B.A., M.A., Girton and Edinburgh, "a genuine British Empire product, like the plaid woolen scarves you bore home from a steamer excursion to Victoria" (147), who could turn the Gallic wars into a novel about Caesar, master alike of warfare and prose, and noble, doomed Vercingetorix. And Miss Dorothy Atkinson, a Vassar woman, blonde bun and pince-nez, who embodied "the critical spirit, wit, cool learning, detachment—everything I suddenly wished to have and to be, from the moment I first heard her light, precise, cutting voice score some pretension, slatternly phrase or construction" ("Vassar Girl" 196).

And from Annie Wright to Vassar, to Miss Kitchel and Miss Sandison, to the rules of English syntax and the reading of Tolstoy and Turgenev. There is a strong family likeness among these women—dry, precise, but decorously romantic and secretly rebellious; intellectually adventurous, but firmly anchored to caste and class, an aristocratic order of Catholic ladies, Vassar women, Girton College bluestockings. It was a training, or perhaps we should say that McCarthy, looking backward, liked to see it as a training in precisely those literary qualities, those traits of sensibility, which she was to bring down to the great world, meaning New York, as a portion of her personal and literary identity, and, if a portion only, then an important one.

No writer had a surer grasp than she of the signifying detail, but one detail, at least, I think carried a greater weight than she intended for it. She tells us in *Intellectual Memoirs* that her first New York apartment, hers and her husband's, at Beekman Place, was furnished with chairs and a small carved oak table and oriental rugs lent to them by Miss Sandison's sister, who taught Latin at Chapin, and with "a handsome card table with a cherrywood frame and legs and a blue suede top," which Miss Sandison had given them as a wedding present. These were offset by more contemporary details supplied by the newlyweds, a " 'modernistic' Russel Wright cocktail shaker," and a chromium hors d'oeuvres tray (12–13). It seems to me fitting, if not downright portentous, that Miss Sandison should have followed her into Beekman Place, and with her those ghostly sisters, Miss Sandison's colleague Miss Kitchel and Miss Gowrie and Madame MacIllvra and Madame Barclay. The aluminum cocktail shaker seems an insignificant echo of Bob Berdan and the front seat of Forrest Crosby's Marmon.

I have gone a long way round in order to suggest that Mary McCarthy was, as her writings make abundantly evident, a genuinely learned writer, erudite and in easy command of her erudition. She was a bookish writer, who never exhausted the energies, delights, and enthusiasms both foolish and wise that reading first aroused in her. Her Northcliffe lectures, for example, published later as *Ideas and the Novel*, move easily among the novels of Balzac, Stendhal, Victor Hugo, Tolstoy, Dostoievsky, Dickens, George Eliot, and that (to me) incomprehensible enthusiasm of hers, Manzoni. Or a 1969 essay which concerns itself with the disappearance from novels of descriptions of nature:

We have almost forgotten that descriptions of sunsets, storms, rivers, lakes, mountains, valleys used to be one of the staple ingredients of fiction, not merely a painted backdrop for action but a component evidently held to be necessary to the art. . . . We have come a long way from the time when the skill of an author was felt to be demonstrated by his descriptive prowess: Dickens' fogs, Fenimore Cooper's waterfalls, forests, prairie, Emily Bronte's moors, Hardy's heath and milky vales, Melville's Pacific ("One Touch" 189).

And she reminds us of "the hunts of Turgenev and Tolstoy, the forest rides of Madame Bovary, Tolstoy's peasants reaping and threshing, the sawmill in Stendhal" (190).

Here as elsewhere she makes her points by drawing not only upon what we used to call the "great novels," but also, with a careless exactitude, upon *Green Mansions, Typee, Moll Flanders, The Unfortunate Traveller, The Ordeal of Richard Feverel, The Blithedale Romance*, and *Manon Lescaut*. She nearly always remembers the right things from a novel. Julien Sorel at the sawmill, Vronsky's large, even teeth, Prince Andrei's small, white hands. The special world which had been opened to her by her reading and by the several disciplines which had guided her quest, which had been opened to her perhaps by history (one of her favorite words), was her particular terrain, her chosen landscape, the world of the novel, of reading.

Madame Bovary, she says in her marvelous essay on that novel, is one of a series of novels—including *Don Quixote* and *Northanger Abbey*—that illustrate the evil effects of reading. All reading, in the case of *Madame Bovary*, not simply the reading of romances. "The books Emma fed on were not pure trash by any means; in the convent she had read Chateaubriand; as a girl on the farm, she read *Paul et Virginie*." So too is her lover Leon addicted to books, and the awful Monsieur Homais "is another illustration of the evil effects of reading" (79). She reminds us of the exchange of platitudes between Leon and Emma, at dinner at the Lion d'Or: " 'is there anything better, really, than sitting by the fire with a book while the wind beats on your window panes and the lamp is burning?' " (78). The central tension of Madame Bovary, her essay suggests, is between Flaubert's susceptibilities to the pleasures of reading and his recognition of their dangers.

This seems to me a not implausible nor indeed even an idiosyncratic reading of the book, and it could even be called, to what I am sure must be her posthumous dismay, a currently fashionable notion of texts thriving upon themselves and each other, cannibalistically. She herself was forever, both with respect to her own art and that of others, watchful, busy with the pruning shears of wit, irony, and skepticism. But she was, for all that, certain, as earlier generations were, her generation and my own, that art opens out upon life, books upon experience. She saw the relationship between the two as endlessly dialectical.

To indulge the kind of closing sentimentality which she, like Miss Dorothy Atkinson of the Annie Wright School, would have been swift to deride, a part of her remained in the wide, dull main street of Great Falls, Montana, poised between Bob Berdan and the girls in the touring car and the boxed, deluxe edition of James Branch Cabell.

WORKS CITED

Gelderman, Carol. *Mary McCarthy: A Life.* New York: St. Martin's, 1988.

McCarthy, Mary. *Ideas and the Novel.* New York: Harcourt, 1980.

————. *Intellectual Memoirs: New York 1936–1938.* New York: Harcourt, 1992.

————. *Memories of a Catholic Girlhood.* 1957. New York: Harvest/Harcourt, 1981.

————. "On *Madame Bovary.*" 1964. *The Writing on the Wall and Other Literary Essays.* New York: Harcourt, 1970. 72–94.

————. "One Touch of Nature." 1969. *The Writing on the Wall.* 189–213.

————. "The Vassar Girl." 1951. *On the Contrary.* New York: Farrar, 1961. 193–214.

Smith, Logan Pearsall. "Myself." *Afterthoughts.* 1931. *Columbia Dictionary of Quotations.* New York: Columbia University Press, 1993.

2

Of Academics and Intellectuals

Terry A. Cooney

In the climactic last sentence of a short piece reflecting on Gandhi's death, Mary McCarthy likened the killings of Gandhi, Leon Trotsky, and Carlo Tresca to acts of "intellectual and artistic criticism." Assassins eliminated those men from the human scene, she suggested, just as "the modern academic critic dismisses the 'good' characters in a novel—glaring improbabilities" ("Gandhi" 23). For many writers it would have been this comparison that was improbable, or perhaps quite literally, inconceivable. For McCarthy, the linkage between killer and critic offered a handy vehicle to convey both her sharp skepticism toward the "academic" and her stalwart insistence on human possibility, including the possibility of goodness.

The striking comparison, the characterizing phrase, the unexpected adjective: these were the deftly handled tools of Mary McCarthy's attitudes and her judgments. From them we learn a good deal about a particular temperament; and in them we catch reflections and refractions of the intellectual culture of her time. McCarthy's essays, especially those from the 1940s and 1950s, can offer a case in point. And perhaps we can keep in mind our own status and presumptions as we consider McCarthy's disposition toward ideas, and her dispositions of them.

The ready use of "academic" as a negative term was well established in the New York circles of Mary McCarthy's early career. Philip Rahv and William

Phillips in the mid-1930s found in academic writing "a content marginal to important literary problems" and "a pedantic treatment of minor ideas" (17). As the editorial board of *Partisan Review* split over its response to World War II, Rahv charged Dwight Macdonald and Clement Greenberg with advocating an "academic revolutionism" that valued formulaic ideas over actual events (499). Lionel Trilling, responding to a gentle criticism from Phillips that his *Matthew Arnold* was too long and rather diffuse, agreed with that judgment and blamed these faults on the "dead hand of academicism" (Letter to Dupee). The "academic," it seemed, did not provoke or enliven thought but caused it to ossify.

McCarthy's own reservations about the academic and its intellectual off-shoots remained clear throughout her career. The Gandhi piece appeared toward the end of the 1940s. In a single essay a decade later, McCarthy dismissed the purveyors of the "guilty-liberal racket and the mass-culture racket"; galloped quickly over a host of "professional intellectuals" in the social sciences and the arts who were simply "the tour-directors of modern society on a cruise looking for itself"; compared one essayist's straightforward verve to the "spectral death-in-life of other contemporary critics"; and consigned minor works of art to the "populous cemetery of the Academy" ("Academy of Risk" (245–48). Later still, in 1973, McCarthy located "some of the worst sinners against language" among intellectuals: "the fall-out in academic circles is asphyxiating," she remarked, "and some of this must be the result of speciali-zation, the loss of touch with common everyday utterance implied by the delegation of powers" ("Language and Politics" 99).

The notions of deadness, of formulaic response, of a distancing from experience, come through again and again as charges against the academic in particular, and as defects of intellectual life more generally. Such complaints could draw on well-rehearsed strains of cultural rebellion against gentility and stuffiness, and the McCarthy of the 1930s was conscious of these possibilities; but that was not the source from which her enduring concerns took their force. Her affiliation with the anti-Stalinist left no doubt strengthened her antipathy to political stances that seemed to close down the possibilities of thought; but McCarthy's reactions were both deeper and wider than this. Her critiques echo, at times, the familiar objections to commercialism, commodification, and consumption that have been a staple of this century's intellectual economy; but her angle of approach provides a distinctive twist.

Although she may share certain of her assumptions with others in the New York intellectual circle, there is always a particular person involved in McCarthy's work: a person who is no friend of elaborate theoretical construc-tions; who rejects intellectual commitments that restrict the mind's vision to seeing only what is expected; who eschews both inappropriate simplification and unnecessary complication as retreats from actuality. These, for McCarthy, are well-worn paths toward deadness and isolation.

A few examples suggest the pattern. Simone de Beauvoir, expecting to find in the United States a "symbol" of something to be "repudiated," can only discover on her visit, according to McCarthy, a country "just as she had imagined it": de Beauvoir's "recoil from American actuality," her "pathetic . . . credulity" amounting to "superstition," can only lead to "a result . . . so predictable that one might say she willed it" ("Mlle. Gulliver" 26–27). In the era of another McCarthy in 1952, Mary McCarthy suggested provocatively that allegiances to particular opinions demanded informally within intellectual circles both right and left constituted "private forms of the loyalty oath," comparable to the official kind ("No News" 39). Lundberg and Farnham's *Modern Woman* McCarthy judged to offer a "mechanical view" that "uses its own hypothesis as proof" and avoids the introduction of "any evidence into the sanctuary of the assertion" ("Tyranny" 172–73). Finally, like these other ways of avoiding actual confrontations with experience, literary symbolism "as taught in the schools and practiced by certain fashionable writers," McCarthy remarked, "flees from the object, the event, into incorporeal distance, where concepts are taken for substance and floating ideas and archetypes assume a hieratic authority" ("Settling" 232).

McCarthy's objections to the prevailing uses of literary symbolism led further, to comments capturing some of her fundamental resistance to theoretical models both cultural and political. In the practice of such criticism, she argued, "symbols become arbitrary; all counters are interchangeable; . . . qualitative differences vanish, and there is only a single monotonous story" ("Settling" 232). Whether the story was literary, social, economic, or political, the concern remained in principle the same for McCarthy, that the object, the event, qualitative differences, real people, and the particularities of actual life should not be obscured by the automatic workings of formula and expectation.

McCarthy sometimes made her own work the subject of such examination. From the viewpoint of twenty years later, she expressed a certain dismay at her apparent late-thirties notion that "abstract reasoning can crush a fact," a notion that she attributed to both "period and person." Her own judgments had not been reached through "relentless logic and lawyer's points," she had decided, even though she had tried to sway others by such means. Her aesthetic judgments had really depended on her ears, on the perception of bad writing or "false notes" that relied on a quality of hearing, not of argument ("Introduction" xvi). Although these reflections came in the 1960s, an inclination to doubt the sufficiency unto themselves of analytical dissections of ideas was clearly evident by the mid-1940s. *The Oasis*, for example, suggested that "realist" left intellectuals who supported the war showed "far less restraint in characterizing opponents . . . as childish, unrealistic, unhistorical, etc., than in formulating a rhetoric of democratic ideals" (19). In 1947 McCarthy described American intellectuals in general as "dissident but inactive," "critical and rather unproductive," inclined to leave it to others to create ("America the Beautiful" 16).

What, then, were the characteristics of worthy intellectuals and worthy ideas? What traits might be valued among intellectuals? In Hannah Arendt, McCarthy found a combination of "tremendous intellectual power with great common sense," and it was clear that for McCarthy the latter quality was as important as the former ("*Vita Activa*" 156). Common sense anchored intelligence to human experience, whereas "abstruse interpretation" left to its own devices, McCarthy suggested elsewhere, would "only lead the reader away from . . . reality" ("Settling" 235). In another instance, McCarthy declared an intellectual saved from "being mastered by one of his ideas so that he would fail to see its implications" because he was possessed of a strong "sense of proportion and balance" ("Academy of Risk" 245). Balance accompanied true vitality; convolution and faddishness were the way of insignificance and death.

As a young theater reviewer, McCarthy could skewer pretense in a second and then drop her scathing witticisms instantly for the sake of broad human themes given honest treatment. Her own deep sense of positive values made McCarthy a frequent scourge of the gimmicky, the flamboyant, and the fashionable. The method of Orson Welles, according to McCarthy, was to "find a modern formula into which a classic can somehow be squeezed" and then apply "strenuous showmanship." Welles's Harlem *Macbeth* stacked up as "at best a pleasant bit of legerdemain"; his *Caesar* offended. Shakespeare's *Julius Caesar*, in McCarthy's eyes, offered an exploration of the tragic relationship between idealism and action; it endured in part because the play insisted "on playing fair with all its characters." In not playing fair, Welles lost any richness of human meaning and offered only a simple "anti-fascist melodrama" ("Elizabethan Revivals" 17–20).

The ILGWU's production of *Pins and Needles*, McCarthy noted, claimed to be "working class drama" but offered only "bourgeois-Democratic" diversion filled with "irresponsible good humor" and "polysyllabic playfulness." Marc Blitzstein's *The Cradle Will Rock* revealed itself to be "abstract and heartless," a "triumph of theatrical goose-stepping" lacking moral struggle or significant conflict ("Class Angles" 21–25). By contrast with these efforts, Thornton Wilder's *Our Town* examined the "tragic velocity of life, the elusive nature of experience." And McCarthy, who dismissed the "sterile cleverness" of many contemporary experiments ("Elizabethan Revivals" 20), found that

Wilder had abandoned "almost all the conventions of the theatre" for the right reasons ("Class Angles" 26–29).

If lively ideas and ethical seriousness often won McCarthy's approval, the drawn-out elaboration of argument and documentation did not. Harold Rosenberg's "eagle-eye view of the twentieth century" had made him the first to see many tendencies, McCarthy insisted; and in a 1940 essay Rosenberg had rapidly sketched out the "whole idea" of André Malraux's 1949 book, *Musée Imaginaire* (*The Museum of the Imagination*). "It might be objected," McCarthy remarked, "that Mr. Rosenberg did not 'do' anything with his idea while Malraux made a book out of it, but a better way of putting it is that Malraux 'got' a book out of it, i.e., labored it to yield him a return" ("Academy of Risk" 244). She expressed similar skepticism toward scholars and critics who "labored" novels less for insight than "a return." It did far less damage to the integrity of art, McCarthy declared, "to disentangle a moral philosophy from a work that evidently contains one" than to undertake a tendentious dissection "as though reading a novel were a sort of paper-chase" ("Settling" 237). We can let these two comments lead us uncomfortably back to the "academic," whether found in universities or not, and to questions of intellectual culture.

Let me offer a bit of speculation on one impetus for McCarthy's ideas within her own realm of experience. By the end of the 1930s, some of those in the *Partisan Review* circle were beginning to suggest, in effect, that the critic might be just as important, or more important, than the poet or novelist (and such ideas were not found in *Partisan Review* alone). William Phillips attempted to argue, for example, that the moment was right for criticism to assert itself, and that "criticism should share in the imaginative possibilities that literature has always enjoyed" (21). Whatever the implications of such a notion in its immediate context, it may have foreshadowed an expanding empire of analysis and reanalysis, an emphasis on the clever construction and reconstruction of ideas about ideas. Might not this tendency have been a part of what Mary McCarthy recognized at some level as early as the 1940s? Might this have been a source of her objections to the flight from event and experience—to intellectuals' removal to a distance "where concepts are taken for substance"? Theory and analysis too easily become forms of intellectual gamesmanship, McCarthy seems to suggest, that lead away from central human issues and from reality.

Parenthetically, we might note that McCarthy finds occasional company in her concern on both the right and the left. The need to echo her fundamental complaint against a too common intellectual practice has not gone away. Henry Louis Gates, for example, without entirely sparing himself, has recently commented on "academic critics" who deliver "readings" of literature in which the "forces of oppression are subverted by the countless powers of irony and allegory," even as those same critics lose track almost completely of "the distance from the classroom to the streets" (19).

We can also approach the basic issue in another way. Taking his cue "from W. H. Auden's remark that a real book reads us," Lionel Trilling once spoke of texts that at first "rejected me" but that later came to "understand my hidden meanings" as age and experience deepened the relationship ("On the Teaching" 7). To think in this way reverses the polarities of what may be a common and too little acknowledged assumption in our "intellectual culture": the assumption that power derives from the commentator, that meanings are provided by analysts, and even, to quote a disapproving Trilling, that "little can be experienced unless it is validated by some established intellectual discipline" ("On the Teaching" 9). McCarthy preferred a different assumption, aptly framed in a remark she attributed to Hegel: the notion that "the tree of life . . . is greener than the tree of thought" ("Settling" 241). In one way or another, McCarthy delivered this message again and again.

What then do we do, for the most part as academics ourselves, with this person who spoke dismissively of intellectual rackets, who cared about everyday utterance, who criticized the camp mentality in matters of opinion, who worried over qualitative differences, who remained cautious before abstract reasoning, and who rejected abstruse interpretation? Do we largely ignore such attitudes as having little to do with us? (And it is easy enough to deflect the bite of McCarthy's opinions by talking about her own contradictions and limitations.) Do we praise McCarthy's wit and style, and then smugly repeat her own observation that "an arresting performance" was often "taken by the Vassar mind to be synonymous with true accomplishment" ("Vassar Girl" 203)? Do we conquer her skepticism through our own transforming analyses?

We will no doubt attempt to do all these things and more. For my part I will only suggest that we may do best, in taking up Mary McCarthy's essays, if we allow the barbs to stick; if we pause in offering our readings until we have allowed ourselves to be read.

WORKS CITED

Gates, Henry Louis, Jr. *Loose Canons: Notes on the Culture Wars*. New York: Oxford University Press, 1992.

McCarthy, Mary. "An Academy of Risk." *On the Contrary*. New York: Farrar, 1962. 242–48.

———. "America the Beautiful: The Humanist in the Bathtub." *On the Contrary*. 6–19.

———. "Class Angles and a Wilder Classic." *Mary McCarthy's Theatre Chronicles 1937–1962*. New York: Farrar, 1963. 21–29.

———— . "Elizabethan Revivals." *Mary McCarthy's Theatre Chronicles.* 13–20.

———— . "Gandhi." *On the Contrary.* 20–23.

———— . "Introduction." *Mary McCarthy's Theatre Chronicles.* vii–xxi.

———— . "Language and Politics." *Occasional Prose.* San Diego: Harcourt, 1985. 83–100.

———— . "Mlle. Gulliver en Amérique." *On the Contrary.* 24–31.

———— . "No News, or, What Killed the Dog." *On the Contrary.* 32–42.

———— . *The Oasis.* New York: Random House, 1949.

———— . "Settling the Colonel's Hash." *On the Contrary.* 225–41.

———— . "Tyranny of the Orgasm." *On the Contrary.* 167–73.

———— . "The Vassar Girl." *On the Contrary.* 193–214.

———— . "The *Vita Activa.*" *On the Contrary.* 155–64.

Phillips, William. "The Esthetic of the Founding Fathers." *Partisan Review* 4.4 (1937–1938): 11–21.

Phillips, Williams, and Philip Rahv. "Criticism." *Partisan Review* 2.7 (1935): 16–24.

Rahv, Philip. "10 Propositions and 8 Errors." *Partisan Review* 8 (1941): 499–506.

Trilling, Lionel. Letter to F. W. Dupee. May 23, 1939. F. W. Dupee Collection. Columbia University, New York.

———— . "On the Teaching of Modern Literature." *Beyond Culture: Essays on Literature and Learning.* 1965. New York: Harvest/Harcourt, 1979. 3–27.

3

A Glint of Malice

Morris Dickstein

For at least a quarter of a century, from the late 1940s to the early 1970s, Mary McCarthy was more than an author, even more than a cultural figure. To the sophisticated, college-educated young of that time she was a byword, even a role model: the bad girl who got away with it, the wicked satirist who held everyone up to ridicule, the Vassar girl who instructed us in worldliness and sexual sophistication, the brilliant critic and essayist whose work exploded the stereotypes of feminine sensibility—in short, the fastest gun in the intellectual world, daringly sexual yet crisply intelligent.

This formidable presence was very much on my mind when I found myself teaching in Paris in the fall of 1980, a figure compounded from innumerable essays and interviews; from the barbed stories in her first book, *The Company She Keeps*, and the shallower, more condescending mockery of her best-selling novel *The Group*; from her trenchant Vietnam reportage of the late 1960s, but also my vivid memories of a recent summer spent in Italy with *The Stones of Florence* as a favorite guide. But this mental image had no resemblance to the dignified, gray-haired lady I finally met in January 1981, shortly before I returned to New York, when she invited me first to tea, then to a larger party at her comfortable flat on the rue de Rennes. There she played the role of Mrs. James West, the perfectly correct wife of a recently retired foreign service officer.

At first our conversation was flat and formal. I had no real reason for calling on her except to meet an icon of my youth, a writer I had intensely admired who was now our last well-known expatriate author in Paris. But how long could we go on talking about the names for different fish in French and English? After three-quarters of an hour things took a different turn when I happened to mention the recent adventures, sexual and political, of some of her old friends in New York. A glint of malice lit up her eyes. She was hungry for details. "Oh, that would make a wonderful story," she said more than once. Not quite, I thought: a wonderful Mary McCarthy story, something quite different.

After reading and rereading her work over several months, I think I can better understand who Mary McCarthy was, what kind of story she wrote, and why she had disappeared into the gray-haired lady, to burst forth only when our talk turned to the New York types whose foibles had once fed her imagination. Her last two novels, *Birds of America* and *Cannibals and Mission-aries*, had been grave, ponderous affairs, with little of the clever, malicious wit her friends feared and other readers savored. She told interviewers she had given up fiction—she said she lacked the social information. But even the memoirs she went on to write seemed lamely matter-of-fact, even trivial at times, compared to *Memories of a Catholic Girlhood* and such dazzling autobiographical essays from the mid-1950s as "Artists in Uniform," about an unsettling encounter with an anti-Semitic colonel, and "My Confession," which traced her political initiation and concluded with her credo as a historical observer. McCarthy's work always had its detractors, such as Alfred Kazin, who said she had "a wholly destructive critical mind" (155), and Randall Jarrell, who famously lampooned her in his brisk roman à clef, *Pictures from an Institution*, which is almost a second coming of *The Groves of Academe*. In his work *The Truants*, even William Barrett—who describes McCarthy in larger-than-life terms as one of the most extraordinary women of our time—observes that her novels and stories had "wit, sharp observation, extraordinary intelligence, an unflagging brilliance and elegance of language," but lacked "the simple virtue of feeling" (65).

Those who did not know McCarthy in her prime could be less generous. For younger readers who saw her only as the sharp-tongued woman embroiled in a lawsuit with Lillian Hellman, the McCarthy mystique had little meaning. Feminist critics, who have exhaustively promoted and analyzed nearly every other woman writer, have shown remarkably little interest in her. If we can understand why her work has faded, we might learn a great deal about why it mattered in the first place.

The first problem with Mary McCarthy's fiction is that not much happens in it. This above all has prevented most of her books from attracting a wide readership. Also, it is often said that her characters are little more than intricately described specimens, pinned and mounted like butterflies but incapable of growth or change. Her own response, a propos of *The Group* (from a 1962 interview with Elisabeth Niebuhr), is that they are "all essentially comic figures," and hence "it's awfully hard to make anything happen to them" (Gelderman 24); but this dictum is belied by comic novelists from Henry Fielding and Jane Austen to Evelyn Waugh and David Lodge. Like these writers, McCarthy is essentially a novelist of manners, but she lacks much of their gift for mixing flat and round characters—comic stereotypes and three-dimensional beings who can develop by undergoing real experiences.

In satiric works such as *The Oasis* and *The Groves of Academe*, McCarthy is wonderful at setting the stage and inserting the actors as comic props. She has the born essayist's gift for describing a world but not the novelist's power to make it move, or make it moving. Her strength is less for emotion than for the anatomy of emotion, less for personality than for the tics of personality. Like Waugh she has a nose for society—not unconnected with snobbery—and an unerring sense of the ridiculous. Her easily recognizable caricatures achieve a crushing accuracy of outline by flattening her characters' human density. But having laid them out she has no idea of what to do with them, not from lack of talent but out of a dark view of human possibility.

At the end of "Portrait of the Intellectual as a Yale Man," the longest, most ambitious story in *The Company She Keeps*, the blithe, vapid Jim Barnett, who has always skimmed across life's surfaces, has lost his former ease and innocence. He had flirted with politics and ideas as he flirted with women. But his brief infatuation with Meg Sargent, who is McCarthy's surrogate in these stories, has disrupted his smooth life, sexually as well as ideologically, and left him badly frightened and "professionally bewildered," convincing him "that he must keep down his spiritual expenses—or else go under" (243, 245). After the charade of being a serious man, he recoils into his convenient marriage and a convenient job. "It was self-knowledge [Meg Sargent] had taught him; she had showed him the cage of his own nature. He had accommodated himself to it, but he could never forgive her" (246).

Here, for once, McCarthy's analytic touch works beautifully. She is essentially a *moraliste*, a dry, lucid anatomist of human nature in the tradition of Montaigne, La Rochefoucauld, and Benjamin Constant, whose great love story *Adolphe* is one of the most acutely analytical novels ever written—about passion, no less. For McCarthy, self-awareness and lucidity, the very things that descend like such a plague on Jim Barnett, are almost absolute values—and as we all know, her prose is astonishing for its clarity and precision. But far from being healing and therapeutic in the style of popular fiction, this bolt of self-knowledge brings us harsh news of our own limitations, the iron cage of personality. For Jim Barnett this news is deadly. "In some subtle way, Jim had turned into a comfortable man, a man incapable of surprising or being surprised. The hair shirt he wore fitted him snugly now" (244).

McCarthy's critics might say that the decline of Jim Barnett into a rather seedy alcoholic and sellout reveals less about the intractability of human nature than about her superior attitude toward her characters, especially since it is her own alter ego, Meg Sargent, who shows Jim "the cage of his own nature." McCarthy's good friend Dwight Macdonald, who (along with John Chamberlain and Malcolm Cowley) may have been one of the models for Jim Barnett, and who certainly sat for the boisterous and obtuse Macdougal Macdermott in *The Oasis*, would have been sympathetic to the anti-Stalinist polemic of the "Yale Man." But he wondered privately about *The Groves of Academe*:

Why does she have to be so goddamned snooty, is she god or something? You begin to feel sorry for her poor characters, who are always so absurd or rascally or just inferior and damned—she's always telling them their slip's showing. She doesn't *love* them, that's the trouble, in the sense of not feeling a human solidarity or sympathy with them—can't create real characters without love, or hate which is also a human feeling; she had just contempt and her poor puppets just wither on the page. . . . The trouble is she is so damned superior to her characters, sneers at most of them and patronizes the rest (Gelderman 170).

This is as shrewd a comment as any later critic would make, exaggerated perhaps, but not unfair to the brittle writing and impoverished human atmosphere of weaker novels like *The Groves of Academe* and *The Group*. This is why McCarthy needs the autobiographical protagonist, why *The Company She Keeps* and *Memories of a Catholic Girlhood* are much better than the satiric books. McCarthy needs a character to whom she cannot feel superior, someone who can sustain not only her wit and cleverness but her weakness and sense of vulnerability, her second thoughts, misgivings, and mistakes. And she herself was the only candidate.

What McCarthy's work badly needed was the "unfinished woman" that Lillian Hellman evoked, the woman before she became a duchess, a princess among trolls who so emphatically knew her own worth. Just before sitting down with Mary McCarthy last summer, I reread several volumes of Leon Edel's biography of Henry James. I was most struck, especially in the second volume, by the tremendous drama of James before he became Henry James, when he was a struggling journalist just learning to write novels, churning out copy to make ends meet, trying to interest editors in his work and gain a toehold in the social world that would become his subject.

In her two best books, especially *The Company She Keeps*, McCarthy is an unformed character in search of a self, wrestling with knaves and naifs who are not really her equal. Yet she is also troubled, put upon, ambivalent. Always an autobiographical writer, McCarthy needed her personal history to furnish her with a character she would never fully understand, and with a ready-made story that would intrigue and challenge her. Her own story gave her the pieces of a plot she wasn't good at inventing, dealing with a person to whom she *can* make things happen.

From the time she wrote her first book Mary McCarthy set out to shock, and with the story "The Man in the Brooks Brothers Shirt" she fully succeeded. She was after all the shiksa in a group of largely Jewish intellectuals, a scarlet woman in a decade that thought itself more proper and serious than the 1920s. Innocently enough, she needed a slight aura of scandal to set her creative juices flowing. When I first read "The Man in the Brooks Brothers Shirt" twenty years later, this account of Meg Sargent's casual seduction in a Pullman compartment was still a byword for sexual daring and sustained wit and brilliance. For its time, the portrait of the heroine as intransigent intellectual was as original as the heroine as casual (though easily embarrassed) sexual adventurer. Every charge that would later be leveled at McCarthy—her snobbishness, her undue care for social niceties, her wobbly moral compass, her traffic in gossip, her sense of superiority—was not only showcased in this story but became part of its theme as the protagonist constantly probed her own behavior.

If feminist critics show little interest in *The Company She Keeps*, it may be because Meg Sargent is neither a victim nor a role model. The company *she* keeps is entirely male. Her only relationship with other women—including the wives of the men she sleeps with and the women in the radical bohemian milieu in which she has been living—is competitive and dismissive. The wives are caricatures of middle-class respectability; the others offer little competition. "It was not difficult, after all, to be the prettiest girl at a party for the sharecroppers" (112).

Meg is completely oriented toward men yet intensely critical of them. Only they can give her the stage on which to shine, the platform where she can look down on them. Nearly every one of the stories is about the Gifted but Confused Woman who gets embroiled with the Unsatisfactory Male, beginning with the husband and the lover in her first story, "Cruel and Barbarous Treatment," and winding up with her psychiatrist and her second husband in "Ghostly Father, I Confess." The Brooks Brothers man, who seems impossible to begin with—a "self-made man," a Babbitt (83)—turns out to be the least unsatisfactory male in the book, though he shares one quality that disqualifies several of the others: he is simply too nice to her, and claims horribly to see the sweet girl concealed inside her. But in her whirl of projections—and much of the story is the quicksilver flow of her imaginings, her rationalizations—she turns even his vulgarity to advantage. If he is not an intellectual, as she is, then he must somehow represent Ordinary Life, with which intellectuals are always in danger of losing touch. Leapfrogging from one fantasy to another, she sees in him what she misses in all the men she knows in New York, "the shrewd buyer's eye, the swift brutal appraisal" (111). Of the men she had been with, she feels,

In one way or another they were all of them lame ducks. The handsome ones, like her fiancé, were good-for-nothing, the reliable ones, like her husband, were peculiar-look-ing, the well-to-do ones were short and wore lifts in their shoes or fat with glasses, the clever ones were alcoholic or slightly homosexual, the serious ones were foreigners or else wore beards or black shirts or were desperately poor and had no table manners. Somehow each of them was handicapped for American life and therefore humble in love (112).

This brilliant inventory, like the rest of the story, highlights the way McCarthy's judgments—for all her confessional intensity, sexual bravado, and intellectual arrogance—were neither religious, moral, nor political but rather social judgments about class, taste, style, and, above all, appearances. As the love interest of these men she felt somehow devalued. When she left Philip Rahv for Edmund Wilson, she writes much later in the posthumously pub-lished *Intellectual Memoirs*, it was important that he "came from the same stock, Anglo-Saxon, Presbyterian." After years among actors, bohemians, and Jews, "there was a certain feeling of coming home, to my own people" (102).

Meg Sargent hasn't the least *moral* qualm about getting seduced by Babbitt on the train. "Still," she thinks, "the whole thing would be so vulgar; one would expose oneself so to the derision of the other passengers" (83–84). In *Memories of a Catholic Girlhood* McCarthy recalls how, as a schoolgirl, her desire to shine was replaced by the "fear of appearing ridiculous" as a "governing motive" of her life, a motive that no doubt contributed to her lifelong need to highlight the ridiculous in other people's behavior (130).

But in "The Man in the Brooks Brothers Shirt," surprisingly, the romantic side of McCarthy, her tenderness, overcomes this fear, overcomes even her social and intellectual scruples. "For the thing was, the man and the little adventure of being with him had a kind of human appeal that she kept giving in to against her judgment. *She liked him*" (94–95). For once she is unguarded, pleasantly embarrassed, entirely without cunning. Meg Sargent's gloriously tacky adventure on the train is also Mary McCarthy's self-transcendence as a writer. Here she dramatizes and overcomes the defects attributed to her fiction—that she is too judgmental and superior, that she doesn't love any of her characters, that, as Kazin insists, she reserves indulgence only for herself.

McCarthy could not really sustain the benign vein of this story. Malice, mockery, and witty derision would remain essential to her fiction, as in the often inane world of *The Groves of Academe* and *The Group*, where she expertly puts the puppets through their paces. At her best in these books, as in her nonfiction, she could be an amusing satirist and an entertaining reality instructor, enclosing a barbed essay on progressive education in the first book and a daring brief on sexual initiation and contraception in the second. But few readers took much notice when she developed the other crucial vein of *The Company She Keeps*, her sense of the confusion, passivity, insecurity, and entrapment that lay just beneath her heroine's brash confidence. Her tempestuous marriage to Edmund Wilson brought her face to face with these feelings.

Wilson, who figures as Meg's second husband, Frederick, in "Ghostly Father, I Confess," which deals with her analysis, and again in McCarthy's next important story, "The Weeds" (1944), apparently treated her with none of the gentleness and indulgence that elicited her contempt for the other men in *The Company She Keeps*. These two grim stories—the second dealing with her failure to leave Wilson—serve as a bridge from the buoyant sexual comedy of *The Company She Keeps* to the harsh Dickensian upbringing portrayed in *Memories of a Catholic Girlhood*, which she began writing immediately after "The Weeds," just as her unhappy marriage to Wilson was disintegrating.

McCarthy always conceded that Wilson turned her into a "creative" writer by sitting her down in a room—just as Colette's husband had done to her—and telling her, with the authority of not just a husband but of America's leading critic, that she had a talent for imaginative writing. In her final, unfinished memoir she acknowledges this again, but with a surprisingly ambivalent and bittersweet edge: "If he had not shut the door firmly on the little room he had shepherded me into . . . I would not be the 'Mary McCarthy' you are now reading. Yet, awful to say, I am not particularly grateful" (*Intellectual Memoirs* 104).

But the harshness she ascribed to Wilson made her a writer in an even deeper way, for it brought back the vulnerability she had tried to put behind her. In "Ghostly Father, I Confess," Meg Sargent begins by confidently mocking her analyst: his taste is vulgar, his intelligence scarcely matches hers. "She had enjoyed doing that malicious portrait," she thinks. When he questions her about it, she says simply, "I've got a good eye for social types, and I've had a lot of practice" (253). But what she's really doing, it turns out as the story proceeds, is resisting the reflux of her melodramatic past, the burden of a miserable childhood and an unhappy self that she had utterly suppressed until marriage to Wilson made her feel helpless and imprisoned.

Mary McCarthy's parents had both died in the flu epidemic of 1918, when she was six, and until she was rescued, she and her brothers were raised by cold, strict, comically sadistic guardians out of *Nicholas Nickleby*. But this was material for just the kind of Victorian novel she would never dream of writing. "I reject the whole pathos of the changeling, the orphan, the stepchild," thinks Meg ("Ghostly Father" 263). "Her peculiar tragedy (if she had one) was that her temperament was unable to assimilate her experience; the raw melodrama of those early years was a kind of daily affront to her skeptical, prosaic intelligence." Though a lapsed Catholic, McCarthy felt that confession was good for the soul, even confession to an analyst she loathed as her husband's surrogate. Her first story inspired by the marriage to Wilson was also the first story in which she could grapple with her orphaned, emotionally deprived past, and it became a prologue to all her later autobiographical writing.

"Ghostly Father" and "The Weeds" suggest that the humiliation and misery she felt as Wilson's wife brought her close to a breakdown, but also tore down her defenses and gave her access to the vulnerable child behind them. Graham Greene said that an unhappy childhood is a writer's capital for life, but McCarthy drew on this legacy only under the greatest stress. *Memories of a Catholic Girlhood* had the kind of Dickensian plot and characters to be found nowhere else in McCarthy's work. But this dry and preternaturally clear book is anything but Victorian melodrama. In her concern with getting the facts right, in the give and take between the individual memoirs and her interpolated comments and corrections, McCarthy managed to make her improbable past accessible to her skeptical, prosaic intelligence.

Memories was the last book in which McCarthy was fully able to strike this balance between tenderness and intelligence, between "the facts" and the feelings. Some of this can also be found in the essays collected in *On the Contrary* and in her wonderful book on Florence, and it reappears sporadically in her late memoirs and the deeply felt obituary tributes she wrote for her friends in her last years. McCarthy's cool wit and sophistication proved bracing for more than one generation, as her wicked satirical eye influenced writers as different as Philip Roth (in his first collection of stories) and Nabokov (in *Lolita*).

But she was at her best when her intelligent mockery wasn't merely mocking, when she herself was implicated by it. Scornful satire may have been McCarthy's defense against feeling, but at her best the vulnerable woman could be seen behind the highbrow scold. Satire was her vehicle for social observation and the kind of sexual comedy that meant so much to my generation, the generation that came of age just before the Pill, just before the sexual and behavioral revolutions and the 1960s took hold.

For us McCarthy was the chronicler not only of a hard-won sexual freedom—"Get yourself a pessary" (*Group* 476)—but also of social discomfort and sexual embarrassment: the foolish display, the drunken seduction, the safety pin on the underwear. Her best heroines were those who not only flouted conventions but had a hard time getting away with it, who did things against their better judgment and often found themselves in tight situations largely of their own making. It would be too simple to say that the Pill did her in by altering sexual mores forever, that she lost her subject and her audience when these matters became too easy, too free of conflict and misgivings. In truth, they are never easy; life always provides us with rich complications.

Only comedy can assuage the complications that intelligence can never fully control. Especially for a Catholic, comedy hints at forgiveness, implies an act without consequences. Meg Sargent's episode on the train only eases up when she sees it as farce rather than high drama, vulgar or tender seduction rather than self-betrayal. For, as she says, "The world of farce was a sort of moral underworld, a cheerful, well-lit hell where a Fall was only a prat-fall after all" (*The Company She Keeps* 111).

WORKS CITED

Barrett, William. *The Truants: Adventures among the Intellectuals*. New York: Anchor/Doubleday, 1982.

Edel, Leon. *Henry James*. 5 vols. Philadelphia: Lippincott, 1953–1972.

Gelderman, Carol. *Mary McCarthy: A Life*. New York: St. Martin's, 1988.

————, ed. *Conversations with Mary McCarthy*. Jackson: University Press of Mississippi, 1991.

Jarrell, Randall. *Pictures from an Institution*. 1954. Chicago: University of Chicago Press, 1986.

Kazin, Alfred. *Starting Out in the Thirties*. Boston: Little, Brown, 1965.

Macdonald, Dwight. Letter to Nicola Chiaromonte. February 14, 1952. Macdonald Papers, Box 10, Folder 242. Quoted in Gelderman, Carol. *Mary McCarthy: A Life*. 170.

McCarthy, Mary. *Birds of America*. New York: Harcourt, 1971.

————. *Cannibals and Missionaries*. New York: Harcourt, 1979.

————. *Cast a Cold Eye*. 1950. New York: Harcourt, 1972.

————. *The Company She Keeps*. 1942. New York: Harcourt, 1967.

————. "Cruel and Barbarous Treatment." *The Company She Keeps*. 3–21.

————. "Ghostly Father, I Confess." *The Company She Keeps*. 249–304.

————. *The Group*. New York: Harcourt, 1963.

————. *The Groves of Academe*. New York: Harcourt, 1952.

————. *Intellectual Memoirs: New York 1936–1938*. New York: Harcourt, 1992.

————. Interview with Elisabeth Niebuhr. Gelderman, Carol, ed. *Conversations with Mary McCarthy*. Jackson: University Press of Mississippi, 1991. Also collected in *Writers at Work*, 2nd series. New York: Viking, 1963.

————. "The Man in the Brooks Brothers Shirt." *The Company She Keeps*. 81–134.

————. *Memories of a Catholic Girlhood*. New York: Harcourt, 1957.

————. *The Oasis*. New York: Random House, 1949.

————. *On the Contrary*. New York: Farrar, 1961.

————. "Portrait of the Intellectual as a Yale Man." *The Company She Keeps*. 167–246.

————. *The Stones of Florence*. New York: Harcourt, 1959.

4

Our Leading Bitch Intellectual

Beverly Gross

A classroom discussion of *The Group* a couple of years ago got me thinking about the word "bitch." I had told the class that Carol Gelderman, McCarthy's biographer, was intrigued by the frequent labeling of McCarthy as such. "Her novels are crammed with cerebration and bitchiness," she quoted John Aldridge; "Her approach to writing [is] reflective of the modern American bitch," she quoted Paul Schlueter (Gelderman xi). Since this was a women's studies course the word "bitch" resonated powerfully, and we became fruitfully sidetracked in considering what it might mean about McCarthy that the word was so frequently applied to her, and what its application means and does to women generally.

I wound up writing an essay about the signification and impact of this epithet which has served the English language for a thousand years as the primary term of abuse against women. Its meaning has changed dramatically, depending on and reflecting what an era deems most threatening in a woman. "Bitch" has sometimes meant a lewd woman, an unfaithful woman, a frigid woman, a malicious woman, a powerful woman. Essentially the word is a misogynistic club that is intended to shackle women's actions and impulses.

But returning to the initial question: why did McCarthy so readily incite the word "bitch" in discussions of her works and her person? Clearly she had a penchant for wickedness, even malice, and a combativeness that made for trouble all through her life. Doris Grumbach called her "compulsively frank" (36). McCarthy had a satirical bent, a tough critical outlook, an adversarial habit of mind, influence in the world of letters, confidence in style and manner. Above all, she was a woman who had a mind and spoke it. In a man, power, assertiveness, and contentiousness are laudable. A woman with the same traits is domineering, threatening, castrating—in a word, a bitch. Much of the extraordinary ire McCarthy aroused among critics and commentators had to do with being the wrong kind of woman, indeed a woman in the first place.

Biographical remembrances of McCarthy by members of the male intelligentsia are replete with images of physical vulnerability, particularly in the genital region. Alfred Kazin's account of meeting McCarthy in Provincetown in 1940 provides a singularly antagonistic portrayal:

She had, I thought, a wholly destructive critical mind, shown in her unerring ability to spot the hidden weakness or inconsistency in any literary effort and every person. To this weakness she instinctively leaped with cries of pleasure—surprised that her victim, as he lay torn and bleeding, did not applaud her perspicacity (155).

William Barrett's *The Truants*, though largely an affectionate and respectful account, nevertheless alludes to McCarthy's "acid pen," "her hatchet," and "her stinging whip":

She rather struck terror into some male bosoms. I remember being at some party or other, sitting beside two older men who suddenly froze as she entered the room. . . . here was this attractive and engaging woman, all smiles, and their recoil was as if an ogress, booted and spurred, had entered the room, brandishing her whips (67).

Dwight Macdonald, a good friend, described McCarthy's smile as "rather sharkish. When most pretty girls smile at you, you feel terrific. When Mary smiles at you, you look to see if your fly is open" (Gelderman 184).

McCarthy's biographers remark on the recurrent imagery of sharp instruments when critics talk of her work. "Scissors, swords, and knives" are noted by Carol Brightman (xxiv). Carol Gelderman quotes a Ph.D. candidate who wondered at the frequent references made by critics of McCarthy to "knives, stilettos, switch-blades" as well as the adjectives they commonly bestow: "cold, heartless, clever, cerebral, cutting, acid, acidulous" (xi). "Cutting," interestingly, is a word that McCarthy herself could use quite positively. An illuminating glimpse of character formation can be found in Mary McCarthy's account of herself as a student at fourteen, swept by adulation for her English teacher, who was "everything I suddenly wished to have and be, from the moment I first heard her light, precise, cutting voice score some pretense" ("Vassar Girl" 196).

Compare McCarthy's expression of delight in a voice that is "light, precise, cutting" with the tone of one of McCarthy's critics talking about "the sharp, ruthless, satiric touch" of McCarthy's novels, "the clinical, dispassionate, acerbic dissection Miss McCarthy performs on her fellow human beings" turned into a "collection of ugly cadavers on which Miss McCarthy has unleashed her fury" (Schlueter 61, 64).

McCarthy's own cutting voice, whether as narrator or (her term) ventriloquist, is strongly discernible in her novels. It was as a satirist rather than a fabulist that McCarthy wrote fiction. Her six novels seem less acts of imagination than of social and intellectual criticism, scoring the pretentious vulgarity of American life and the treachery of doctrinal thinking. She was hard on everything and everybody but hard most of all on herself. "The heroine is presented as a perfect bitch" (Brightman 208), Malcolm Cowley wrote about Margaret Sargent in *The Company She Keeps*, McCarthy's most recognizable persona. "You use your wonderful scruples as an excuse for acting like a bitch," Margaret's husband tells her in the story "Ghostly Father, I Confess" (*The Company She Keeps* 276). His term for her is "a natural-born bitch" (295). In *A Charmed Life* the husband of Martha Sinnott, another heroine closely modeled on the author,

was startled by the laughing sharpness with which she spoke of the local people. . . . He was a critical man himself, but she made him feel old and tolerant by contrast. Yet it puzzled him to remember, as he listened, that it was Martha's arrogant intolerance that he had loved most about her (75).

McCarthy the novelist was frequently charged with malice for her habit of mining her life for her fiction—friends, husbands, lovers, neighbors, colleagues, and classmates were all fair game. This fictionalizing often involved betraying intimacies and stomping on weaknesses. (In June 1993 when members of the Vassar class of 1933 celebrated their sixtieth reunion the *New York Times* reported that they were still fuming about McCarthy's act of exposure and betrayal in *The Group*.) Her friend Dwight Macdonald, who served as the model for the satiric portrait of Macdougal Macdermott in *The Oasis*, commented about her next novel, *The Groves of Academe*:

Why does she have to be so goddamned snooty, is she god or something? You begin to feel sorry for her poor characters, who are always so absurd or rascally or just inferior and damned—she's always telling them their slip's showing. . . . Is she really like that? Or is she just kidding *me* along too, and making all sorts of snooty little footnotes in her head as we talk (Gelderman 170)?

McCarthy at seventy wondered about the "excessive anger, ferocity, vehe-mence" behind her adolescent writings, described in *How I Grew* as satires on "triteness and self-deception." Of herself at fourteen, she says, "I was rubbing my heroines' noses in [the truth]" (101–102). McCarthy spoke in similar terms of her adult novels, admitting for example to being "awfully mean to those girls" in *The Group*. "I felt that I was just whacking those girls over the head and making them parrot this terrible nonsense. Not that they didn't, in reality, parrot a lot of nonsense" (Kufrin 84–85).

McCarthy seemed genuinely troubled by her own unstoppable satiric and critical impulses. She was painfully aware of the limitations of satiric fiction and the unending criticism that her work elicited for its aura of authorial superiority and supercilious disapproval. In midlife McCarthy seemed to be struggling to surmount her predilections. "My intention is not satirical," she stated in her application for a Guggenheim to complete the writing of *The Groves of Academe*. "In fact, I am trying to curb an overly satirical and self-recriminating tendency in my work" (Gelderman 167). She wrote similarly in another application (1959) for a Guggenheim to finish *The Group*, "The book is not meant to be . . . a satire," adding however, "It is a crazy quilt of *clichés*, platitudes, and *idées réçues*" (Gelderman 253). The curious contradic-tion suggests how inescapable for her was the satiric habit of mind.

It is fair to say that McCarthy never quite succeeded in expunging the satiric impulse, though it was considerably curbed in her last two major novels, *The Group* and *Birds of America*. No matter—the critics damned her anyway. Dwight Macdonald remarked that "most of the intellectuals I've talked to, or read, about *The Group* think it is the old Mary, cold and bitchy and superior," though he himself saw "a quite new note of sympathy and concern" (Gelder-man 254). "Our leading bitch-intellectual" is how Hilton Kramer's review (*Bookworld*, May 23, 1971) referred to the author of *Birds of America*, which, ironically, McCarthy called her favorite book. "I like the hero. I like the ideas. Well, it's close to my heart" (Kufrin 82). There is far more love in this than in any of her other novels, especially for the main character, young Peter Levi, who with all his foibles clearly has the author's affection and admiration.

"Our leading bitch-intellectual": the phrase is startling in its bald misogyny and what it reveals about the wellspring of antagonism to McCarthy. She was a lightning rod for the blatant and subtle misogyny of commentators, male and female. "A career of candor and dissent is not an easy one for a woman," Elizabeth Hardwick writes in her essay "Mary McCarthy" (35), explaining that "a great measure of personal attractiveness and a high degree of romantic singularity" in McCarthy enabled her "to step free of the mundane, the governessy, the threat of earnestness and dryness." The implication is that

McCarthy attained her eminence in the male province of America's intelligentsia because she was a good-looking, sexually venturesome woman—someone plainer and primmer would not have gotten away with McCarthy's kind of bitchiness. (The spirit of that judgment is echoed in Hardwick's review of *The Second Sex*, in which she compliments Simone de Beauvoir for "miraculously . . . not giv[ing] to me, at least, the impression of being a masochist, a Lesbian, a termagant, or a man-hater" [170].)

A similar exemption occurs in a 1962 piece in *Esquire* called "Mary McCarthyism," which defends McCarthy against "her hostile critics [who] claim that what she has really defined, for all men to know, is the Modern American Bitch." But no, says the author, Brock Brower: "Bitchiness is hardly a fair estimate of her critical, imperious, yet highly feminine sensibility" (65). A lovely paradox: McCarthy is here deemed too feminine to be really a bitch, an epithet presumably better suited to the above-mentioned triad of Lesbians, termagants and man-haters.

Elsewhere, however, traits of femininity are cited to bolster allegations of McCarthy's malice and treachery. How frequently allusions are made, gratuitously it would seem, and often in combination, to McCarthy's comeliness and Vassar background. The combination is invoked as a polite way of conjuring up the kind of bitch who is a heartless *femme fatale* with overtones (by way of Vassar) of female privilege, snobbery, and overeducation. In his angry portrayal of McCarthy in *Starting Out in the Thirties*, Alfred Kazin writes, "Truth, in the person of this sharply handsome twenty-eight-year-old Vassar graduate, had come to pass judgment on the damned in Provincetown" (155). In *Making It*, Norman Podhoretz alludes to the "wicked pen" of this "Vassar girl, and a very pretty one at that" (127). Later in the book and a few decades later in time, in a most extraordinary passage Podhoretz suggests that Susan Sontag has taken over McCarthy's position as "the Dark Lady of American Letters," a position left vacant by McCarthy's—not demise—but aging:

Miss McCarthy no longer occupied it, having recently been promoted to the more dignified status of Grande Dame as a reward for her long years of brilliant service. The next Dark Lady would have to be, like her, clever, learned, good-looking, capable of writing . . . criticism as well as fiction with a strong trace of naughtiness (154).

In support of his contention, Podhoretz notes that Sontag's "figure mystically resembled that of the young Mary McCarthy and she had the same black hair" (155). Imagine such comparisons being made of male intellectuals. Did Podhoretz's "figure" resemble that of the young Lionel Trilling?

Podhoretz's anatomical tributes were probably supposed to pass as chivalry, but they are more demeaning and denigrating than Norman Mailer's out-and-out assault in his review of *The Group*, entitled "The Case Against McCarthy" when it was reprinted in *Cannibals and Christians*. Mailer's review is peppered with an assortment of female bogeys referring to author, work, and characters ("witch," "bitchery," "princess," "dyke," "old-maid," "broad"), coupled with a panoply of excretory allusions. A strange benediction ends the review, with Mailer softening his case against McCarthy by offering the prospect "that McCarthy [to whom he has referred until this point as "Mary"] may finally get tough enough to go with the boys. She has been a very bad girl these years, mean and silly, postured and overpetted, petty in the extreme." But someday, Mailer says, the saints may "bless her with a book that can comprehend a man" (140).

This is worth trying to decipher. "Comprehend a man"? Apparently eight women are not sufficient and fitting protagonists. "Bless her with a book"? Apparently McCarthy, should she achieve the miracle of producing a book that the masculine mind could respect, would create it not as a writer but as the Virgin Mother carrying God's incarnation in her womb. This silliness still amounts to uncustomary praise from Mailer, who, in "Some Chlidren of the Goddess," his essay about the state of the novel in the mid-1960s, had dismissed "all the lady writers, bless them" because "one cannot speak of a woman having a piece of the Bitch" (105)—in Mailerspeak the novelist's obsessive passion to write the great book is likened to his desire to fuck the Bitch Goddess of success. Women writers, of course, are anatomically disqualified.

McCarthy may be the only contemporary woman writer whom Mailer cannot totally dismiss. She presents him with too many challenges and paradoxes which may explain in part why his review is so undecipherable. "The First Lady of Letters," as he calls McCarthy, has written in *The Group* what he calls a "lady-book," but, significantly, Mailer stops short of labeling McCarthy with the dread term "lady writer." He can still put her down in a note that sounds like Kazin's and Macdonald's: "she failed out of vanity, the accumulated vanity of being overpraised through the years for too little . . . she failed out of snobbery." For Mailer this adds up to her being "simply not a good enough woman to write a major novel, not yet" (138–39). The entire review is ugly, brutal, and insulting, but Mailer pays a backhanded tribute by his inability to call McCarthy a lady. About McCarthy he has to use the word "woman," even though she is "not yet" a good enough one. A lady could never be a bitch—it takes a woman.

The implicit and explicit imputations of "bitch" by Mailer and others, though not exactly a compliment to McCarthy, are surely an acknowledgment of her singular authority, courage, and self-possession. There weren't many like her, certainly not in the 1940s and 1950s. She had the courage to kill off at a very early age the Angel in the House of her brain. She did not live or write to please. There may be much to dislike in McCarthy as a person and a writer. But there is much to admire in her capacity to break the mold of female expectations, subservience, politeness, and respectability. And much to admire in her refusal to be tamed and muzzled by the number one weapon in the verbal arsenal that has kept women in their place.

WORKS CITED

Barrett, William. *The Truants: Adventures among the Intellectuals*. New York: Anchor/
    Doubleday, 1982.
Brightman, Carol. *Writing Dangerously: Mary McCarthy and Her World*. New York:
    Clarkson Potter, 1992.
Brower, Brock. "Mary McCarthyism." *Esquire* 58 (July 1962): 60–65.
Gelderman, Carol. *Mary McCarthy: A Life*. New York: St. Martin's, 1988.
Gross, Beverly. "Bitch." *Salmagundi* 103 (Summer 1994): 146–56.
Grumbach, Doris. "The Subject Objected." *New York Times Book Review* (June 11,
    1967): 36.
Hardwick, Elizabeth. *A View of My Own*. New York: Farrar, 1962.
Kazin, Alfred. *Starting Out in the Thirties*. Boston: Little, Brown, 1965.
Kufrin, Joan. *Uncommon Women*. New York: New Century, 1981.
Mailer, Norman. "The Case against McCarthy: A Review of *The Group*." *Cannibals
    and Christians*. New York: Dial, 1966. 133–40.
————. "Some Children of the Goddess." *Cannibals and Christians*. 104–130.
McCarthy, Mary. *A Charmed Life*. New York: Harcourt, 1955.
————. *The Company She Keeps*. 1942. New York: Harcourt, 1967.
————. *How I Grew*. New York: Harcourt, 1987.
————. "The Vassar Girl." *On the Contrary*. New York: Farrar, 1961. 193–214.
Podhoretz, Norman. *Making It*. New York: Random House, 1969.
Schlueter, Paul. "The Dissections of Mary McCarthy." Moore, Harry T., ed. *Con-
    temporary American Novelists*. Carbondale: Southern Illinois University
    Press, 1964. 61–64.

5

Terrorists, Artists, and Intellectuals

Margaret Scanlan

In his notes for "The World Is a Wedding," Delmore Schwartz observed of a thinly disguised Mary McCarthy figure that she "wants to get married again so that she can once again have someone to whom to be unfaithful" (Brightman 396). As character analysis, the remark is doubtless more cruel than just, but it aptly describes McCarthy the writer, who like other satirists found permanent, unconditional loyalty to most persons, groups, and ideologies impossible. Catholics and Stalinists, Trotskyites and Freudians, all felt the sting of her rejections. In the heyday of the blacklist, her cold eye turned to the victims of Joe McCarthy and, against her own political sympathies, found much to ridicule. No sentimental patriotism would deter her in 1968, as a cosseted guest of the local government, from meeting captured U.S. pilots in Hanoi. She might love Philip Rahv, yet caricature him mercilessly in the fictional Will Taub; not all of her octogenarian classmates who still feel "exposed and violated" by *The Group* were personal enemies (Kiernan 57).

Yet for most of her adult life McCarthy remained faithful to a set of liberal intellectual convictions about the moral worth of art and education and about the need for a progressive politics. What makes her last novel, *Cannibals and Missionaries*, remarkable is that in it the satirist turns on these long-held values, systematically revealing them as foolish, futile, even dangerous. After her novel appeared in 1979 to lukewarm reviews, McCarthy defended it against charges that readers don't care about the characters by remarking that "you're not meant to . . . the emotional depth of the book is extremely shallow" (Brightman 594). The defense seems strange if we read the book for realism, but is eminently understandable if we see McCarthy as blending two genres, the thriller and the novel of ideas, neither notable for realistic characterization, in order to explore the responses of liberal intellectuals to actual violence. The novel's "anointed band of liberals" (*Cannibals and Missionaries* 297) is made up of people closely modeled on her own friends and acquaintances and, one suspects, herself; and their failures, successes, and especially their shallowness embody the author's own responses to her generation's role in U.S. political life.

The plot comes from the thriller: a committee of high-minded liberals "in the American sense, i.e., slightly to the left in politics and devoted to human rights," undertakes a fact-finding mission to the Shah's Iran. They are hijacked, along with a tour group of rich art collectors, by pro-Palestinian terrorists, and held hostage in a farmhouse in Flevoland, the new Dutch province reclaimed from the sea. In time the collectors are exchanged for the masterpieces of their collections; thus, in a farmhouse in an obscure corner of Europe, as devoid of European history as Utah, the author assembles people and paintings who represent the West's artistic, intellectual, political, and social elites. McCarthy found such "isolation" "crucial" to traditional novels of ideas such as *The Magic Mountain* or *The First Circle*, and for the most part *Cannibals and Missionaries* reads like them: highly articulate people spend hours discussing their theories in the shadow of historical catastrophe (*Ideas and the Novel* 20).

McCarthy's portrait of liberals is all the more devastating in the end because they are allowed many positive characteristics. Detached from their ordinary lives, they work out a group identity, though some are far more likeable than others. The retired bishop from Missouri is a virtual saint; the Dutch poet and parliamentary deputy, Henk Van Vliet de Jonghe, is consistently warm and sympathetic; on the other hand, the college president, Aileen Simmons, talks nonstop in kittenish self-preoccupation, and Frank Barber, the foolishly optimistic Episcopal rector, is someone whom, as Mary Gordon remarks, one can hate from the first page. Yet all share the historical situation that puts the liberal American intellectual in a position once occupied by the clergy, a point McCarthy underscores by arranging for the bishop to die early. Their kidnappers believe they represent the national conscience, that violating them will provoke the sense of "sacrilege" essential to terror (220). Engaged on a "mission," liberals have inherited from their evangelical predecessors an ambivalent identity as potential martyrs and unconscious colonialists, "salesm[e]n for Western democratic merchandise" (5).

McCarthy's liberals are remarkably courageous, partly because they are resourceful, able to impose structure and therefore meaning on their captivity. A petulant sense of injustice leads Aileen half advertently to finger the collectors in first class; it is the only significant exception to their general decency and courtesy. They impose on degrading conditions the rituals of upper-class life, so that the reader, hearing their witty conversation or watching them play bridge with cleverly decorated cards cut from magazines, forgets how long it has been since they have had a change of underwear.

Yet mental worlds can be frighteningly detached from reality. Early in the novel Senator Carey, the Eugene McCarthy clone, notices how a trivial misunderstanding spreads through the group until everyone assumes that it is a fact and reflects on the "gravity-defying power of ideas to stand unsupported by evidence" (68). Unsupported constructions like Henk's fantasy that Holland is an imaginary country have dangerous consequences; this whimsy leads him to ignore two Dutch-speakers on the plane, and thus to lose a chance to eavesdrop on its hijackers. When the bishop dies of a stroke and their captors pump his body full of bullets in order to pressure the Dutch government, the committee quickly rationalizes the terrorists' action as a humane alternative to killing one of them, almost as if it ensured their safety.

The intellectuals' capacity for detachment makes them adept at self-criticism: Aileen knows that her motives for going to Iran include a desire to cultivate the eligible senator, Frank suspects that he is running away from his pregnant wife, and Victor Lenz, the CIA stringer sent to watch the others, has no illusions of nobility. Yet self-criticism can paralyze, as Jim Carey knows too well: he was "wary . . . of his brain. . . . It had deterred him, too often, from action by showing him the futility of it" (305). Besides, it has its blind spots. Striving for empathy with the Third World, the American intellectuals usually recast it in their own image as easily as their compatriot Charles Tennant does when he compares a SAVAK torturing device to a toaster (239).

But even Henk, who criticizes Americans for "taking their country for the world" (82), recasts his captors in his image. During his captivity, the married Dutchman falls in love with the American journalist Sophie Weil, but both circumstance and temperament constrain passion. That both agree they will never consummate their love because they do not want it to be "messy" may help explain why readers find the characters shallow. Yet perhaps the point is that Henk, who can submit his own passion to rational discipline, believes that the terrorists can also do so. Fatally, he urges their leader, Jeroen, to discontinue the siege because the Dutch government cannot possibly give in to the demand that it withdraw from NATO and sever diplomatic ties with Israel. What he cannot feel is the suicidal despair this insight induces.

Perhaps like her own characters McCarthy recasts the terrorist in her image; Brightman may be right to find her portrayal of Jeroen romantic (Brightman 594). But the resemblance is not altogether unconvincing, for terrorists often are well-educated people who have lost faith in conventional politics; as Lenin put it scornfully, "Terrorism is the violence of intellectuals." There is an affinity between this man and the committee members; he too is used to thinking in terms of theories and entertaining what may well be delusional notions of changing the world. Jim, at least, thinks so, reflecting on his 1968 challenge to Lyndon Johnson: "He had been as much of a millennialist in hopes as any 'misguided' terrorist. . . . terror was only the kid brother of minority electoral politics" (312). On one Marxist view missionaries and cannibals are much the same species; neither can leave other people alone. However, this rapprochement can only go so far; and oddly we see the critical difference between terrorists and intellectuals in their response to art, rather than in their methods.

As we know, McCarthy was drawn to write about works of art held hostage by the IRA's theft of the "Kenwood House Vermeer" in 1978 and by a series of physical attacks on artworks, including the Mona Lisa and Michelangelo's Pietà, in the 1970s. McCarthy speculated in a lecture that such attacks were fueled by press reports about inflated art prices, which underscored the Marxist perception that artworks are loot. Meditating on whether being surrounded by beautiful objects improves one's character, she concluded that art, unlike music or poetry, induces possessiveness: "the eye is a jealous, concupiscent organ . . . a natural collector, acquisitive, undemocratic, loath to share" ("Living with Beautiful Things" 111). Our subjective experience of joy when we see beauty makes us imagine that we not only feel good but actually are good (122). Yet McCarthy does not need Hermann Goering to discredit this view; look, she says, at museum guards, at art historians, at collectors and critics; look even at people who live in scenic parts of the United States. "Quite poisonous people . . . are attracted by the visual arts and can become very knowledgeable about them"; the residents of Carmel Valley are "vicious" (120, 123).

Why should art, rather than literature, attract poisonous people? The answer for McCarthy lies in the materiality of art, its embodiment in unique objects, in originals. No one minds if other people read Jane Austen; no one expects to be the only person in the audience for Mozart. Yet, as anyone who saw this year's Magritte exhibit can testify, large crowds diminish our pleasure in visual art.

One would expect that Cannibals and Missionaries, which incorporates the themes and language of McCarthy's lecture, would be equally negative about art collectors. But from the beginning they are more silly than despicable, representatives of "old money" who seem even in comparison with college presidents and senators to come from a claustrophobic world of privilege, where everybody has known everybody since their undemanding days at Saint Timothy's. Unlike the terrorists and intellectuals, who focus on the world scene, on food supplies and prison conditions and foreign elections, the collectors lead intensely private lives, their minds filled with impractical and useless knowledge, with, for example, the names of dozens of hybrid roses.

If living with their Vermeers and Cézannes hasn't made them charitable to the poor, their passion for these paintings, which "makes reasoning useless," goes deeper than a desire to preserve negotiable assets (256). Early on it enables them to grasp intuitively that Jeroen will exchange them for their collections, a "nutty example of group-think," to Henk's mind: "these people had become *possessed* by the notion that their art treasures were in danger, without . . . considering it aloud as an objective proposition" (248). It leads Helen Potter, at first glance a mildly ridiculous woman with a "muffin" head, to beg the terrorists to take her whole fortune rather than her Vermeer; when she refuses to comply with their demands, "her dumpy form seem[s] to . . . gain a full inch and not only in moral stature" (249, 256). That she relents when the terrorists threaten her husband increases, rather than diminishes, our admiration. Then, too, McCarthy shows the collectors generally growing throughout the siege: "there was more to [Lily] mentally than had ever been suspected" (287). Freed from the time-consuming tasks of the leisure class—dressing, getting their hair done, having a massage—they finally have the "leisure" to get to know themselves, "which was like making a new acquaintance" (287).

The collectors, in other words, learn to acquire some of the more admirable qualities of McCarthy's intellectuals. Unfortunately, at the same time, Jeroen is becoming more like the jealous concupiscent collectors of her lecture. Before he was a terrorist Jeroen was an artist, an electrician with a love of drawing in whom the masterpieces of the Rijksmuseum inspired "a feeling close to worship" (205). Failing as an artist, he gradually grew to dislike "art for art's sake" and turned instead to the Communist Party and action. But the aesthetic theory he rejected became a political theory he embraced. Although the text seems to be contradictory, occasionally speaking of the hijacking as though it had a practical goal, much of the time Jeroen thinks of terrorism as the political equivalent of art for art's sake. The bourgeoisie, as he sees it, like "*e*volution," but true revolution describes a circle: "the purpose served by the capture of the Boeing was simply the continuance of . . . the original thrust" (226). As committed as any modernist to the autotelic object, he wants nothing from his plot but its perfect embodiment in the world, its "sheer beauty" (227). Specifically, the hijacking is "a work of art," and he is gratified when the "raw materials of bourgeois life, of their own initiative, spr[i]ng forward to collaborate in a revolutionary design" (215).

What undermines this pure commitment to the revolutionary deed is the presence of real art, which McCarthy finds powerful and distinctive. "You have gone back to your first love," his formidable lover, Greet, warns when he decides to take the collectors hostage (224). In a sense, the greatest masterpiece, Helen's beloved Vermeer *Girl*, corrupts this terrorist and sways him from the purity of his design. He falls in love with it, as the Palestinian Ahmed says, "like a bride," spending hours staring at it obsessively. And when Henk produces his reasonable argument for negotiating with the government, Jeroen chooses to blow himself up with the painting in a classic murder-suicide that Ahmed calls "*le geste sublime d'un grand révolutionnaire*" (358); although he does not mean to, he also kills ten other people.

Ahmed's language tells us what Edmund Burke meant when he treated the sublime as an effect of terror: "whatever is fitted in any sort to excite the ideas of pain, and danger . . . or operates in a manner analogous to terror, is a source of the *sublime*; that is, it is productive of the strongest emotion which the mind is capable of feeling." Now in choosing a Vermeer as Jeroen's love object, rather than, say, a Munch or even a Turner, McCarthy deliberately chooses a painter who never strives for the effects of the romantic sublime, a painter of domestic tranquillity. Yet she suggests that the aura of this original, its rarity and unobtainability—only the very rich or a museum can hope to buy a Vermeer— induces a sublime and terrible gesture in a susceptible man. The Basho poem that Henk, Jim, and Ahmed all know by heart offers a momentary sense of unity, encouraging them to transcend their differences. But the rare original, through no fault of its creator, is a costly object that engenders possessive passion.

Now McCarthy's intellectuals, once the exchange of collectors for paintings takes place, also live in the presence of these beautiful objects. But unlike Helen or Jeroen, they remain singularly unaffected; instead of falling in love, or even seeming deeply moved, they conduct lengthy disquisitions about the moral effects of art. Frank relativizes its value—an African might not admire a Vermeer—and finds a cult of originals problematic. Sophie and Henk develop a theory of why a Vermeer painting resembles a photograph; Jim can't appreciate a Cézanne once someone shows him that a figure's arm is "out of drawing" (307). The point is not that McCarthy disagrees; they are parroting ideas she had already set forth in her lecture; but she measures their ineffectuality by the distance separating them from the passions of other people.

In the end, the thriller overtakes the novel of ideas, and violence explodes the decorous mental world the characters have created. The "mayhem," as Brightman notes, seems "incongruous in what is essentially a novel of manners" (593). But then, of course, terrorism always changes the tone, turning a day of shopping at Harrods or a cruise on the *Achille Lauro* into a lurid scene from an alien world. But this ending also shocks because the emotional "shallowness" of McCarthy's characters has given them an air of invulnerability.

Liberals, like terrorists, seem in this novel to make nothing happen; Aileen and Frank, the only two to survive unscathed, are also unchanged. In the novel's last paragraph they are flying back to America, entertained by a movie that features David Niven in a tropical helmet, fighting off urban guerrillas. Doubtless this pessimistic ending echoes McCarthy's own disillusionment in the late 1970s. This traveler to Vietnam knew well the missionary impulse that drives her fictional liberals; yet a decade later, disillusioned not only with North Vietnam but with "politics in general," she told Miriam Gross that "America is horribly sad and discouraging"; though she still believed in "socialism with a human face" she was convinced that "nobody will ever give it a chance" to work (Gross 174). After this *Götterdämmerung* of progressive politics she wrote no more novels; perhaps there was nothing left to be unfaithful to.

WORKS CITED

Brightman, Carol. *Writing Dangerously: Mary McCarthy and Her World.* New York: Clarkson Potter, 1992.

Gross, Miriam. "A World out of Joint." Interview with Mary McCarthy. *The Observer.* (October 14, 1979): 35. Reprinted in Carol Gelderman, *Conversations with Mary McCarthy.* Jackson: University Press of Mississippi, 1991. 170–78.

Kiernan, Frances. "Group Encounter." *The New Yorker.* (June 7, 1993): 56–61.

McCarthy, Mary. *Cannibals and Missionaries.* 1979. New York: Harvest/Harcourt, 1991.

————. *Ideas and the Novel.* New York: Harcourt, 1980.

————. "Living with Beautiful Things." *Occasional Prose.* New York: Harcourt, 1985. 101–126.

6

"*Knowing* Concerns Me": The Female Intellectual and the Consumer Idiom

Jill Wacker

"A good deal of education consists of *un*-learning—the breaking of bad habits as with a tennis serve," wrote Mary McCarthy of the Vassar education that she sometimes felt consisted of little more than smart talk, labels, and pseudo-cleverness (*How I Grew* 203). Many of McCarthy's conclusions about Vassar are more laudatory, yet all are juxtaposed with exhaustive and self-conscious asides about the "right" baked potatoes, baseball players, and rail lines. Some of the class-bound consumer lessons of childhood, for McCarthy, could not be unlearned, even at Vassar. The result is lists. In the autobiographical *How I Grew*, McCarthy lists the books she read as a girl, in school, and at college. She lists train schedules and catalogues the boys she went out with, including one she fell in love with not only because of his "bright-blue eyes," "crisp hair," and "amused mouth," but also as a result of his car, his pipe, and the shoes and socks he wore. "It was his accessories that seduced me," she admits, "as in an advertisement, and they included his name, which, like so many names in Seattle (Armour Spaulding!), seemed pseudonymous, creations of a press agent" (84). When we look to *How I Grew* for a thoughtful tale of artistic development, McCarthy regales us with lists, lessons, and commercial inventories.

Which education is the "real" education for McCarthy—the Vassar education of which she says, "They were trying to teach us to stand on our own" (206), or the consumer education to conformity McCarthy self-deprecatingly concedes that she cannot forget: "how can I as long as *knowing* concerns me" (238)? Are McCarthy and the women she creates in fiction simply bourgeois materialists, or do requests for Log Cabin syrup and Del Monte peaches signal some more complex politics? Again and again, her writing depends on educated young women with the ability to learn the consumer idiom. This chapter explores the connections between testifying to materialism or admitting to educated consumerism and female self-making in much of McCarthy's work. Its inspiration comes from a passage near the end of *How I Grew* that describes the pleasures of transcontinental rail service in the 1930s and outlines McCarthy's negotiation of the politics of consumer education.

All our railroads were proud of their linen napery and the hotcakes they served for breakfast with sausages and lots of maple syrup. Real? I now ask myself. No; most likely, imitation. Probably the catering services reckoned that Far Westerners could not tell the difference. Certainly I myself did not know the difference then between Log Cabin and the real thing. Indeed I thought that Log Cabin *was* the real thing and would faithfully ask for it by name in a grocery store, the way I asked for Del Monte peaches, testifying to my consumer education. (As you can see, Reader, I do not care for that side of myself, which I have not completely shed, however; how can I as long as *knowing* concerns me?) And while we are on that subject, I can quote from Proust, speaking of Swann as one who inherited from a rich and respectable middle-class family "the knowledge of the 'right places' and the art of ordering things from shops" (237).

What some have criticized as the "obsessive irrelevant detail" of McCarthy's autobiographical writing I see as the communication of a specifically female and American idea of intellect.[1] McCarthy was certainly not the first American woman to write about the kinds of limited and limiting empowerment offered by knowledge of brand names, but she wrote much more about the links between female reading, materialism, and politics than most critics seem to have noticed. What is at work here is the tension that McCarthy sensed between the mass-produced nature of the commodity and society's claim that it could represent or express a unique subjectivity for women. McCarthy's reliance on products as referents suggests her acknowledgment of the tensions between the idea of the uniqueness of the intellectual woman, and the idea that her unique subjectivity could be expressed through the purchase and use of mass-produced goods.

Part of the strategy of brand names in her writing is a call for authenticity, a love of detail like that she wrote about in the essay "Fact in Fiction." The language of brand names here is the language of good taste, expert knowledge, "originality," and social distinction. Distinctions between things mirror the kinds of distinctions McCarthy makes between people. The same questions are asked, and copies, forgeries, and fakes are forbidden. The only way to represent an authentic, intelligent American woman is to create an educated consumer. McCarthy did not believe in the kind of democratizing rhetoric employed in advertising and other texts which, through detail, created women as consumers and claimed to be at work democratizing fashion; rather, she challenged such rhetoric, but used consumerist claims to understand herself in autobiography and to create others in fiction. The knowledge that McCarthy details in consumption, including its often technical, mythological, and evaluative components, deserves a less contemptuous and more political interpretation.

Most interesting are the terms in which McCarthy chooses to relate this confession to educated consumerism. Why must she legalize a taste for canned peaches with the word "testify," imply a systematic instruction with careful and limiting modification of "education," and, as if in a final admission of guilt, admit "I do not care for that side of myself"? McCarthy *does* care for that side of herself, and in this chapter I choose to ignore her ironic distance from this kind of commodified communication and instead excavate its origins—the careful cultivation of a kind of knowing that is at base an act of public participation, of enfranchisement offered to those who would otherwise be exiles in the larger consumer society. It is also a kind of class certification. Brand names become passwords for those at the edge. When McCarthy admits that "*knowing* concerns me," she does so in a culpable and proprietary way, and the property at stake in this testimony is the "inheritance" of the trade school of American womanhood. Finally, in that passage from *How I Grew*, McCarthy self-deprecatingly validates her own consumerism with a reminder that she is also a consumer of high culture. This reference to Proust signals more than mastery of some long-ago reading list or insecurity. Not coincidentally, the moment of Proust (the 1910s and 1920s) is the moment of McCarthy's own childhood reading, a moment when the world, especially the American world, was turning to mass production and mass markets.

Locating both McCarthy's guilt about and joy in commodity culture participation historically suggests links to the political climate of the 1930s, an easing of the transition from that era's depression-bred psychology of scarcity to an acceptance of spending in a mid-century culture which insisted on women's primary role as consumers, and finally, the unselfconscious celebration of consumerism that has become the American norm. In *The Company She Keeps*, McCarthy presents the pathetic, poverty-stricken Margaret Sargent as the desperate intellectual woman of the depression era. Her apartment is dingy, her underwear held together with a safety pin. At this point in McCarthy's career, the educated woman must suffer and almost starve to justify her cosmopolitanism, her insistent ignorance of consumer culture. Sargent's reliance on taste without money, finally, has a sort of anorexic middle-class pathos. Her carefully assembled veneer of nonparticipation, McCarthy shows, is just another kind of consumerism. "The Man in the Brooks Brothers Shirt" appears to Sargent "like something in a seed catalogue," yet even he has the skill to choose brand names which win and impress her: Brooks Brothers clothing and a Vassar wife (*The Company She Keeps* 81).

"The Man in the Brooks Brothers Shirt," while not a tale of consumer education, relies on a structure of the kinds of knowing available to women. The story is an inventory of Margaret Sargent's passive knowledge: she *knew* now that New York was not what it had appeared from the viewpoint of a western childhood; she *knew* that there in that rail car she was beautiful and witty, and *knew* that she did not know how to refuse. Instead, she and the avant-garde novel she holds as a prop fall victim to a more ruthless consumer, the suited man whose "connoisseurship" she locates at the "center of things where choice is unlimited" and who chooses her (113). In the absence of self-knowledge, McCarthy's young women construct themselves as consumable. The only feelings Sargent does know are materialized in the objects which surround her and help to create in her the lasting memory value offered by an exquisite product. From the 1930s onward, as many among the vanguard of American industrial designers laid out their personal recipes for a successful styling strategy, one necessary ingredient was mentioned repeatedly—"memory value."[2] Industrial design was largely a task of creating commercially appealing surfaces, but its effectiveness depended upon its ability to touch something deep in the consumer. Product designs, packages, and corporate symbols had to be able to be impressed on the memory, had to endure in the minds of prospective consumers. McCarthy assigns some of this strategy to Margaret Sargent. "She could not be accused of insincerity," argues McCarthy, "unless it could be that her whole way of life had been assumed for purposes of ostentation . . . if it had not been this book, it would have been something else, which would have served equally well to impress a pink middle-aged stranger" (84). The crowning blow in "The Man in the Brooks Brothers Shirt" is the man's self-assurance as shopper, his insistence that Sargent is merely a nice normal girl in exile among misfit intellectuals. For him, her self-creation has no "memory value."

The real interest in "The Man in the Brooks Brothers Shirt" is the memory value assigned minor objects. The brass safety pin Sargent scrambles for the morning after once again symbolizes this woman's participation in consumer culture through lack of participation. Failure to mend becomes a statement of politics. In the bath after her escape from the man's compartment, Sargent experiences a revulsion for the American ethos of consumerism:

All the pretty things she had seen in shops and coveted appeared to her suddenly gross, superfatted, fleshly, even, strangely, unclean. By a queer reversal, the very safety pin in her underwear, which she had blushed for earlier in the morning, came to look to her now like a symbol of moral fastidiousness, just as the sores of a mendicant saint can, if thought of in the right way, testify to his spiritual health (117).

The image of the brass safety pin appears again in McCarthy's work. In "The Fact in Fiction," an essay from a series of talks McCarthy gave in Europe many years after "The Man in the Brooks Brothers Shirt," she recalls questions about the mechanics of her writing practice. This is a pointless question, she says, as boring as the story of flour or the story of a brass safety pin. These stories of the manufacture and marketing of the literary product, McCarthy claims, do not interest her, are at odds with the great books "of a certain thickness" that tell "the story of real life" (*On the Contrary* 250). Yet McCarthy *is* interested in the story of a brass safety pin, telling as it does of the crucial interactions of people with products, the "fetishism of fact" that creates the whaling chapter of *Moby Dick* and the best work of Balzac. Both McCarthy's fiction and McCarthy's autobiography are thick with the things of real life.

One of the things real to McCarthy as an American woman was the proliferation of magazines aimed at selling things to women. In the summer of 1950, McCarthy published a literary history of the supposed democratization of the fashion press in an article called "Up the Ladder from *Charm* to *Vogue*." In this essay, McCarthy creates a taxonomy of women's reading and suggests some of the ideological links between reading and consumerism. She celebrates the unreality of the condescending *Vogue*, where "the actual habits of the American young girl, who smoked and wore lipstick, were excised from consideration and reality was inferior to style" (176). Buying, she argues, is the key to confidence and a stable identity. McCarthy sees through the "rhetoric of fashion as democracy, as an inherent right or manufacturer's guarantee," and has no illusions about the fact that style is still, in 1950, contained in the labor of many hands. Down the ladder from an editorial which rails against fashion and urges readers to determine their own proper style and body weight, a letter from the editor of *Glamour* that suggests "the American girl lives too much on dreams and illusions and proposing impersonal goals" has, according to McCarthy, "the gently remonstrative seriousness of a young woman dean exhorting her alumnae" (190). At the bottom of McCarthy's ladder are magazines like *Charm*, in which editorial content steers toward "a preoccupation with deodorants and personal hygiene." McCarthy's analysis of women's magazines ends with the observation that the idea of women's relationship to the commodification of beauty is an idea of national identity, a "tribute to be extorted from others . . . laid down as an American right, to be fought for, creamed for, depilated and massaged for—more than that, as duty, with ostracism threatened for slackers" (192).

McCarthy's novel *The Group* was published at a very important moment in the history of consumer discourse in America. Written in the 1950s about a group of Vassar College graduates of the 1930s, *The Group* was published in 1963, some four years after Vice President Richard Nixon's Moscow "kitchen debate" with Soviet premier Nikita Khrushchev. Arguing the virtues of American and Soviet washing machines and color televisions in a kitchen set, Nixon and Khrushchev created in the public mind the so-called commodity gap. "We welcome this kind of competition because when we engage in it, no one loses, everyone wins," said Nixon.[3] I will not suggest that the materiality of *The Group* is a direct result of the consumer politics of the Cold War, yet *The Group* does reflect a population fixated on consumption. If McCarthy was unwilling to dismiss consumerism in an era in which William Whyte called thrift "un-American," it was not because her sympathies had suddenly veered toward the consensus. Rather, she was as unwilling as ever to dismiss one of the only areas of knowledge and economic power that had been offered to women. *The Group*'s Kay (who is, to a certain extent, modeled on McCarthy) becomes an insider when a flair for consumer culture and a job at Macy's offer a short-lived sense of belonging. McCarthy's autobiographical sketch of Kay's democratic snobbery, her naive feelings of well-being brought on by new recipes for canned beans or a fresh pot of Maxwell House coffee, ultimately signal the insecurities of women whose intelligence is kept small and tamed, linked to goods. Yet when all else falls apart, there is a solidarity of truth in the fact of commodities. Canned beans become the communicable substance of identity in much of this writing.

The Group has prompted many a contemptuous observation about its domestic details—its recipes and furnishings, from Harald's chili con carne to Norine's conscientiously bohemian lair. Goods surround people with a discourse of their own. Details not only contribute to the reality of the novel but are part of its subject. Kay has, she realizes, "tried to bind [Harald] with possessions."[4] A lot of Kay's talk is about her acquisitions, including Harald, whose brilliance is one of her attributes, part of the success story she sends home. Kay, like Margaret Sargent, has trouble coming to terms with the niceties of things: her seams are crooked at her wedding, and she dies without a suitable dress for burial. Instead, her consumer expertise expresses her ambition, as she keeps up with the latest trends in manufacturing, display, and design. Equally keen is Kay's acceptance of new products, the result of new innovations in industrial design, men "using industrial materials, like the wonderful new spun aluminum, to make all sorts of useful objects like cheese trays and water carafes" (13). Rather than considering her job secondary to her role as consumer. Kay's expertise and enthusiasm inspire her in the work of re-creating Macy's as a cultural institution, "something more than a business, something closer to a civic center or permanent fairgrounds, with educational exhibits, like the old Crystal Palace" (77). In the changing styles of automobiles, appliances, clothing, and department stores, we confront a visual representation of passing time in McCarthy's work. Fragmentary and essentially stylistic representations of an era, these transvaluations of memory are significant. As style becomes a rendition of social history, it silently and ineluctably transforms that history from a process of human conflict and motivations, an engagement between social interests and forces, into a market mechanism, a fashion show.

The world of *The Group* is a world in which style has emerged as the predominant expression of meaning. Kay's apartment reflects a bad marriage, and the Group reads its deficit in its inadequacies: no rugs, blinds instead of curtains, ivy instead of flowers, a mattress and box spring instead of a bed. These Vassar girls are able to express what they find missing only in identifying material lack. Similarly, the apartment attributed to Norine, a predator who derides materialism, is a place where

every item in it seemed to be saying something, asserting something, pontificating; Norine and Put were surrounded by articles of belief, down to the last can of evaporated milk and the single, monastic pillow on the double bed. It was different from Kay's apartment, where the furniture was only asking to be admired or talked *about*. . . . But here in this dogmatic lair, nothing had been admitted that did not make a "relevant statement" (162).

When one of the Group challenges Norine to clean up her act with toilet paper, Clorox, and a new dress, Norine strikes back. "Notice your stress on bourgeois acquisition, on mere things" she says. "You don't touch on the basic things. The intangibles" (180). As a form of information (or disinformation), style places these women on slippery and dangerous ground. Where style has become a visible world of memorable "facts," easily appended as a facade to almost anything, it has emerged as a powerful element in what Herbert Marcuse once described as "the closing of the universe of discourse."[5] As style becomes increasingly ubiquitous, other ways of knowing, alternative ways of seeing, become scarce. As Norine tells the Group, "You're hipped on forms, while I'm concerned with meanings," McCarthy sketches the ground zero of noncommunication (180).

The Group is rife with the life histories of objects. Perhaps the most memorable is that of the contraceptive device procured by Dottie, a commodity which negotiates the gendering of consumer education. Convinced that a man's instruction to "get herself a pessary" signals "the language of love," Dottie sets out for what will be an enlightening lesson in consumerism and conspicuous consumption (59). Thinking about the fellow's definition of women as those fond of "money, change, excitement, things, clothes, and possessions," she wonders whether she has lost her virginity to a man "who sounded, from his own description, like a pretty bad hat" (62). McCarthy surrounds this entire episode with a rhetoric of knowing and education drawn from the counters of the department store. The man argues that he hates possessions, while Dottie is perfectly content to see herself as an acquisition, the right kind of possession, what she calls a "true" possession, or incentive. Without possessions as incentives, she says, people would still be living in caves. The man laughs and says, "You must be the fiftieth woman who has said that to me. It's a credit to universal education that whenever a girl meets Dick Brown she begins to talk about the wheel and the lever" (63).

Later, at the clinic where Dottie goes to procure the diaphragm, she sees her own consumer zealotry reflected in the furnishings of the doctor's office, full of copies of magazines like *Harper's* and *Consumer's Research Bulletin*. "Knowledge was responsible for her composure," McCarthy reminds us, providing a history of the device, which "had the backing of the whole US medical profession; it had been found by Margaret Sanger in Holland and was now for the first time being imported in quantity into the USA, where our own manufacturers could copy it" (64). The whole trip to the birth control clinic, tagged by Kay's husband Harald as "profiteering" for women of their class, in fact mimics the luxury of the labor of many hands such women might feel at a dressmaker's in its trappings: the fitting, the advice of several experts, instruction, and personal attention. The exotic, imported device is tailored, specially cared for, a perfect fit. The scene is as antidemocratic as the fashion McCarthy describes in "Up the Ladder from *Charm* to *Vogue*." "This sense of the accrued labor of others as a complement to one's personality," writes McCarthy, "as tribute in a double sense, is intrinsic to the fashionable imagination, which desires to feel that labor next to its skin, in the hidden stitching of its underwear—hence the passion for handmade lingerie even among women whose outer clothing comes off the budget rack" (*On the Contrary* 177). The contraceptive is the thing that will tie Dottie both to her lover and to the rest of society. Kay's husband Harald provides an analysis of the diaphragm as signifier. This he calls "the fetishism of property" (69). One of the novel's long-standing resentments is the men who trespass the halls of female consumer education. Nothing is more preposterous than the rhetoric of progress and class eclipse surrounding Harald's discussion of canned goods.

To have a man, an "eternal pedagogue," as McCarthy would say, claim to have discovered the new Corn Niblets is the final affront (*How I Grew* 209).

This economy of things, this narrowing of communication, becomes, in McCarthy's world, a gendered language, and a language of life experience. I take McCarthy's testifying to consumer education as a historical statement, a contextualization that returns, at base, to a childhood reading of magazines. The magazine fiction of McCarthy's childhood often focused on teaching readers, especially female readers, to read possessions for clues to character and status. This publishing explosion of the early twentieth century also encouraged readers to buy the products that would create them as capable consumers and readers of this language of signs. What this literature aimed at girls and young women sold was not just a single product, or even a group of products, but the role of consumer. The kind of reading McCarthy so exhaustively recounts in memoirs like *How I Grew* was instrumental in creating the McCarthy sensibility, a sensibility evolved to offer at once a valorization of consumerist choice making and the often unflattering portraits of young women with knowledge and authority who self-deprecatingly communicate their intellect through the savvy of smart shoppers.

McCarthy's autobiographical lists record shortages and surfeits of reading matter. The shortage of books in her grandmother's Minneapolis house was compensated for by other kinds of reading matter: funny papers, the Sunday magazine section, religious periodicals like *Extension* and *Our Sunday Visitor*. This same world of book hunger is a world constructed by an ungiving grandmother who populates her world with inviolable things, the self-creation of a woman whose "home was a center of power, and she would not allow it to be derogated by easy or democratic usage" (*Memories of a Catholic Girlhood* 34). Here, McCarthy describes a childhood of Catholicism "cheapened and debased by mass production" and peppered with attempts to secrete magazines of Catholic fiction under her mattress. The prohibition against reading laid out by McCarthy's Minneapolis relatives is matched in Seattle by McCarthy's other grandmother, who spends every afternoon shopping, and is interested only in "the latest wrinkle," news from the fashion front. In Seattle, McCarthy gobbled books and magazines, her omnivorous appetite for literary consumption pushing her to make her grandfather subscribe for her (in his name) to a magazine called *The American Boy*. Later, she admits, she turned to the more adult reading of the mass market: *True Story, True Confessions,* and movie magazines, in which she studied ads for trusses and bust cream (*Memories of a Catholic Girlhood* 26). These lists of childhood books are McCarthy's memories of herself as a consumer. Just as no Vassar girl could be the same after consuming the name brands "Kitchel's English" and "Sandison's Shakespeare," no American girl could be the same after assimilating the stuff of magazine advertisements. She creates an identity through consumption, translating her story into the communicable substance of the books on her shelf.

McCarthy's work raises questions about the kinds of knowledge which have offered women legitimacy in America. For most of the century, with the exception of avant-garde intellectuals and a small number of politically active feminists, few women were able to articulate alternatives to a consciousness hung up on "knowing" about brand names or to resist attempts to alleviate misery with goods. McCarthy expresses an unabashed joy at being able to enact her childhood study of *Vogue*, yet her resilient belief in the potential for individualism and upward mobility stand in contrast to the painful contradictions of a society in which female success and enculturation are measured by the depth with which women assimilate and learn to surround themselves with the right commodities. In the piecing together of *How I Grew*, we see the framing of McCarthy's perverse pride in her knowledge of brand names as a complicated acceptance of models of selfhood from a culture in which limits are put on the female intellect.

NOTES

1. Sonya Rudikoff recounts the irritation of reviewers who found *How I Grew* inconsequential, citing the memoir's "obsessive irrelevant detail" in "An American Woman of Letters," *Hudson Review* 42 (1989–1990): 53.

2. On the subject see critiques of the mid-century culture of consumption, such as Vance Packard, *Hidden Persuaders* (New York: D. McKay, 1957), and Walter Teague, *Land of Plenty* (New York: Hall, 1947).

3. See Elaine Tyler May's reading of the "kitchen debate" in *Homeward Bound: American Families in the Cold War Era* (New York: Basic Books, 1988), 162–64.

4. Mary McCarthy, *The Group* (New York: Harcourt, Brace, Jovanovich, 1963), 14. All further references will be to this edition and will be documented in the text.

5. Herbert Marcuse, "The Closing of the Universe of Discourse," in *One Dimensional Man: Studies in the Ideology of Advanced Industrial Society* (Boston: Beacon, 1964), 84–122.

WORKS CITED

McCarthy, Mary. *The Company She Keeps*. New York: Harcourt, 1942.
———. *How I Grew*. New York: Harcourt, 1987.
———. *Memories of a Catholic Girlhood*. New York: Harcourt, 1957.
———. *On the Contrary*. New York: Farrar, 1962.

II

Questions of Politics
and Religion

7

Nicola Chiaromonte, the *politics* Circle, and the Search for a Postwar "Third Camp"

Gregory D. Sumner

Historians have long been accustomed to viewing the middle and late 1940s as a period of retrenchment and defeat for the American Left, a time when "deradicalized" intellectuals, bereft of new ideas, moved quickly to embrace the liberal anticommunist consensus solidifying by the end of the decade. But although World War II did irreparable damage to the Old Left's dreams of working-class revolution, this did not mean the end of all hope for fundamental challenges to the status quo. One group that tried, for a time, to mount such a challenge, to articulate a peaceful and democratic "third camp" alternative to what they called the "monstrous inertia" of the developing Cold War, was the transatlantic network of writers gathered around Dwight Macdonald's "little magazine," *politics*. Inspired by the ethos of the European antifascist resistance, as personified by figures like George Orwell, Albert Camus, and Hannah Arendt, this group recognized that the preceding years of violence and upheaval had perhaps, paradoxically, fostered unique opportunities for a fresh start. Mary McCarthy, Macdonald's friend and confidant since their days together at *Partisan Review*, spoke for others in their circle when she recalled,

After the war was the very best period, politically, that I've been through. The war was over! Certain mistakes had been realized. The political scene looked free. It seemed possible still, utopian but possible, to change the world on a small scale (Gelderman, *Conversations* 15–16).

McCarthy's ideas about small-scale change began to take shape during the last stages of World War II, when the conflict seemed to degenerate into a mindless orgy of violence beyond all constraint, producing, in Macdonald's memorable formulation, "the maximum devastation accompanied by the minimum human meaning" ("Atrocities" 227). As the terror bombing of civilians escalated, and the dimensions of the Nazi Holocaust became unavoidable, the faith in inevitable human "progress" axiomatic to the dominant ideologies of the day, conservative, liberal, and Marxist alike, appeared more and more bankrupt to the members of the *politics* community. In flight from old orthodoxies, and looking for ways to oppose the forces of a catastrophic history, McCarthy and Macdonald encountered Nicola Chiaromonte, an Italian refugee writer whose impact was to prove lasting and profound. As McCarthy later told biographer Carol Brightman, "talking with . . . Chiaromonte was an absolute awakening, and I never got over it" (*Conversations* 241).

It was during a holiday retreat on Cape Cod in the late summer of 1945—the "Hiroshima summer," which McCarthy would remember as "a watershed, a dividing line"—that she and Macdonald became enthralled by the quiet wisdom of this "dark, handsome man who looked like a monk" (Gelderman, *Mary McCarthy* 122–123). They enjoyed their respite from New York City and from the relentless headlines of the war by sharing moonlit picnics on the beach, reading Shakespeare, and discussing modern literature and philosophy. In this "monastic" isolation, Chiaromonte found a receptive audience for his passions: the ethical vision of Tolstoy, the anarchism of Proudhon, and the classical Greek conception of limit eloquently defended in an age of totalitarianism by Simone Weil, an obscure French writer whose works he had discovered while on the run from Hitler's armies in 1940. Carol Gelderman describes how on many days McCarthy "could be spotted on the beach with her typewriter, pounding out a translation of Weil's essay *The 'Iliad,' or the Poem of Force*" (Gelderman, *Mary McCarthy* 123) a critique of ideological messianism that appeared in Macdonald's journal several months later, symbolic of *politics*' new direction.

What was it these Americans found so compelling in Chiaromonte? For McCarthy, as presumably also for Macdonald, it was "a kind of seriousness, a kind of thoughtfulness" she found lacking in the internecine feuds of the New York literary world, insulated as it was from direct exposure to the radical evil at large across the Atlantic. Chiaromonte exhibited the same bracing moral "seriousness" characteristic of another émigré she befriended in the 1940s,

Hannah Arendt. "[W]hat I was listening to on the beach," McCarthy later concluded, "was Europe" (Gelderman, *Conversations* 241, 249).

What was Chiaromonte's "program"? Amid a world of technological and bureaucratic dehumanization, of superstates engaged in wars of mutual annihilation, he asserted that "mass" political organization was corrupting and counterproductive, and that traditional romantic notions about violent revolution were now more dangerously obsolete than ever. In this "zero hour" for Western civilization, Chiaromonte offered a strategy for resistance modeled upon the clandestine international networks he had been involved with since his youthful days in the anti-Mussolini underground. The place to begin working for a better future, he insisted, was in the realm of civil society, the intimate sphere of human relationships "outside"—or "beneath"—the arena of conventional power politics. A post-Marxist "new left" had to start small and work organically, across national boundaries and other artificial barriers, to promote changes in the moral and social climate as a precondition to genuine institutional reforms. Chiaromonte's mentor, the anarchist Andrea Caffi, summarized this approach in a 1947 letter from Paris:

Today the multiplication of groups of friends, sharing the same anxieties and united by respect for the same values, would have much more importance than a huge propaganda machine (Caffi 28).

Chiaromonte's message about the need to create human-scaled, grassroots, *transnational* communities of dialogue and solidarity as a counterweight to centralized aggregations of power received ominous confirmation in early August, when word of the atomic bomb shattered the tranquillity of the Cape Cod retreat. McCarthy's shock and disorientation at that moment were undoubtedly typical:

I remember reading the news of Hiroshima in a little general store on Cape Cod . . . , and saying to myself as I moved up to the counter, "What am I doing buying a loaf of bread?" The coexistence of the great world and us, when contemplated, appears impossible ("The Fact in Fiction" 267).

McCarthy and her friends returned home with a heightened sense of urgency about the need to transform and reconstruct modern society from the ground up.

In the months that followed the war's demoralizing conclusion, the members of the *politics* circle thought hard about how to create the basis for an international "new left" along the lines Chiaromonte (and Caffi) envisioned. The initiative they decided upon emerged from a series of discussions between

Chiaromonte, Dwight Macdonald, and Albert Camus, who visited New York in the spring of 1946 on a fund-raising tour for the French government. Camus, the young writer who embodied the aspirations of the "Resistance" generation in Europe, had for some time been pondering his own version of a third-camp "peace movement," made up of diverse "communities of thought," existing "outside of parties and governments," linked together across national boundaries (Camus 141).

Macdonald enthusiastically offered the resources of *politics* magazine for the project, and by early 1948 he had drafted, with Mary McCarthy, a statement of principles for an organization they called "Europe-America Groups" (EAG). Chiaromonte, returning to the continent after years of exile, agreed to serve as EAG's foreign liaison. Various New York intellectuals, representing a wide ideological spectrum, signed a document that began as follows:

We are a group of individuals . . . who have gotten together to provide some center of solidarity with and support for intellectuals in Europe who find themselves outside the mass parties. Like ourselves [they] are isolated not only from the great power blocs that divide the world, but also to a large extent from each other (Lottman 458–59).

The founders intended Europe-America Groups to provide the informal lines of communication and mutual assistance necessary for a cosmopolitan, dissident subculture to take root and mature. Through its multiplying networks, EAG would be devoted to defending human rights, to keeping institutional power in check, and, above all, to challenging the nationalist polarization that seemed to be dragging the world toward a final nuclear conflagration.

The project began with a flurry of activity in the spring of 1948. With McCarthy as chairperson, EAG held meetings, sponsored public debates, and raised funds, which were sent to Chiaromonte to be distributed as he reestablished contacts with his Resistance friends from before the war. But despite its early promise, and numerous expressions of interest from Europe, the initiative foundered, due to a lack of internal consensus about its goals. The familiar and irreconcilable split quickly manifested itself. The Macdonald-McCarthy-Chiaromonte faction was sincerely interested in a nonaligned alternative to the Cold War, one that would be critical of the West as well as the Soviet bloc. Those gathered around *Partisan Review* editors Philip Rahv and William Phillips, in contrast, were already by this time well on the way to the "vital center" of liberal anticommunism. The "*PR* Boys" did their best at every turn to either sabotage EAG or take it over for their own ends, to remake it into a vehicle like the Congress for Cultural Freedom (launched two years later). The hoped-for collaboration with Camus and his circle broke down as well. He was too involved in other activities in Paris to devote much attention to building a transatlantic "new left," and his *Groupes de Liaison Internationale* disintegrated with the same kind of factional squabbling that destroyed its sister organization in New York.

The collapse of Europe-America Groups caused especially deep anguish for Mary McCarthy. In July 1958 she wrote to Macdonald of her "shame at the seriousness of the European response to our very trivial and muddling efforts." Her words poignantly convey the sense of paralysis many others must have felt in that period. "Our American political condition [is] appallingly inert and footless," she continued.

I am absolutely sick of the way I am living, the lack of accomplishment . . . , and one year succeeding another with nothing's being changed. . . . [S]omething must be done; this *drift* is fearfully demoralizing (Letter).

McCarthy took out her frustrations at the aborted project by satirizing the experience. Her 1949 novel *The Oasis* chronicled the attempt by a group of urban intellectuals to establish a model cooperative community in the backwoods of New England, an endeavor inspired by the ideals of a heroic Italian anarchist named "Monteverdi." The experiment was doomed from the start, however, by the disputes that inevitably arose between a "Utopian" faction headed by "Macdougal Macdermott," the combative editor of a libertarian magazine, and the "Realists" aligned behind "Will Taub," a thinly disguised and not especially flattering version of Philip Rahv. In the end, McCarthy's message seemed to be that moral action, problematic enough on an individual level, remained an even more complex and elusive affair in the context of social relations.

By 1950 the Cold War appeared firmly entrenched, and Macdonald's *politics* magazine was among the casualties of the exhaustion of hopes for a way out. McCarthy's efforts in 1953 to revive discussion of "utopian" alternatives through a new, internationally oriented monthly, *Critic*, came to naught because of funding problems, and for the next decade she, Macdonald, and Chiaromonte each turned away from public engagement with the arid world of politics to focus on cultural criticism. Through it all they maintained, across the Atlantic, the kind of intimate "sibling" relationship they had forged during that fateful summer at the Cape in the mid-1940s, sharing vacations, exchanging gossip, and debating the latest issues. During the turbulent 1960s the three returned to the arena of political controversy. They concurred on the egregious folly of Vietnam, but Chiaromonte disagreed sharply with Macdonald's qualified sympathy for the student New Left, which he saw as merely another expression of reflexive, nihilistic rebellion, given its penchant for glib slogans and violent rhetoric. Chiaromonte's brand of humanism was a more demanding one. After

his death in 1972, McCarthy aptly wrote of her mentor, "His ideas did not fit
into an established category: he was neither on the left nor on the right. Nor
did it follow that he was in the middle; he was alone ("Preface" xv).

Like other "third camp" initiatives of the postwar years, Europe-America
Groups, the *politics* circle's effort to lay the foundations for a transatlantic "new
left," failed almost before it began. But Chiaromonte's idea of an international
dissident subculture, devoted to certain principles of dialogue and flourishing
"outside" official institutions, still has merit—especially now that the Cold War
has finally ended. This approach bears striking affinities to the "antipolitical"
strategies recently pursued, with stunning success, by Central European activ-
ists like Vaclav Havel and Gyorgy Konrad, and it certainly holds lessons for us
as we confront the crisis of democracy that is everywhere so apparent today. As
the new order proceeds through its traumatic birth, driven "from above" by
the often dehumanizing imperatives of state and corporate power, it may be
time to explore once again the possibilities for activity on a "small scale" that
so captured the imagination of Mary McCarthy and her friends on that
summer holiday half a century ago.

WORKS CITED

Caffi, Andrea. "Violence and Sociability." *politics* 4 (January 1947): 23–28.
Camus, Albert. "Neither Victims nor Executioners." *politics* 4 (July/August 1947):
    141–47.
Chiaromonte, Nicola. *The Worm of Consciousness and Other Essays*. New York:
    Harcourt, 1976.
Gelderman, Carol, ed. *Conversations with Mary McCarthy*. Jackson: University Press
    of Mississippi, 1991.
———. *Mary McCarthy: A Life*. New York: St. Martin's, 1988.
Lottman, Herbert. *Albert Camus: A Biography*. Garden City, New York: Doubleday,
    1979.
Macdonald, Dwight. "Atrocities of the Mind." *politics* 2 (August 1945): 227.
———. "Comment." *politics* 1 (May 1944): 102.
McCarthy, Mary. "The Fact in Fiction." *On the Contrary*. New York: Farrar, 1961.
    249–270.
———. Letter to Dwight and Nancy Macdonald. July 1948. Dwight Macdonald
    Papers, Yale University.
———. *The Oasis*. New York: Random House, 1949.
———. "Preface." Chiaromonte, Nicola. *The Worm of Consciousness*. xiii–xvi.
———, trans. *The "Iliad," or the Poem of Force*. By Simone Weil. *politics* 2 (Novem-
    ber 1945): 321–31; *politics* Pamphlet 1 (1945).
Weil, Simone. *The "Iliad," or the Poem of Force*. Translated by Mary McCarthy.
    politics 2 (November 1945): 321–31; *politics* Pamphlet 1 (1945).

8

Reimagining Politics
Harvey Teres

In his minor classic *Politics and the Novel,* published in 1957 and recently reissued, the late and sorely missed Irving Howe endorsed the Jamesian thesis concerning the thinness of American culture and its inability to sustain a rich novelistic tradition. Very "few American writers," observed Howe,

have tried to see politics as a distinctive mode of social existence, with values and manners of its own. . . . Those massive political institutions, parties, and movements which in the European novel occupy the space between the abstractions of ideology and the intimacies of personal life are barely present in America.

Americans, Howe claimed, were "bored or repelled" by politics, however tempted they may have been:

The Americans failed, and they could not help but fail, to see political life as an autonomous field of action. . . . Personalizing everything, they could not quite do justice to the life of politics in its own right, certainly not the kind of justice done by the European novelists. Personalizing everything, they could brilliantly observe how social and individual experience melt into one another so that the deformations of the one soon become the deformations of the other (162–63).

Howe went on to discuss whatever circumscribed political life there was to be found in Hawthorne's *The Blithedale Romance,* Henry Adams's *Democracy,* and Henry James's *The Bostonians*. He brought his account into the twentieth century with some very brief remarks on Dos Passos's *USA*, Trilling's *The Middle of the Journey*, and Robert Penn Warren's *All the King's Men*. The chapter in which these novels were discussed was duly entitled "The Politics of Isolation."

Howe's understanding of politics gave priority to the often violent, sometimes cataclysmic confrontation between ideologies, movements, parties, and powerful individuals. Since his study was written in the wake of totalitarian violence and during the depths of the Cold War, this should not surprise us. But this concern with apocalyptic politics foreclosed other possibilities, as Howe himself has acknowledged in the preface to the 1992 edition. Here he expresses regret over having neglected the novels of Eliot, Meredith, and Trollope—"which portray the political life of a settled society, that is, a society in which the usual interplay of group conflicts is regulated by democratic procedures" (7–8). Had he examined these writers, no doubt his vision of the political novel would have been enhanced by greater attention to the nuances of politics in ordinary life.

But there is another category of experience—the ordinariness of political life—that seems to elude even this approach. For Howe, even the novel about settled societies "still tests extreme situations, the drama of harsh and ultimate conflicts." Yet what of the common situations, the drama of harsh and seemingly *trivial* conflicts, the small but salient encounters among the politically involved that allow us to take the measure of their ideals in light of their personal lives, instead of vice versa?

It seems to me that Mary McCarthy performed this political task exceedingly well. How ironic that this so-called dark lady was so named because, to paraphrase Adorno, she insisted upon illuminating the crevices of the body politic. She showed us life before and life after the climaxes: not the manifesto but the writing of it; not the political rally but the trip home. From her unique vantage point she observed from below the people who claimed to observe history from below. She demonstrated that politics is ordinary. Not only does she deserve to be taken seriously as a writer of political fiction, but she should be given credit for having deepened and enlarged the very tradition of political fiction Irving Howe has adumbrated.

I want to touch on these distinctive attributes of Mary McCarthy's fiction, especially as they shaped her understanding of the dynamics and liabilities of American literary radicalism. This may strike some as an unpromising framework within which to discuss McCarthy, since much of her critical and imaginative work has been thought to fall outside of this political rubric. Yet I would argue that a fundamental implication of much of McCarthy's fiction is that our normative understanding of political life has been too narrow. It has excluded experience that in reality not only shapes politics from without but informs it from within.

As I have suggested, it is with the everyday that McCarthy's fiction dwells, where contingency mixes with chance, determinism combines with will, convention merges with dissent, and ideals run into practicalities. It is the personal side of politics she has explored, in the process giving meaning *avant la lettre* to the phrase "the personal is political." In doing so, however, she has not simply portrayed private life as ideological epiphenomena; rather she has turned life loose on the ideological, revealing the chinks in the armor of radical intellectuals whose personal lives have been riven by lapses of character. This "dark lady" sheds light on a great deal: marriage, divorce, sexuality, abortion, maternity, adultery—in short, the quality of personal interaction among progressive intellectuals and the texture of the culture they surround themselves with. It goes without saying that such an exploration challenges abstraction, dogmatism, and arrogance on the Left. It also inquires into the manner in which the Left, always concerned with organizing others, organizes itself.

Among McCarthy's many books that deal with the interaction between politics and personal life, *The Oasis* is perhaps the most direct. (Unfortunately, this "veritable little masterpiece," in the words of Hannah Arendt, remains out of print.) As is well known, two of the novella's main characters, leaders of factions within a New England utopian community, were modeled after prominent New York intellectuals: Macdougal Macdermott, head of the purists, was Dwight Macdonald in disguise; Will Taub, head of the realists, was Philip Rahv. Indeed the two factions, as Alan Wald has pointed out, resemble somewhat the two groups that formed within the *Partisan Review* circle over the issue of whether and how to support the Allied war effort during World II (241). More recently, Carol Gelderman (139–48) and Carol Brightman (305–17) have suggested that the two wings of the Europe-America Groups, with their differences on how to create a third alternative to capitalism and communism, provide the more relevant context.

At any rate, in the novel these matters are transmuted into the less portentous but in many ways more revealing debates over whether the utopians should admit a businessman into their midst, and how the group should deal with an impoverished family who trespasses onto their property and picks their ripe, wild strawberries. Like so much effective satire, the exquisite humor of the novel derives precisely from the incongruity between grandiose ideals on the one hand, and mundane circumstances on the other. In the end it is not the circumstances that seem trivial at all, but rather the leaders with their self-important pronouncements and endless machinations. By thus preferring to explore the consequences of ideas rather than simply their content, and by insisting on inquiring into the motives, styles, and attitudes of those who hold them, McCarthy presents the reader with one of our most discerning and comprehensive examinations of the morals and manners of the American Left, or at least an important portion thereof.

For McCarthy, morals and manners inevitably involve gender. Although never explicitly stated in the novel, the incessant discussions and debates that take place among the utopians constitute a masculine discourse, one that prevails until the story's heroine, Katy Norell, offers an alternative at the very end. Until then, women are obviously subordinated by the commune's male leaders. When Eleanor Macdermott, for example, interjects her opinion into the discussion about whether to admit the businessman Joe Lockman into the community (her rather vapid contribution is "And what is Utopia but the right to a human existence?"), her husband responds enthusiastically: " 'Eleanor's right!' Mac shouted, slapping his knee in delighted admiration. He applauded his wife thunderously, as if she were a team of acrobats, whenever she performed what to him was the extraordinary feat of arriving at a balanced opinion" (11). The wife of the other leader, Will Taub, is also regularly diminished by her husband. Taub exits the same discussion, his wife in tow, as follows: " 'We'll go,' he abruptly announced, tapping his wife familiarly on the shoulder, as if to apprise her that a show was about to begin into which he had privately written a sardonic star part for himself. His wife, inured to surprises, merely raised her penciled eyebrows" (14). When the men consider expelling Joe Lockman for jokingly sneaking up on Taub with a gun and embarrassing him, the wives are not included (although Susan Hapgood, a wide-eyed young novelist who venerates Taub, is). When it is suggested that the next meeting be held in "the chieftain's living-room" (Taub's), his "male associates rumina-tively nodded their large heads in concord" at the prospect of stacking the meeting against Macdermott, who usually succeeds in meeting at his home because of his children (apparently his wife attends the meetings). One of the men readily volunteers his wife's services: "[Danny] Furnas now spoke up to remind them that his wife was assistant to a pediatrician. . . . 'Helen will be glad to stay with the kids' " (46).

But McCarthy goes beyond depicting the men's complicity in subordinating and objectifying women. Indeed, one gathers from McCarthy's fiction that such dynamics are so pervasive and commonplace in society that calling attention to them with any regularity leads to predictability, stridency, and boredom, all enemies of good writing. Nor is she given to depicting women who resist patriarchal power and are therefore to be taken as inspiring heroines. Most of her women, as critics have long noted, have internalized their inferior status, and are plagued by self-doubt, self-contempt, guilt, dependence, and competition with other women. Nonetheless, some of McCarthy's profoundly conflicted women manage to create for themselves a degree of independence and self-knowledge that is, for the most part, admirable.

In *The Oasis*, it is Katy Norell who is capable of bringing fresh insights to bear on the stale alternatives proffered by the men. To be sure, she is hardly a tower of strength. In one of the novel's more important incidents she is singed when she attempts to light a stove, which Joe Lockman has mistakenly filled with oil. Instead of taking full responsibility for the accident and thereby protecting from possible expulsion the man whom she and her husband are in effect sponsoring, she tries to minimize what remains his mistake: " 'It was only an accident,' she said finally, in a feeble and unveracious voice. 'Somebody was careless and left the oil turned up without lighting the stove' " (37). Her husband Preston is furious with her:

Preston Norell's long fingers dropped from his wife's arm, and he pushed his way out in disgust. For those words *only* and *somebody*, he wished her in hell. . . .

She was following him out now; he could hear her footsteps running behind him; she caught him just beyond the lawn, her face distorted with tears, which he could envision with perfect distinctness while keeping his eyes averted. "Forgive me," she cried. "Forgive me!" Plainly, she was not going to pretend, as she sometimes did, not to know how she had offended; the others were watching curiously, and he perceived, with a certain savage satisfaction, that she felt she must deflect him from whatever course he was planning, before their rupture was public. "Go in and get the breakfast," he said sternly, shaking his arm free. "Pull yourself together. You disgust me" (38–39).

Yet Katy Norell's greatest humiliation comes when she is forgiven. Despite the fact that following her husband's outburst she "had made a great resolution to resign herself to his condemnation . . . to take it, that is, seriously," when he suddenly decides to forgive her (wickedly portrayed by McCarthy as the result of being inspired on the porch as he gazes into the New England sublime), she immediately relents:

She did not know what to say. "Do I really disgust you?" she whispered, looking nervously behind her in the direction of Eleanor Macdermott. "Yes!" he cried emphatically, but with a shout of laughter; the conspiratorial manner of the question struck him as splendidly farcical—in his very tenderest moments, he looked upon Katy as a comedian. He now relented and patted her sharply on the buttocks. Katy returned to her work, in some peculiar fashion well pleased; though she had broken her resolution and come off with nothing to show for it, it seemed to her undeniable that she had acted for the best (44).

These painful passages are typical of McCarthy, who out of hatred of oppression and impatience with women exposes with relentless and morbid exactitude every grim inflicted and self-inflicted wound. As indicated earlier, this is perhaps especially true when the wounds result in destructive behavior. This is a concern and at times an obsession in McCarthy that can be taken as misogynistic, but which does after all describe some women. Moreover, because McCarthy's men are often more seriously flawed and certainly more dangerous than her women, one needs to take care when arguing that McCarthy's interest in women's weaknesses can be understood as mysogynistic. But surely McCarthy sometimes suggests that weakness can become a source of strength. In the case of Katy Norell, weakness provides the basis for uncommon insight and even evolving character. It is Katy's voice, after all, sometimes alone and sometimes in close association with the narrator's, with which the novel ends. Her voice represents a third alternative to what Marguerite Duras has called "the theoretical rattle of men" (100). The stale debate among the men is over how to handle the poachers—by threatening force or pacifically. Unlike the voices of the men, Katy's projects understanding and composure (maybe too much composure due to her state of inebriation). At any rate hers is a voice that is by all appearances sincere. Her ideas seem to emerge directly out of her feelings, and thus there is no hint that they are manufactured by a haunted intellect. Able to silence Taub for the first time, she declares,

"You conceive the problem incorrectly. . . . If the problem is to get rid of the berry-pickers, it follows that force is the answer—to that extent, you are right. Ultimately, it will have to be resorted to, if they will not respond to moral coercion, which is simply force still withheld. But," she went on, growing more excited, "supposing there is no problem, but simply an event: the berry-pickers are in the meadow; the sun is in the sky. If you do not wish to eject them, there is no problem, there is only an occurrence."

Taub shrugged; he did not understand what she was getting at (91).

Katy goes on to claim as virtuous "the body and the body's objects," until, that is, they become the object of "a mental desire"—presumably any abstract, doctrinal, possessive, or power-enhancing desire. Lying on the grass, her hand entwined with her husband's,

[S]he recognized, with a new equanimity, that her behavior would never suit her requirements, not to mention the requirements of others; and while she did not propose to sink, therefore, into inequity or to institutionalize her frailties in the manner of the realist faction, still, seen in this unaccustomed light, the desire to *embody* virtue appeared a shallow and vulgar craving, the refracted error of a naive and acquisitive culture which imagined that there was nothing—beauty, honor, titles of nobility, charm, youth, happiness—which persistency could not secure (93).

In the end she sees the colony itself, with its "cycles of recession and recovery," as "a kind of factory or business for the manufacture and export of morality." Although she envisions no alternative, it is hard to believe she will remain the cooperative, subordinate citizen she has been in the past.

How much of the "manufacture and export of morality" we are meant to associate with male domination remains unclear. Certainly McCarthy has not gone as far as contemporary feminists in their efforts to demarcate what is masculine and deficient about the dominant culture (and, for that matter, adversary cultures). Nor has she been as interested in defining what is unique and salutary about the experiences women share.

Nevertheless, McCarthy's critique in *The Oasis* runs deep, and its consequences spread to wherever gender touches upon the culture of radicalism. It calls attention to the exclusion of women, to the enfeebling of women, to the unhappiness of women. It mocks habits of mind such as abstraction, idealism, combativeness, and rigidity, which, if they are not necessarily shown to originate in male prerogative, nonetheless enhance it.

So let us, finally, put behind us those words that have been used to characterize McCarthy in the past, "words like knives, stilettos, switch-blades, cold, heartless, clever, cerebral, cutting, acid, or acidulous" (Gelderman xi). In *The Oasis* Mary McCarthy performed precise surgery on the American Left, and she found malignancies. Today the patient is barely alive, not because McCarthy's care constituted malpractice, but because the Left has since replaced her with more benign physicians who avoid surgery at all costs. Suffice it to say, there is a great need today for those with talent and courage to emulate McCarthy by wielding the life-saving knife.

WORKS CITED

Brightman, Carol. *Writing Dangerously: Mary McCarthy and Her World*. New York: Clarkson Potter, 1992.

Duras, Marguerite. *La Création étouffée*. Quoted in Gayle Greene and Coppelia Kahn, *Making a Difference*. New York: Routledge, 1981.

Gelderman, Carol. *Mary McCarthy: A Life*. New York: St. Martin's, 1988.

Howe, Irving. *Politics and the Novel*. 1957. New York: Columbia University Press, 1992.

McCarthy, Mary. *The Oasis*. 1949. New York: Bard/Avon, 1981.

Wald, Alan M. *The New York Intellectuals: The Rise and Decline of the Anti-Stalinist Left from the 1930s to the 1980s*. Chapel Hill: University of North Carolina Press, 1987.

9

The Left Reconsidered

Alan Wald

To newly consider Mary McCarthy and the U.S. literary Left from the perspective of the 1990s, one must seek to avoid repetition of the already familiar clichés. I think this can only be done if we devote special attention to at least three areas.

First, I think that such a reconsideration can strike out in a new direction if it offers a fair assessment of the character and quality of the scholarship to date about the political and cultural trajectory of Mary McCarthy.

Second, I think that a fresh approach must be forthright about the specific areas in which the rethinking needs to be undertaken, which also means a very straightforward statement of the reasons for this revisionary effort.

And third, the effort must be candid about the criteria by which any fresh, contemporary judgments are to be reached. We cannot simply rely on the conventional abstractions about integrity, honesty, independence, and critical-mindedness. These ideals are universally endorsed, along with Mom and apple pie, by the entire political spectrum from socialist-internationalists to neocon-servative ideologues. But clearly these worthy abstract values mean wildly different things in the contexts of diverse political projects.

Basically, scholarship to date on Mary McCarthy and her politics is quite solid in comparison to extant studies of many of her contemporaries. Thus I'm arguing that a revisionary effort is required more in the way of expansion and

elaboration, particularly on a comparative plane, than of a rethinking, refor-
mulation, and factual correction of the foundation. In contrast, no book-
length study exists at all, for example, on the life and literary-political career
of McCarthy's long-time associate Philip Rahv, although there is an oft-cited
1977 dissertation by Andrew Dvosin. By now it may well be too late to unearth
the thick description required to explain many facets of Rahv's unusual and
contradictory politicocultural itinerary.

Equally troubling, there is no balanced book on Irving Howe. Moreover,
following his recent death, we seem to be trapped among the rather unproductive poles of near adulation that have appeared in the *New Republic*, the *New
York Times Magazine*, and Howe's own *Dissent*, and the intemperately one-
sided bashing provided by Alexander Cockburn in the *Nation*.

To take another example, much more scholarship exists on Lionel Trilling
than on Howe, Rahv, or McCarthy. But despite some very impressive cultural
critique, too many of the biographical elements are heavily based on anecdotes,
the sole source of authentication of which is Trilling's widow.

The case of McCarthy, however, is very different from all three of these, for
at least two reasons, First, McCarthy was extraordinarily candid about the
details of her life in her autobiography, fiction, and interviews. A good deal of
her recollections has received verification through documents and other primary sources.

Second, there has often been a salutary critical distance from the charming
and attractive subject of McCarthy on the part of most of those scholars who
have scrutinized her life and work. This critical distance is due, I think, to the
fact that McCarthy naturally attracts the interests of feminists, yet she herself
denied an allegiance to feminism, as Carol Brightman graphically documents
in *Writing Dangerously*. The critical distance exists also because McCarthy's life
and work attract the interest of leftists, yet her unregenerate elitism and her
uninspiring behavior during the Cold War grate against the values of most of
us on the Left.

What, then, needs to be done in the area of expansion and augmentation?
More, I think, than may seem to be required from an initial glance. This is
because all of the serious scholarship on McCarthy—with the exception of
more purely literary studies such as the books by Barbara McKenzie and
Willene Schaefer Hardy—proceeds accurately by treating McCarthy within a
network or framework of an intense milieu of highly politicized writers
generally referred to as "the New York Intellectuals."

This network, however, was hardly McCarthy's only subject position. She
was also a daughter, a Vassar graduate, and a lover (many times over), and she
played many other parts. Even in regard to her role in the construction of the

famous political and cultural trend of the New York intellectuals, one needs to recognize that that phenomenon itself is complex and contradictory. For example, the New York Intellectuals' tradition has been theorized variously as largely the product of upwardly mobile Jews; as the transit of utopian-sectarian radicals into the world of critical realism; and, by myself, among others, as the bifurcated movement of onetime rebels from a counterhegemonic stance as allies of working-class agency to a tragic incorporation into the structures of political and cultural domination.

Moreover, to that tradition McCarthy, like just about all the others among what Harold Rosenberg so aptly called "the Herd of Independent Minds," had an individualized and often eccentric relation. Still, it is worth recalling that, very much like the case of most of her colleagues, it was the very early stages of this journey that gave distinctive and memorable character to her achievement.

I myself feel that it was these early stages that were recalled in the heroic moments of McCarthy's later years, as in her 1964 defense of Hannah Arendt's *Eichmann in Jerusalem* ("The Hue and Cry"). And also in McCarthy's excoriation of what she regarded as the insincere opponents of the Vietnam War, such as Diana Trilling and Arthur Schlesinger, Jr., in the writings published in her 1974 volume *The Seventeenth Degree*.

In her formative period, McCarthy was writing from within the framework of a revolutionary politics, which lasted from the mid-1930s through World War II. In these years, McCarthy promoted in her fiction perhaps the most corrosive and searing critical assault on the contradictions, pretensions, and hypocrisies of the middle-class radical intellectual ever to have appeared in U.S. radical literature.

Moreover, McCarthy's effectiveness was not just due to literary skill, since this skill was unevenly applied (*The Oasis*, for example, just doesn't "work" for many readers). That effectiveness was largely from McCarthy's location inside, and very sincerely inside, the politicized class fraction that she set out to skewer.

For me, the high point significantly remains the 1942 collection *The Company She Keeps*, treated very accurately as an example of women's revolutionary literature within Paula Rabinowitz's 1991 study, *Labor and Desire*. In this work, McCarthy's autobiographical persona, Meg Sargent, is quite capable of saying, in one breath, that she stands "for the Fourth International" (152)—and in the next breath that "I'm not even political" (194).

Although the fellow-traveling progressives of the early 1940s saw mainly the first statement, and her liberal admirers of later years saw mainly the second, the fuller reconstructions of her life that have appeared in recent years make it clear that both statements are true . . . and yet not true. She was and she wasn't for the Fourth International; she was and she wasn't "not really political." The dialectically intertwined functional relationships of these statements are aptly explained in Meg's closing plea, "Preserve me in disunity" (304).

This is a critically conscious outlook, I think, of enormous value when harnessed to a militant campaign for social emancipation. But, of course, it can easily degenerate into dull narcissism in the context of a life shaped over decades by "summers on the Cape" and other accoutrements of the cultural elite.

It is true that there remains a considerable amount of unfinished business on the whole subject of the tradition of the New York intellectuals and McCarthy's complex relation to it. McCarthy certainly, along with Dwight Macdonald, represents one of the more attractive and recuperable components of that tradition. Yet, on the whole, this is not a group of intellectual role models who grew wiser and more admirable with age, experience, and increasing influence.

This "group"—as I have argued elsewhere, it is highly problematic even to talk of the New York Intellectuals as a group—was certainly accurate in its appreciation of mid-to-late 1930s Stalinism. And Macdonald and McCarthy were right on the mark in their appreciation of the meaning of U.S. imperial and inhuman objectives in World War II (though I do not agree with their semipacifist response to fascism, which McCarthy later repudiated although she threw out much of the baby along with the bathwater).

On the other hand, as we now ought to see more clearly with the hindsight of about five decades from those crucial early attitudes and positions, to be "right" on questions *A* and *B* does not guarantee correct answers to problems *C* and *D*.

In fact, there really is very little here in the tradition of the New York Intellectuals for young people, critical, as they should be, of the oppressive features and injustices of our society. For those searching for a tradition of militant antiracism, cultural egalitarianism, anticolonialism, uncompromising internationalism, and, in general, for examples of lives devoted to the cause of social emancipation through the empowerment of social movements, the literary and cultural practice becomes more miseducational than educational after the 1930s.

That is why I surmise that young rebels, who are the hope of today as they were in the 1960s and the 1930s, have not looked, nor do I believe that they will ever look, to that later New York Intellectuals' tradition, at least since the time of its transmogrification after World War II. I think that this will remain the case, even though some of these intellectuals became brief allies of the radical student movement of the 1960s (F. W. Dupee and Macdonald during the Columbia student strike, for example; Rahv pontificating on, of all things, the need for a Leninist Party shortly before his death).

Of course, individuals variously connected with this tradition wrote scathing and sometimes brilliant essays on particular topics that ought to be part of any left cultural tradition in the United States—Hannah Arendt on the Eichmann trial, Irving Howe's fine Modern Masters book on Trotsky, and Alfred Kazin's wonderful polemic against the Committee for the Free World ("Saving My Soul at the Plaza," March 1983 *New York Review of Books*) are just a few of those that I treasure.

Still, we are not really talking about anything very much that a new generation of socialist-feminist-antiracist rebels will treasure, no matter how eloquently we strain to give a liberatory politicocultural content to that legacy. Mary McCarthy, Dwight Macdonald, and Irving Howe—these are clearly the "best" of a promising generation that won the intellectual lottery and pulled all the gold rings, yet came to a bad end.

For the most part, the above three names somewhat excepted, they destroyed, debased, and defamed the progressive social movements of workers, the racially oppressed, and the colonized, as they capitulated increasingly to the Cold War and cultural elitism, finally ending up on the opposite side of the barricades from the student radicals of the 1960s. Yet these were originally the social struggles that gave these intellectuals their vision and identity, and provided many themes of their literary work at the outset, and to which they should have felt a kind of debt to repay. Thus I conclude that the most crucial component of rethinking McCarthy and the U.S. literary Left requires bringing back into the picture the fuller context of the broader literary Left against which she and her associates began to define themselves in the 1930s.

I'm referring here to that majority in radical cultural circles that eventually became a persecuted minority, and which lived on in myth as the justification or rationalization for the route taken by McCarthy and her associates in the 1950s. In reality, it was these others who carried on the fight in the hard times: the Meridel Le Sueurs, Jessica Mitfords, Shirley Graham DuBoises, Eve Merriams, John O. Killenses, Julian Mayfields, Lorraine Hansberrys, and Jesus Colons.

These writers, after World War II, peopled the picket lines, protested the lynchings, opposed the Korean War, and suffered the moral and intellectual humiliation of having their delusions about the Soviet Union exploded in 1956 with Hungary and the Khrushchev revelations. I am talking here of that unconscionably silenced "other," that defamed and traduced generation of peers seen so often as the "literary losers" in contrast to Mary McCarthy; the writers, women and men, who must first be returned from the netherworld of caricature to become at least part of the screen against which McCarthy is refigured and rethought.

It is not at all that I object to the reconstruction of McCarthy's life and career as it has been done, mainly in the framework of her friends, lovers, and rivals in the circle of New York Intellectuals; indeed, how could I object, having contributed so heavily to that approach? Yet it is now time to move forward, beyond that tightly circumscribed world, which tautologically refuses validation and verification in terms that offer a way out of the trap, out of what I've called the cul-de-sac, of the New York Intellectuals' tradition (Wald 311–43).

With the collapse of the Stalinist system, which the New York Intellectuals mostly insisted could not be democratically destroyed from within, that tradition is at present largely dead and dishonored as a force in radical intellectual life. With the exception of some crucial moments, such as Macdonald and McCarthy's revolutionary opposition to World War II, it is a tradition that really has little to say about racism, sexism, imperialism, and the need for an equalitarian alternative to the New World Order.

Let me end by just making a few observations on the alternative, silenced tradition of the so-called literary losers, of the thirty to forty women of the Marxist literary Left who were productive during and after the 1930s. At least a dozen have birth dates very close to that of Mary McCarthy (1912), which could be one way of comparing their politicocultural trajectories. For example, Henrietta Buckmaster (1909), Josephine Johnson (1910), Katya Gilden (1910), Ruth McKenney (1911), Tillie Olsen (1913), Muriel Rukeyser (mainly a poet but also novelist, essayist, and biographer, 1913), Margaret Walker (1915), and Helen Yglesias (1915).

Clearly there are fascinating tales to be told here in a collective story of literary women on the Left. Ruth McKenney, for example, has striking similarities to McCarthy in her Irish background; her journey from the provinces to New York City; her rise to fame for satiric short stories of New York bohemian life (McKenney's were mainly about her sister Eileen, and appeared in the fellow-traveling *New Yorker*, not *Partisan Review* or *Horizon*); her production of less successful "serious" novels such as *Jake Home* (1943) and *Mirage* (1956), although her documentary proletarian novel, *Industrial Valley* (1939), was a success; and her numerous satiric autobiographies such as *Love Study* (1950) and *Far, Far from Home* (1954).

McKenney's fate coupled with her husband's suicide and her own madness, brilliantly chronicled in Christina Stead's posthumously published novel *I'm Dying Laughing* (1986), certainly makes McCarthy's career seem enviable. But things look different when we look at other turns of fate, such as the heroic resurgence of Tillie Olsen from promising proletarian short story writer "Tillie Lerner" in the mid-1930s to the inspirational figure she is today; the mysterious career of Josephine Johnson, youngest writer ever to win the Pulitzer Prize (in

1932 for *Now in November*), and steadily productive in obscurity for decades after; and Katya Gilden, who coauthored *Between the Hills and the Sea* (1971), a work that, in my view, far outdistances any other text produced by a man or woman of that literary-political generation.

As these too-brief remarks indicate, the effort here is not to trounce McCarthy by scoring her failings in contrast to more honorable sisters. On the contrary, McCarthy's contribution will do well as a thread within this richer fabric of literary history. There will be weak moments when she is comparatively assessed as artist and political engagée, especially when it comes to her record on racism, class exploitation, and the horrific 1950s. But the McCarthy we know today, re-created by scholars who have perhaps spent enough time by now demonstrating which lovers were partial role models for which literary characters, and treating the New York Intellectuals as the only meaningful political milieu, will become increasingly boring and useless if considerations of her life and work do not now move beyond, into a broader context.

There certainly is a risk in constructing a new Mary McCarthy—a vision of her career that circumspectly takes into account what we know, but rethinks this against a broader and better-informed context of what really happened in her generation by restoring the forgotten and caricatured women of the Left. In the end, however, unless one is mistakenly looking for the individual heroic role model, the McCarthy who will be understood as part of a collective experience, who will emerge from such a group effort at recovering and revisioning, is one who may be appropriated more usefully, in line with political and cultural concerns of the 1990s.

McCarthy will then be seen as one who contributed some of the answers to a meaningful life in the movement for collective and egalitarian social emancipation. More importantly, perhaps, she will be regarded as one who, like all the rest of us, could learn much from rivals and even the supposed political and literary "losers" of that generation that created the literary and political foundation of mid-twentieth-century intellectual life.

WORKS CITED

Brightman, Carol. *Writing Dangerously: Mary McCarthy and Her World*. New York: Clarkson Potter, 1992.

Dvosin, Andrew J. "Literature in a Political World." Doctoral dissertation. New York University, 1977.

Hardy, Willene Schaefer. *Mary McCarthy*. New York: Ungar, 1981.

McCarthy, Mary. *The Company She Keeps*. 1942. New York: Harcourt, 1967.

————. "The Hue and Cry." *The Writing on the Wall and Other Literary Essays*. New York: Harcourt, 1970. 54–71.

————. *The Seventeenth Degree*. New York: Harcourt, 1974.

McKenzie, Barbara. *Mary McCarthy*. New York: Twayne, 1960.

Rabinowitz, Paula. *Labor and Desire: Women's Revolutionary Fiction in Depression America*. Chapel Hill: University of North Carolina Press, 1991.

Rosenberg, Harold. "The Herd of Independent Minds." *Discovering the Present Three Decades in Art, Culture and Politics*. Chicago: University of Chicago Press, 1973. 15–28.

Wald, Alan M. *The New York Intellectuals: The Rise and Decline of the Anti-Stalinist Left from the 1930s to the 1980s*. Chapel Hill: University of North Carolina Press, 1987.

10

"A Very Narrow Range of Choice": Political Dilemma in *The Groves of Academe*

Timothy F. Waples

In his *Perspectives USA* review of Mary McCarthy's 1952 novel *The Groves of Academe*, Albert Guerard snipes, "Does Miss McCarthy (making her choice within a very narrow range of choice) realize how conservative a book she has written?" (169). Guerard's presumptions that the novel can simply be labeled "conservative" and that its conservatism is the consequence of a narrow range of choices available to her reflect habits of thought that plagued McCarthy and other New York intellectuals in the years following World War II—habits that still influence our understanding of the politics and literature of Cold War America. Guerard's sharply limited, if not binaristic, political and literary assessments deserve to be challenged. In her best moments as a critic and novelist, McCarthy makes just such a challenge; at crucial moments, however, she does not.

One such moment of challenge appears in "America the Beautiful," a 1947 essay in which McCarthy struggles against atomic age fatalism. While the A-bomb represents an overpowering symbol of U.S. military might, its presence need not necessarily also demonstrate a unified expression of American political will. McCarthy holds a set of cultural imperatives which she seeks to "differentiate" from the geopolitical givens of American foreign and—as the 1940s freeze into the 1950s—domestic Cold War policy.

It seems likely at this moment that we will find no way of not using the [atomic] bomb, yet those who argue theoretically that this machine is the true expression of our society leave us, in practice, with no means of opposing it. We must differentiate ourselves from the bomb if we are to avoid using it, and in private thought, we do (15).

McCarthy understands that a blanket condemnation of American culture provides no resistance to the wielders of the A-bomb. Her differentiating position pursues a critique of the imperial mind-set that admires atomic displays of power, but this position sometimes falters in its search for generative cultural elements that might offer American resistance against U.S. imperialism. If McCarthy has a knack for differentiating, she is also prone to pondering the limits of differentiation, to demonstrating moments when overlapping political and cultural concerns display the coercion exerted by the ideological center on and within American culture. The following passage from a 1946 letter to Dwight Macdonald, the editor of *politics*, provides a clear example:

The point is that *The New Yorker* cannot be against the atom bomb, no matter how hard it tries, just as it could not, even in this moral "emergency," eliminate the cigarette and perfume advertising that accompanied Mr. Hersey's text [regarding Hiroshima's devastation]. Since *The New Yorker* has not, so far as we know, had a rupture with the government, the scientists, and the boys in the bomber, it can only assimilate the atom bomb to itself, to Westchester County, to smoked turkey, and the Hotel Carlyle. ("Whenever I stay at the Carlyle, I feel like sending it a thank-you note," says a middle-aged lady in an advertisement.) It is all one world (4–5).

"[N]o matter how hard it tries," according to McCarthy, *The New Yorker* cannot differentiate itself from the A-bomb, and its synecdochical relationship to American imperialism; or from the Hotel Carlyle, and its synecdochical relationship to bourgeois individualism. These are the twin foundations of the American Cold War effort, and as early as 1946, McCarthy had grave doubts that its momentum could be halted or even slowed.

An important source of McCarthy's doubts is the shifting landscape of opinion among her collection of friends and associates known widely as "the New York Intellectuals." Literary historian Alan Wald notes the most significant change: "Many of the New York intellectuals came to dismiss the reality of American imperialism during the late 1940s and the 1950s" (217). Because these intellectuals first came to prominence in the 1930s by championing leftist critiques of American politics and culture, they struggled to frame their new perspectives as continuations and advancements of their previous views. Wald argues,

They did so by reorganizing their thought around a cluster of key terms that began to appear increasingly in their writing. . . . these coinages were utilized to convince the intellectuals as well as their audiences that they had moved forward rather than backward (217–18).

"Forward" for the New York Intellectuals—Wald is thinking specifically of editor and critic Philip Rahv in this context—in terms of literary form means moving from a socially oriented, ideologically explicit writing associated with the 1930s to individually oriented narratives that assert the complexity of experience and disavow ideology. Rahv is indeed a prime example by which to trace this trend, as he is one of the earliest and most insistent advocates of this line: in 1939, he writes,

The revolution may have sunk out of sight . . . but the impulse to represent experience truthfully persists. The impulse persists, even though the job of judgment and representation has seldom been so arduous, so perplexing, so enmeshed in ambiguous claims and counterclaims (308).

By relating "experience" to ambiguity, and by emphasizing the impulse toward "truthful representation" over the social role of art or literature, Rahv establishes an unlikely alliance with New Criticism; as Wald observes more generally about Rahv's circle, "Proclaimers of a selective skepticism, they had produced nothing less than a sui generis ideology that seemed to suit the very institutions they had sought to abolish" (230).

In this context, McCarthy's desire to "differentiate" becomes clearer. When looking to the examples of more critical, less accommodating New York intellectuals, such as McCarthy, Wald sees them responding to the beginnings of the Cold War with "a phase of erratic and personalized dissidence" (227). His phrase captures McCarthy's political dilemma in the era, when so many colleagues and friends were on the move ideologically. Indeed, McCarthy's writings are addressed more directly to the shifting politics of her circle of friends and acquaintances (as in *The Oasis*, where a Philip Rahv caricature takes center stage) than to a larger view of U.S. imperialism; her irony is sharpest when it is directed at those closest at hand, including herself. McCarthy's literary politics in this era are thus not, as Guerard insists, "conservative," but are instead the product of leftist self-critique. To the extent that McCarthy's writing operates "within a very narrow range of choice," to borrow Guerard's phrase once again, it is a strategy that reflects the poverty of the choices being made by McCarthy's intellectual intimates. At the same time, if Wald's characterization is apt, one should not be surprised to find a sense of ideological claustrophobia in McCarthy's "erratic and personalized dissidence" (227).

The novel Guerard was responding to, *The Groves of Academe*, seems uniquely designed to demonstrate McCarthy's position of being both against and within the growing Cold War consensus. The novel's setting is Jocelyn College, a small, experimental liberal arts college—not unlike Bard or Sarah Lawrence, where McCarthy taught in the late 1940s. When an unsuccessful English instructor named Henry Mulcahy learns that his contract will not be renewed, he concocts for himself a history of Communist Party membership. By spreading this falsehood, he hopes to make it politically unwise for Maynard Hoar, his liberal college president already on record against the Red Scare, to dismiss him. To prosper in this ruse, Mulcahy must win the support of his English department colleagues, which he does by manipulating the confidence of young, idealistic Domna Rejnev. Mulcahy preys on Domna's sympathy by inventing for his wife Cathy a life-threatening illness, and telling Domna he is protecting Cathy from worry by withholding from her the knowledge of her own illness. To complete his bogus drama of politically correct injustice, 1950s-style, Mulcahy ties the false secret of Cathy's illness to the false secret of his Communist Party membership by fabricating the college president's silent, knowing complicity regarding both secrets.

This silent complicity is the genius of Mulcahy's scheme, and a coup on McCarthy's part as well. Domna's silence, necessary to protect Mulcahy's web of lies, is ensured by his insistence that Maynard Hoar already knows all while Cathy knows, and must know, nothing. By the same token, McCarthy invites her readers to know all: to assume that those at the helm of the "real" Red Scare are silently, knowingly complicit in their anticommunist fictions, deliberately withholding systemic falsehoods from the citizens they purportedly represent. Cathy and the body politic are really healthy, but it does not suit Mulcahy and his scheming analogues to acknowledge that fact.

Having knowledge and acting on it are two different things, as McCarthy's fiction always demonstrates (an important reason why her fiction is often short on plot and long on talk). McCarthy's characters—in her autobiographical prose as well as her fiction—frequently know who their enemies are, but find themselves inextricably linked to these enemies. This is Domna's dilemma, because she discovers Mulcahy's duplicity barely halfway through the novel. Interestingly, her eyes are opened by Cathy Mulcahy, who reveals that she knows too much about her husband's machinations to be the untroubled, sick, passive housewife of his fiction. The male paradigm that dominates the action for the first half of the book is broken by the bond between two women, as Mulcahy himself observes while raging at his wife:

I'll tell you why you did it [why you revealed your knowledge to Domna]. You hate to be left out of anything. You couldn't stand the idea that these discussions were going on every day and you were supposed to be kept in the dark. You resented the implication that you were stupid and didn't have the mother-wit to guess your husband's troubles. And you're jealous of my relation with Domna. You want to have her all cosy to yourself with your lace tablecloths and your confidences. You're dying for an aristocratic friendship. Everything has changed here since you met her (169).

Mulcahy's class critique of Cathy's friendship is specious, because his manipulations are aimed at preserving a position in the bourgeois institution of Jocelyn College. What rings through much more honestly is Cathy's rejection of the passive, stupid role devised for her. In fact, that role is not even stereotypically feminine, as Mulcahy must acknowledge that his fiction does not grant her the "mother-wit" to divine his masculine protectiveness. Cathy's willful slip of the lip, her knowing too much for the male paradigm, allows Domna to see through Mulcahy's patriarchal fictions.

From this point in the novel, Domna is clearly the center of McCarthy's attention. Focusing on Mulcahy as protagonist, as the con artist trying to pull off a heist, turns the novel into a generic crime story, where right and wrong are clearly delineated, and the only suspense is whether the robber will elude the cops. Such a reading is also politically centrist: by figuring Mulcahy as an aberrant individual operating outside the system, the system is implicitly approved. If he succeeds, then Mulcahy becomes the rugged individual, the heroic exception that proves the rule by outstripping it in an isolated case; if he fails, then justice will have been served and order preserved. Thus, it is important instead to see Domna as protagonist, the figure against the ground of Mulcahy as system—Mulcahy as the rule of corruption and coercion, not the exception.[1] By the time Domna takes center stage, Mulcahy's manipulations have firmly established his agency and compel the thoughts and actions of all characters great and small. At this point, the "very narrow range of choice" Guerard complacently laments in his review becomes a more insistent dilemma, as Domna must ponder how to act on her new political understanding of Henry Mulcahy.

Domna's ally in her struggle is Alma Fortune, a more experienced colleague in the department. As they meet in Alma's room to plot strategy, McCarthy inserts a description, almost circular and at least partially sardonic, of their difficulties as liberal intellectuals in search of a strategy to resist Mulcahy's power play:

They were conscious of owing a duty to the students to protect them from the eccentricities of a teacher whom they themselves had sponsored, but they could not be sure how far this duty extended and where it conflicted with their duty to Mulcahy as a fellow-being with certain gifts and certain handicaps, for which due allowance must be made. There was also, they could not help but feel, a duty to themselves, a duty not to spy, not to be underhanded, not to encourage informers or welcome irresponsible gossip, but this duty, likewise, was in conflict with both the other two, for how were they to determine the limits of their responsibilities if they did not inform themselves precisely as to what was going on (211)?

McCarthy sharply contrasts this liberal muddle, this paralysis of ethical analysis, with Mulcahy's less inhibited *Realpolitik*, by a conjecture Domna offers Alma: "I sometimes think Henry knows us better than we know ourselves. He forces us to choose whenever we see him. He asks only one question, 'Are you with me or against me?' " (218). While the women wring their hands over moral principles, Mulcahy proceeds by the loyalty oath's aggressive binarism.

Unfortunately, Domna and Alma do not proceed at all. They find themselves thwarted, more by their own tangle of duties and obligations than by Mulcahy's unscrupulous initiatives. And, perhaps, by a couple of McCarthy's novelistic trademarks that ultimately contain the resistances her texts identify. Domna and Alma's dilemma is abruptly set aside to present the satiric trivialities of an academic conference on poetry. McCarthy's shift of scene presents the trademark outside observer to comment objectively upon the fray, a scruffy proletarian poet named Keogh, who gives himself advice authorized by its placement so close to the end of the novel:

Keogh, keep out of this, or they will get you. . . . Within twenty hours, he perceived, they had succeeded in leading him up the garden path into one of their academic mazes, where a man could wander for eternity, meeting himself in mirrors (249).

Keogh's insistence on remaining apart, or differentiating himself, from the struggle against Mulcahy removes the hope of an effective challenge to Mulcahy's paradigm. With Keogh's condemnation of academia as labyrinth—which, after all, was originally designed for containment of the Other—McCarthy effectively concedes victory to Mulcahy. She provides no Theseus, nor are Domna and Alma able to act as more independent Ariadnes. McCarthy's retreat indicates the limits of differentiation within the ideological conflicts set into motion on the Jocelyn campus. This shortfall is another McCarthy trademark: her fiction is peopled with smart, brassy women who find themselves overmatched by their conditions.

Perhaps, however, McCarthy had other options she might have exercised. Alma Fortune is a character marked with signs of possibility, a path of greater resistance down which McCarthy could have traveled farther. To do so, one would start with the overbrief description of Alma's sexual history, which blurs gender and challenges the assumed hierarchy and permanence inherent in marriage:

[S]he had not been altered either by marriage or by the death of her life-companion—it was as though she had lost a congenial sister or a woman colleague with whom she had shared a flat and a small collection of books, bibelots, and common habits; having lived together with Mr. Fortune by a continuous stipulation of mutual consent, she had allowed him his independence in departing (98–99).

Alma's niche at Jocelyn also appears to be one she has consciously and somewhat independently contrived, an alternative arrangement of privacy and affiliation, with an authority Alma does not hesitate to employ:

She was both extremely outspoken and extremely reserved; her personality was posted with all sorts of No Trespassing signs and crisscrossed with electric fences, which repelled the intruder with a smart shock. To men, in particular, the protocol of her nature was bewildering, like court etiquette; like a queen, too, she had her favorites, who were granted familiarities and indulgences not granted to their superiors in rank or outward attainments (99).

Early in the novel, when the English department is still naively gathering support for Mulcahy, Domna is shocked, both admiring and a bit jealous, to learn that Alma's zeal exceeds her own: Alma has already prepared a letter of resignation. Even Mulcahy is surprised by her action, and prefers that her resignation be provisional, a negotiation with authority. Alma's response is intriguing.

[M]y feminine instinct tells me that he [college president Maynard Hoar] responds only to the irrevocable, to a *fait accompli*. It's a defect of imagination; you and I have too much; Maynard has too little. Tomorrow is never present to him until it becomes yesterday. My father was such a man. I left home for good when I was fifteen and went to work as a stack-girl in a library—my sisters reaped the benefits of his repentance (130).

Alma's reply provides a thumbnail sketch of an ideological continuum: on one level, she and Mulcahy, as radical and reactionary extremists, respectively, stand against Maynard's centrist lack of imagination. On another level, Alma positions herself as bellwether for Domna and other women to reap the benefits of her opposition to patriarchy. To radical Alma, tomorrow is present today when she thinks of her sisters. It is a shame that *The Groves of Academe* does not offer more of Alma's story, but her presence nevertheless complicates the "narrow range of choice" the novel supposedly reflects. Alma's ready defiance, and Mulcahy's anger at his wife Cathy's bond with Domna ("Everything has changed here since you met her" [169]), are the text's most promising, most radical moments.

However, it is Domna's character that offers the best perspective on McCarthy's own sense of political agency in the Cold War. Domna's true colors are revealed in her first conversation with Mulcahy, as we share his sense of her reaction to his fabrications:

This new admission, he saw with relief and a certain misanthropy, had put her altogether in his hands; his malfeasance would make her submit to his better judgment as to ways and means, as she would submit to the superior knowledge of a criminal whom she was concealing in her house. At bottom, he reminded himself, she was conventional, believing in a conventional moral order and shocked by deviations from it into a sense of helpless guilt toward the deviator. In other words, she was a true liberal, as he had always suspected (51).

This definition of the "true liberal" in Chapter 3 explains Domna's immobility in Chapter 11. When Domna, a liberal like Jocelyn president Maynard Hoar, finally sees the fait accompli of Mulcahy's entrenched power, she lacks the imagination to find alternative strategies of resistance. Domna's strongest reaction is an immobilizing, blanket self-condemnation: "You know what Tolstoy would have said? . . . He would have said we are all fools" (213).

The line might as well be McCarthy's, whose oft remarked-upon "cold eye" and bitter irony are sharpest when they are cast upon herself. As critic Paula Rabinowitz says about an earlier McCarthy persona, Margaret Sargent of *The Company She Keeps*, "Even when 'she' is the focus of a vignette, she is observed from without by an intimate, knowing narrator . . . whose ironic tone distances her story from its teller" (13). Rabinowitz's observation allows us to see that what Wald reads as a post–World War II "phase of erratic and personalized dissidence" is at the same time vintage McCarthy. Although so much of her fiction features an intimate, insular setting, from Utopia in *The Oasis* to New Leeds in *A Charmed Life* to the circle of women who form *The Group* to Jocelyn College in *The Groves of Academe*, these small spaces rarely provide the sort of haven an Alma Fortune might fashion. They become instead microcosms, in which the power of a consensus can be portrayed in all its ugliness, an ugliness that ultimately, despite the scattered glimmerings of hope and resistance, condemns the victims almost as harshly as the victors.

NOTE

1. In a letter to Hannah Arendt a few months after the publication of *Groves of Academe*, McCarthy connects Richard Nixon, then campaigning for vice president, with Mulcahy, noting that they share a "groveling sense of justification and threatening inferiority" (Brightman, ed. 8).

WORKS CITED

Brightman, Carol, ed. *Between Friends: The Correspondence of Hannah Arendt and Mary McCarthy, 1949–1975.* New York: Harcourt, 1995.

Guerard, Albert. "Some Recent Novels." *Perspectives USA* 1 (Fall 1952): 168–69.

McCarthy, Mary. "America the Beautiful: The Humanist in the Bathtub." *On the Contrary.* New York: Farrar, 1961. 6–19.

———. *The Groves of Academe.* 1952. New York: Signet, 1953.

———. "A Letter to the Editor of *politics.*" *On the Contrary.* 3–5.

Rabinowitz, Paula. *Labor and Desire: Women's Revolutionary Fiction in Depression America.* Chapel Hill: University of North Carolina Press, 1991.

Rahv, Philip. *Essays on Literature and Politics, 1932–1972.* Edited by Arabel J. Porter and Andrew J. Dvosin. Boston: Houghton Mifflin, 1978.

Wald, Alan M. *The New York Intellectuals: The Rise and Decline of the Anti-Stalinist Left, from the 1930s to the 1980s.* Chapel Hill: University of North Carolina Press, 1987.

11

Reluctant Radical:
The Irish-Catholic Element

Stacey Lee Donohue

The Irish-Catholic-American sensibility is broad. James T. Farrell, F. Scott Fitzgerald, Eugene O'Neill, Mary McCarthy, Flannery O'Connor, and Mary Gordon might not appear to have much in common, but they do. A particularly Irish brand of Catholicism hangs like a shroud. The humor is often dark, cruel, biting, and self-deprecating. The politics are generally liberal with paradoxical conservative views, or conservative with paradoxical liberal views. There is usually a conflict between the flesh and the intellect. The plot is often centered on family relationships and gatherings to illustrate their power on each character. There is often a self-loathing, similar to what we find in Jewish-American writers of this century; however, Irish-American writers combine this self-loathing with a distrust of free will that often results in a tragic, fatalistic outlook on life. There is an idealism that flourished despite years of colonization and emigrated along with millions of Irish men and women to the United States, creating in their literature a disorienting sensibility of romanticism tinged with paradoxical fatalism.

Mary McCarthy is identifiably a Catholic writer, writing in the Irish-American literary tradition, although I certainly would not want to limit her to that identity. She broke away from an anti-intellectual, puritan, sexist Irish-Catholicism, succeeding as a writer, participating in the sexual, political, and intellectual freedom of the 1930s and 1940s, but still struggling with the Church's restrictive definition of women, and a historically and culturally Irish fatalism. In her fiction, McCarthy was unable to fully reject or replace these sensibilities: her heroines are often foiled by a stereotypically Irish-Catholic idealization of suffering and penance, and the desire to be seen as good girls; and because they are out of the context of a traditional Irish-Catholic environment, their self-sacrifices are meaningless.

Another Irish-American writer, Mary Gordon, has noted that there are many heroic women in Catholic history:

It occurs to me that one good fortune in being brought up a Catholic and a woman was that you did have images of heroic women. And that's not frequently the case in other religious traditions. In the tradition of Catholicism you have a poem spoken by the Virgin Mary which points out her place in the divine order. And she speaks with pride ("Getting Here" 169).

But this "divine order" is still male dominated. Catholic women are encouraged to participate in the servitude of God, but only to a well-defined point. Roles and images offered to good Catholic girls are varied, yet ultimately limiting for the woman who wants to be creative, intellectual, and physical: Mary the Blessed Virgin, Mary the Blessed Mother, Mary Magdalene the witch, who cured Jesus of evil spirits, Mary Magdalene the prostitute, Martha, sister of Lazarus, the household drudge. There is also Mary, sister of Martha, who is acceptable as an intelligent woman, but only if her intellect is used to serve Jesus. Stories of female saints offer conflicting images of heroism and suffering. As a young, intelligent girl, McCarthy read about saints and martyrs where the love of God is expressed through masochism: Agatha's breast is cut off; Catherine is broken at the wheel; and many were burned. McCarthy notes in her autobiography *How I Grew* (1987) that it was during Sunday Mass in Minneapolis that she was introduced to stories such as these: "Catholics had a great appetite for reading about gruesome diseases, especially those involving the rotting or falling off of parts of the body"(12). Perhaps this explains McCarthy's infamous obsession with the physical: in *How I Grew* McCarthy's portrait of her early intellectual growth is juxtaposed with vivid descriptions of a penis and its jism; in *The Company She Keeps* Meg is shamed yet turned on by the light sadomasochistic sex with the Man in the Brooks Brothers Shirt; and *The Group* shocked readers with details of Dottie's pelvic exam and flying diaphragm. McCarthy admitted on the *Jack Paar Show* in 1963 that sex is either comedy or grotesque: it is "indecent to write about happy sex." As a result of historical and economic forces, and the puritanical influences of Jansenism, the Irish were the only Catholic nation to uncritically adopt an almost Calvinistic position on issues relating to sex. Jansenism was imported to Ireland by French clerics after the French Revolution, and its doctrine appealed to the Irish because it confirmed their experiences as colonized peoples on a poor, isolated island. The principal Jansenist teaching is that man is naturally depraved, and that only God's grace can save him: human will is powerless. Jansenism distrusts human instincts and desires, and obviously sexual desires are included. Distrust of and distaste for the physical, as well as sexual or physical inhibitions, pervade Irish-American literature, and McCarthy's fiction is no exception.

Mary Gordon has criticized the false stereotypes of the Irish as garrulous, witty storytellers when what she hears from her family is, "Don't tell anyone our secrets. Laugh and smile and lie" ("I Can't Stand" 201). This echoes Joyce's *Portrait of the Artist as a Young Man*, when Stephen Daedalus realizes that silence, exile, and cunning are the only way to survive as an Irish-Catholic artist. The history of the Irish supports this: first colonized by Roman Catholicism, then the British, then forced into exile where they were treated poorly, the Irish, as many oppressed groups, have had to adopt a victim's distrust of others, and a way of distancing themselves with humor and stories that deflect any real intimacy. McCarthy reveals this in *How I Grew*, perhaps responding to the criticism that her writing is dry and unemotional. After depicting a series of painful incidents with her Uncle Myers, she reserves the right to laugh at her past rather than fall into self-pity: "Laughter is the great antidote for self-pity, maybe a specific for the malady. Yet probably it does tend to dry one's feelings out a little, as if by exposing them to a vigorous wind. . . . There is no dampness in my emotions, and some moisture is needed to produce the deeper, the tragic notes" (17).

In a closed society such as the Church before Vatican II, which treasured women only as mothers or saints, a woman who wanted to write had even more obstacles than a man. When Irish women did tell stories they were used as correctives. This was a self-preserving instinct, no doubt, ensuring their continued dominance in the house and preparing their children for the worst, passing on a fatalism imbedded in Irish culture. McCarthy wrote of her grandmother McCarthy that "the most trivial reminiscences received from her delivery and from the piety of the context a strongly monitory flavor; they inspired guilt and fear, and one searched uncomfortably for the moral in them, as in a dark and middling fable" ("Yonder Peasant" 162–63). Storytelling is pragmatism, not art, a criticism often applied to a McCarthy novel. As the moral guardians in the family, women are encouraged to tell stories for family and friends. Yet when Irish women write for the world at large, they may use this power of condemnation not only on themselves and others, but on the Church itself. At the 1993 conference on Mary McCarthy held at Bard College, keynote speaker Mary Ann Caws said that McCarthy "had the bravery to draw a moral," and she did, although in some respects she had her Irish heritage to support her. McCarthy has done this in all her fiction, satirizing as the earliest Irish immigrant writers did, moralizing as the nineteenth-century Irish-American writers did, carrying on the Irish-American literary tradition.

As a result of her "bravery to draw a moral," McCarthy made enemies with every organization to which she belonged: the communists denounced her support of Trotsky; her ex-boyfriend from the *Partisan Review* sued her for libel; and the Vassar class of 1933 responded angrily to *The Group*. And McCarthy herself, as much as her writing, was the target of many Catholics who thought she had brought shame to the Church. In Mary Gordon's *The Company of Women*, the heroine, Felicitas, brings McCarthy's book *Vietnam* to the peace rally she secretly attends:

She had been warned against Mary McCarthy for years. Ever since *The Group*, nuns had shaken their heads and breathed her name as a warning to the better students. "What good do all those brains do her? Four husbands and writing filth," they said. It was a comfort to have that book with her; she felt accompanied by a daring older sister whom defiance had made glamorous (90).

Memories of a Catholic Girlhood recounts both the positive (education, love of beauty, Latin) and the negative (vulgarity, lies, hypocrisy) features of McCarthy's Catholic education and upbringing. Yet, although this is her only writing explicitly on the Church, not even a close reading of her fiction and essays is necessary to see the influence of the Church in her writing and thinking: ecclesiastical allusions abound. Like Flannery O'Connor, McCarthy does not directly write about Catholics or the Church, but in her strong sense of morality, of punishment, of self-criticism, McCarthy's sensibilities are clearly Catholic—*Irish* Catholic. There are also Catholic characters, such as Meg Sargent and her vulgar Aunt Clara in *The Company She Keeps*, where Meg's psyche is deformed by her upbringing and she is caught between what Thelma Shinn defines as "two sets of values": the modern, intellectual, bohemian woman that she aspires to be, and the antimodern or "traditional values of feminine stereotypes and Catholic dogma in which she was raised " (91). Her heroines from Meg to Martha Sinnot in *A Charmed Life* to Kay in *The Group* all suffer from this tension, and it is never resolved: Martha and Kay die, and Meg begs for merely the awareness of her fate.

Ironically, although she herself lived the life of a bohemian, sleeping with many men, drinking, traveling, writing, it becomes increasingly clear that McCarthy, like the Church, was quite conservative. Although McCarthy outgrew Catholicism, as an adult she continuously tested and rejected what can be seen as twentieth-century replacements for the authority and promises of religion such as politics and psychoanalysis. In *Memories* she painfully recalls how at age fourteen she got the priest to admit that there is a gap between faith and experience that cannot be filled with reason: " 'Natural reason, Mary,' expatiated Father Heeney, 'will not take you the whole way today. There's a little gap that we have to fill with faith.' I looked up at him measuringly. So there *was* a gap, then. How was it that they had never mentioned this interesting fact to us before?" (123).

This gap both disturbed and obsessed McCarthy. She insisted yet doubted that reason could correct this discrepancy, and this tension is felt in her works and seen in her life. "Faith" by Catholic definition is a virtue that requires God's grace, not man's. McCarthy has written that *The Group* is a novel about the "loss of faith in progress" (quoted in Kakutani 265). With that word, she is, consciously or not, revealing the fatal flaw in belief in any ideology: God's grace is absent in any man-made ideology. A critical response to her Catholic childhood taught McCarthy to be sensitive to the dangers of uncritical faith as portrayed in her novels: faith in political ideology, faith in psychoanalysis, faith in technology, faith in social progress—all are faithfully deconstructed.

As a result of her own lifelong self-examination, McCarthy's critical eye looked coldly on the bohemian, intellectual woman who toys with sex and politics as a form of escape, or as a shield from some essential truth about herself or the world around her. With each heroine—Meg, Martha, Kay—Catholicism plays a smaller role as McCarthy grew further away from her Catholic girlhood, but since McCarthy was an infamously autobiographical writer, portraying herself in each of her heroines, all are effectively Catholic. Like her, all are unable to mediate between the traditional definitions of femininity embraced by the church, and the modern revisioning, an Irish-Catholic fatalism and a belief in free will: Meg tries psychoanalysis but even the psychiatrist becomes terrified at the conclusion that Meg's Catholic childhood and her resulting problems as an adult suggest a mechanical universe; Martha's seemingly moral decision to have an abortion indirectly kills her because it is a misapplied morality in the context of her bohemian environment; and the women of *The Group* all succumb to different but equally unappealing fates, while the structure of the novel forebodes determinism, beginning with Kay's wedding and ending with her wake (a common trope in Irish-American literature).

In *The Company She Keeps*, Meg, the self-proclaimed radical, learns that her freedom from the feminine/bourgeois ideal is lonely, and she feels so guilty about the sex she turns to in order to relieve the loneliness that she idealizes sex into an act of self-sacrifice rather than the sordid mess that is depicted. Since Meg remembers her Catholic childhood as being easy because "the

Church could classify it all for you" by categorizing good and evil, sex with
Mr. Breen must become a sacrifice to qualify as a good act:

The glow of self-sacrifice illuminated her. This, she thought decidedly, is going to be
the only real act of charity I have ever performed in my life; it will be the only time I
have ever given anything when it honestly hurt me to do so . . . it was the mortification
of the flesh achieved through the performance of the act of pleasure (*Company* 114).

Meg thus turns her sexual encounter on the train into a moral and intellectual
choice, an abstraction, so that she does not have to take the responsibility for
her decision.

Much has been written about the passivity of the heroines in *The Group*. In
the novel, Kay marries Harald even after she's realized that it is a mistake
because she's lived with him; Prissy meekly follows the medical advice of her
physician-husband even though she recognizes the sadism inherent in his
prescriptions; and Libby romanticizes what is a terrifying rape. Yet Paul Giles
notes that McCarthy intended them to be products of their time and place,
unable to control their own destinies (457). The novel details the social and
economic lives of a group of upper-middle-class college graduates during the
1930s, and it was criticized for its catalogue of details, from recipes for mixed
drinks to the minutely detailed procedures in a visit to the Margaret Sanger
Clinic. All the girls claim that the worst fate would be to end up like their
bourgeois parents; yet their lives become even more restricted than those of
their more open-minded parents: Dottie's mother begs her daughter to try true
love before marrying for security. Perhaps McCarthy is responding through her
Irish-Catholic fatalism—all the characters, including the men (Harald repeats
his father's professional failure), have little control over their lives: they are fated
to follow the failures of their parents; or the economic, educational, historical,
and social forces are simply too powerful for an individual to overcome.

Meg Sargent desperately tries to gain autonomy, to take herself away from
the comforts and demands of authority, personified in the Man in the Brooks
Brothers Shirt. Yet, in doing so, she falls back on abstractions, rather than taking
responsibility for her own actions and inactions: the seduction is abstracted
into a political or class war, the bourgeois versus the bohemian, while the safety
pin holding together her underwear no longer embarrasses her as it did at first,
but becomes a symbol of her "moral fastidiousness" (*Company* 117). Martha
Sinnot also retreats to the dogmatic, noncontextual response to a moral
dilemma, one which sees the world in the polarities of sin and punishment,
good and evil, and a moral position that is ultimately destructive. According
to Thelma Shinn, "Miles has again enabled Martha to feel evil so that she can

feel good about herself when she makes the grand sacrifice. Deciding to punish herself by having the abortion . . . she admires her internal 'lawgiver' and is in awe of her own integrity" (95–96). Neither Meg nor Martha accepts the responsibility for sex, believing that the men have misunderstood or misread them: Meg did not want to have sex with Mr. Breen, nor did Martha with Miles: both were more than tipsy. Both women punish themselves afterwards—Meg reasons that she must have sex with the man again since she submitted the first time, while Martha, although she wants to have a child, has the abortion rather than face the possible result of her infidelity—yet neither feels absolved. The secular punishment is simply not enough.

Bruce Cook, writing for a conservative Catholic journal, extends the metaphor of the child within the adult beyond her heroines to McCarthy herself. He sees *Memories of a Catholic Girlhood* as an attack on her Grandmother Preston, her Uncle Myers, all the adults of her childhood who failed her: "She has kept alive the twelve-year-old's romantic notions of love and her fear of sex, the scrupulous interest in motivation with its attendant casuistry and passion for analysis. . . . All schoolgirls are Jansenists; some, however, do grow out of it" (41). Yet what Cook fails to see in his attack on McCarthy is that, like her heroines, she was a product of her own time, a time when girls, especially bright girls, were encouraged to look toward men for authority, to please all adults, and to put their own needs on hold. The reason for McCarthy's passive heroines may simply be her way of destroying her past selves, allowing her, in her own life, to move on.

Perhaps this is why McCarthy's satire of her heroines is tempered by her sympathy for them and their modern predicament. She feels that they have lost something—perhaps a sense of utility, or perhaps a sense of knowing what their role as women should be—and the effects of this loss are disastrous. In a Lawrencean sense, their faith in ideology has cut them off from reality and their own natures as women. Oddly, it is still a rather feminist position in the way it acknowledges the tension of women torn between two conflicting ideals. Her heroines declare their sexual freedom and intellectual independence, and are willing to compete in the world with men, but ultimately they are undermined by self-doubt, shame, and an internalization of Catholicism, which lead to a desperate search for someone to tell them what to do, and some structure to tell them how to do it.

Meg is McCarthy's most overtly Catholic heroine. Her every contemplated action is debated first as to whether or not it is moral; every object becomes a potential symbol to guide her in her decisions: the safety pin in her underwear becomes a symbol of moral fastidiousness, with a positive moral value rather than simple carelessness. Along with her sense of sacrificing herself to the Man in the Brooks Brothers Shirt, she gives him the role and power of a priest, confessing her despised middle-class roots to him, and she later turns his harshness into a self-punishment that excites her as much as the masochistic sex that includes spankings and curses: "He spoke harshly: this was the drill sergeant, the voice of authority. . . . This was the first wound he had dealt her, but how deep the sword went in!" (*Company* 115). She accepts his severity and even expects, with excitement, more to follow—this was merely the *first* wound.

Although there are some references to Meg's enjoyment of inflicting emotional pain—particularly in "Cruel and Barbarous Treatment," the monologue about Meg's deliberate withdrawal from her husband-to-be with the lover she is using—most of the time she is the recipient:

This was, she knew, the most profound, the most subtle, the most idyllic experience of her life. All the strings of her nature were, at last, vibrant. She was both doer and sufferer: she inflicted pain and participated in it. And she was, at the same time, physician, for, as she was the weapon that dealt the wound, she was also the balm that could assuage it. Only she could know the hurt that engrossed him, and it was to her that he turned for the sympathy she had ready for him. Finally, though she offered him his discharge slip with one hand, with the other she beckoned him to approach (*Company* 11–12).

McCarthy's heroines masochistically seek dictatorial men, and, as one critic puts it, "submit to a vague standard of values which seem to be measured by the pain or unattractiveness of the moral act" (Shinn 96). McCarthy, accepting criticism like Shinn's, responds that "American Catholicism has that sort of Calvinistic flavor" of self-examination and the belief that the difficult path is the moral path (Newman 81). The self-criticism, the penance, the masochism of McCarthy heroines, and the judgmental critic in McCarthy herself, reflect McCarthy's Irish-Catholicism; a culturally influenced religion, although based on the concept, or ideology, of forgiveness, is transformed in practice into a patriarchal, punishing legacy.

Many Irish women immigrants and their daughters were actively vocal against any discrimination: consider Mary "Mother" Jones and Margaret Sanger. In *The Group* radical politics is intertwined with sexual and personal liberation. William Barrett, fellow *Partisan Review* contributor, writes of McCarthy's first novel, "We did not know it then, but she was in fact firing the first salvo in the feminist war that now rages within our society, though I doubt that the movement has since produced any weapon of equal class and caliber" (67). Many male critics admire McCarthy and declare her a woman extraordinaire; even after her death she succeeds in attracting the admiration of intelligent men. In 1993, John Crowley called her first novel "a pioneering work of feminist fiction" (112). And she impressed Joseph Epstein, who recognizes that McCarthy did not consider herself a feminist: "Like most talented women, Mary McCarthy was no feminist, either when young or in her later years. She felt feminism 'bad for a woman,' for she thought it born of desperation and that 'it induces a bad emotional state' " (43). McCarthy once denounced feminism as "a competitive ideology born of desperation," though she admitted that "I'm sort of Uncle Tom from this point of view" (quoted in Brightman 343). She believed that the successes she had in life were due to men: as Philip Rahv's girlfriend, she got to write for *Partisan Review*; through Edmund Wilson, she started writing fiction; and her third husband Bowden Broadwater took care of life for her while she continued to write: "[H]e fixed the leaky faucets, deployed the hated vacuum cleaner, screened the calls and callers, restored one house, caretook another, and remained throughout a steadfast companion to Reuel" (Brightman, *Mirabella* 142).

As she got older, she got progressively more hostile toward feminism; in a 1979 interview with Miriam Gross she firmly stated:

As for Women's Lib, it bores me. Of course I believe in equal pay and equality before the law and so on, but this whole myth about how different the world would have been if it had been female dominated . . . I've never noticed that women were less warlike than men. And in marriage—an equal division of tasks is impossible—it's a judgment of Solomon (Gross 176).

It is not surprising that McCarthy would reject any philosophy that went against her sense of reality: McCarthy herself was never considered less of an aggressive, or warlike, critic and satirist than any man. Yet McCarthy was often called "bitch" and other feminine pejorative names because she was able to ignore Virginia Woolf's angel of the house. Biographer Carol Brightman believes that McCarthy actually liked being a woman, particularly because of the skills a woman has to learn such as getting her own way "without direct confrontation—which are the gifts of observation and analysis" (343). Her life and her writing, however, are often not the same. The women of *The Group* compete with each other for who gets the best life, the best man, and their juggling of allegiances at Vassar is merely a precursor to their lives; their "friendship" is superficial. Carolyn Heilbrun dismisses McCarthy because in her fiction there are no female friendships, but in *How I Grew* McCarthy wrote that "[i]n the course of history, not love or marriage so much as friendship has promoted [intellectual] growth" (28).

There are some feminists who do admire her, myself included. Martha Duffy wrote that she inspired generations of women because she wrote about "a woman's domestic strategies, her finances, her female friendships, her minute biological concerns. Every syllabus on feminist literature is indebted to her" (87). Alison Lurie looked to McCarthy's life, not her fiction, for a role model:

Before Mary McCarthy, if an educated girl did not simply abdicate all intellectual ambitions and agree to dwindle into a housewife, there seemed to be only two possible roles she could choose: the Wise Virgin and the Romantic Victim. . . . [McCarthy invented her own role] both coolly and professionally intellectual and frankly passionate (19).

In her fiction, however, although her heroines do not achieve her success in life they are painfully, humorously aware of their positions, and that is still a very feminist awareness.

McCarthy's reliance on Catholic allusions and metaphors to make her point can be found on the pages of nearly all of her novels and essays. Even in her nonfiction about her political and social life as an agnostic adult, Catholic metaphors are used almost exclusively. In "My Confession" McCarthy describes the seven days she spent with her fiancé (who soon became an ex-fiancé) and a communist organizer in Southampton as having "a special, still quality, like the days of a novena you make in your childhood; a part of each of them was set aside for the Party's task" (89). Besides the comparison between the Communist Party and the Church, Catholic references are often associated with nostalgia for a lost world or childhood—a time when she was free of many adult responsibilities but also a time of great stress in Uncle Myers's household.

Yet McCarthy's Catholic allusions almost always have positive connotations. Miles Murphy from *A Charmed Life* is only one Catholic character in McCarthy's fiction, and, like another Irishman, Henry Mulcahy of *The Groves of Academe*, his Catholicism is tied up with his villainy. The Church is not only the source of Miles's villainy, but also of his charisma and power. This power is also seen in the "good" characters like Polly from *The Group*, to whom the most space is devoted in that novel, and who is one of the only girls who lives the fairy-tale existence of McCarthy's childhood. As the narrator notes, there is a "Catholic strain in Polly's ancestry" enough perhaps to make her, almost alone of all the other girls, happy with her life.

So the question is, Why did she rely in her fiction and essays on Catholic allusions when she effectively left the church at age fourteen? Why did she maintain that she was a liberal, or libertarian, when she supported a traditional and even conservative position on many issues? For some critics and contemporaries, these gaps and contradictions constitute a major flaw in her work. For others, the gap, which is reflected in the "latent Catholicism" in all her works, reflects her desire to assimilate into the mainstream in conflict with her desire to be the perpetual outsider, outside the ordinary (Giles 458). Most of her allusions to Catholicism are positive; a Catholic heritage greatly informs her writing and ethics, despite her apparent renunciation of Catholicism in *Memories of a Catholic Girlhood*.

Despite her public persona as a radical and her outspokenness against the Catholic Church, McCarthy retained her Catholic sensibility, and was a very reluctant radical. She believed in social change, political change, and freedom for women to reach their potential, yet she retreated whenever these changes threatened her perceptions of the way things ought to be. As in the fiction of other Irish-American writers, the traditions and beliefs of Catholicism are often distorted when applied to a contemporary context. Mary Gordon's Isabel Moore (*Final Payments* 1978) sacrifices herself to her dead father's housekeeper as punishment for an affair with a married man; McCarthy's Martha Sinnot aborts her child rather than succumb to the guilt of her perceived sin. Ignoring contemporary cries of personal freedom, both characters are responding to moral dilemmas with their out-of-context Catholic moral sensibilities.

Alienation from society, of course, is one response to the fragmentation of modern life; yet for many Irish-Catholic fictional characters, the results of these tensions are too often tragic. McCarthy's inability to fully reject her Catholic moral upbringing is apparent in all her fiction; as Norman Podhoretz has written, McCarthy's conservatism "flows from an ineluctable skepticism about [her own destiny] by force of will and idea" (87). In other words, McCarthy's political, sexual, and intellectual radicalism was tempered by the quest she began when she was a child, which she was never able to fully complete: a quest for the reason that can fill the gap between faith and experience.

WORKS CITED

Barrett, William. *The Truants: Adventures among the Intellectuals*. New York: Anchor Press, 1982.

Brightman, Carol. *Writing Dangerously: Mary McCarthy and Her World*. New York: Clarkson Potter, 1992.

————. "Writing Dangerously." *Mirabella*. August 1992: 134–44.

Cook, Rev. Bruce. "Mary McCarthy: One of Ours?" *Catholic World* 199 (1964): 34–42.

Crowley, John. "Mary McCarthy's *The Company She Keeps*." *The Explicator* 51 (Winter 1993): 111–15.

Duffy, Martha. "She Knew What She Wanted." *New York* (November 6, 1989): 87.

Epstein, Joseph. "Mary McCarthy in Retrospect." *Commentary* 94 (May 1993): 41–47.

Giles, Paul. *American Catholic Arts and Fictions: Culture, Ideology, Aesthetics.* Cambridge: Cambridge University Press, 1992.

Gordon, Mary. *The Company of Women.* New York: Random House, 1980.

————. *Final Payments.* New York: Random House, 1978.

————. "Getting Here from There: A Writer's Reflections on a Religious Past." *Good Boys and Dead Girls, and Other Essays.* New York: Viking, 1991. 160–75.

————. "I Can't Stand Your Books: A Writer Goes Home." *New York Times Book Review* 11 (December 1988), p. 1+. Reprinted in *Good Boys and Dead Girls, and Other Essays.* 160–75.

Gross, Miriam. "A World out of Joint." Interview with Mary McCarthy. 1979. Gelderman, Carol, ed. *Conversations with Mary McCarthy.* Jackson: University Press of Mississippi, 1991. 170–78.

Joyce, James. *A Portrait of the Artist as a Young Man.* 1916. New York: Penguin, 1964.

Kakutani, Michiko. "Our Woman of Letters." 1987. Gelderman, Carol, ed. *Conversations with Mary McCarthy.* Jackson: University Press of Mississippi, 1991. 257–67.

Lurie, Alison. "True Confessions." Review of *How I Grew* by Mary McCarthy. *New York Review of Books* 34 (June 11, 1987): 19–20.

McCarthy, Mary. *A Charmed Life.* 1955. New York: Harvest/Harcourt, 1992.

————. *The Company She Keeps.* New York: Harcourt, 1942.

————. *The Group.* 1963. New York: Avon, 1980.

————. *How I Grew.* New York: Harcourt, 1987.

————. Interview with Jack Paar. *The Jack Paar Show.* NBC Television. November 29, 1963.

————. *Memories of a Catholic Girlhood.* New York: Harcourt, 1957.

————. "My Confession." *On the Contrary.* 1953. New York: Farrar. 75–105.

————. "Yonder Peasant, Who Is He?" *Cast a Cold Eye.* 1944. New York: Harvest/Harcourt, 1992. 157–82.

Newman, Edwin. "A Conversation with Mary McCarthy." WNBC-TV interview. December 4, 1966. Reprinted in Gelderman, Carol, ed., *Conversations with Mary McCarthy.* Jackson: University Press of Mississippi, 1991. 68–87.

Podhoretz, Norman. "Miss McCarthy and the Leopard's Spots." *Doings and Undoings.* New York: Farrar, 1964.

Shinn, Thelma. *Radiant Daughters: Fictional American Women.* Westport, Conn.: Greenwood, 1986.

12

The Uses of Ambivalence: Mary McCarthy's Jewish Politics

Rhoda Nathan

Mary McCarthy's "Jewish" politics were both a key to and a reflection of her social and political attitudes. Scrupulously, almost morbidly, honest and projecting a near-clinical detachment about her own and others' positions with respect to controversial issues, she alternately distanced herself from and identified with her Jewish roots and the identities of her colleagues, friends, and lovers. Jewish "issues" did not intrigue her as much as did the phenomenon of anti-Semitism, which she examined frequently in the confessional mode in her memoirs. On occasion, she made the subject a teaching device, most notably in her essay "Settling the Colonel's Hash." In her fiction, she employed the thorny dual problems of anti-Semitism and "passing" in a gentile society, both drawn from intimate experience, as complex metaphors for other forms of social discrimination.

A case in point is the short story "The Friend of the Family," in which she uses anti-Semitism as an analogy for a more tolerable form of social prejudice—the dilemma which decent people face when confronted by an individual who is not high on their list of social priorities. How to include that marginal person without disturbing the social pecking order? How to guarantee his relegation to the fringe without alerting him to his limitations? In this story, Francis Cleary is McCarthy's marginal man, filling a category usually reserved for Jews in entrenched social circles. McCarthy makes her point through not one, but two, analogies drawn from the annals of the more subtle forms of anti-Semitism. When he is invited into the circle, whether as a fraternity pledge, a dinner guest, or a business associate, "the choice of Francis Cleary was not an affirmation of something, but a negation of something else" (59). To explain his position, McCarthy uses the analogy of the anti-Semite who marries a beautiful Jewess "and exempt[s] her from the Jewish race by a kind of personal fiat, declaring over and over to himself and possibly to her that he married her in spite of her relations, her mother, her sisters, her hook-nosed uncles, while in reality he is bored with his wife (who actually does not seem very Jewish), and it is the yearly visit of his mother-in-law to which he looks forward with sadistic zest" (63–64).

To complete the analogy and deepen its complexity, McCarthy offers yet another hypothesis: "A still worse cheat is the anti-Semite who asks a Jewish Francis Cleary . . . time after time to his house so that he may later express the most cruel and hair-raising opinions without being accused of bias" (65). McCarthy is merciless in anatomizing prejudice, casting a very cold eye indeed on social behavior, her own as well as others', which is compensatory for hidden stores of suppressed bias, not exempting even Jews themselves from her scrutiny: for example, "the Jewish banker in the concentration camp [who] forgets the donation he made to the Nazi party fund, back in 1931, when his great fear was communism" (81).

One of the more curious and ultimately unsatisfactory "carriers" of the Jewish identity virus in McCarthy's fiction is Peter Levi, the central character of *Birds of America*, written in 1965. If the book was, indeed, as Brightman suggests, "a catalogue of her tastes" (525), the hero also appears to have been formulated as a repository of her ambivalence. Peter may be "three-quarters Americanized" and a model of the intellectual, political, and social attitudes of his generation—values much admired and espoused by McCarthy at the time—but he is also unaccountably half Jewish, both through his biological Italian-Jewish father and his German-Jewish stepfather. The Jewishness of the hero in this novel would appear to be gratuitous, because it has few reverberations in the tale itself, unless it is there to reinforce the position of the outsider, the otherwise "nice kid" who is also an exile, or a marginal figure. The only conclusion the reader can come to is that the boy, conflated with the character of his mother, is McCarthy herself, in spite of her insistence that he is modeled on her son and his friends, growing up in the Vietnam era. His two internalized monologues, spaced at the beginning and the end of the novel, reinforce that impression. "Being American, he muses, was like being Jewish, only worse. You recognized 'your people' everywhere in their Great Diaspora and you were mortified by them and mortified by being mortified; you were drawn to them, sorry for them, amused by them, nauseated by them. Not only that. They spotted you as one of them, infallibly, just as Jews could always spot other Jews, even when they had had their noses fixed and changed their names" (103).

At the close of the novel, speculating with a mixture of distaste and compassion about the horde of vagabonds littering the streets of Paris, he engages in one more introspection: "They were clever and tightly organized. '*Comme les juifs*,' murmured Peter. And yet maybe it was true. It might even be true what anti-Semites said about Jews sticking together and if-you-knew-one-you-had-to-know-their-friends" (317). The issue of Jewish identity in this case is utilized as a metaphor, communicating the helpless ambivalence but never the resolution to the problem. With clinical detachment McCarthy hung her own dilemma about the necks of her fictional characters in whom she dwelled.

McCarthy spares no one, least of all herself, in scouring the hidden storehouses of the soul for what she terms "pseudo-friendships," the social ploys of those too cowardly to vent their true feelings, and others, like herself, who are guilty of ambivalence. In *Intellectual Memoirs* she reflects with some recoil on her own shameful "prettifying" of her love affair with the very openly Jewish Philip Rahv, whom she truly loved. So much did she admire his powerful identification with his Judaism that she declared him to be "[un]like most of the other Jewish intellectuals around PR, . . . exempt from what is known as Jewish self-hatred" (80). Still, her admiration for the unabashed "tenderness of his feeling" for his Judaism, which she acknowledged to be one of his greatest charms, did not deter her from hedging about her romantic alliance with a Jew. To her mortification she recalls, with characteristic merciless self-castigation, gushing to her friend Nathalie Swann, "My dear, I've got the most *Levantine* lover!" (83). She could not bring herself to admit then that she had a Jewish lover, especially during that period in her life when she was conscious of being "the only non-Jewish person in the room" with a bunch of Jewish Stalinists (61). In those days she went to great lengths to literally expunge her one-quarter Jewish ancestry when it suited her. She conveniently eradicated Grandma Augusta Morganstern in her zeal to separate herself even from the man whom she loved fiercely and frankly and admired for his boasting of Jewish "superiority" in every field of endeavor.

McCarthy's ambivalence about her Jewish identity began very early, as she records in her first two memoirs. In *How I Grew* she reminisces with burning shame about her complicity in the Elinor Coleman affair, in which her guilt lay in the sin of omission. One could not tell that the young Vassar freshman was Jewish, she was so snub-nosed and golden-haired. But when it was discovered, although the young woman made no attempt to conceal her identity, McCarthy recalls that "out of shame we were forced to stay friends with her. . . . But it came up unavoidably, of its own accord, as we got to know her better, as we met her mother and her grandmother, both of whom did look Jewish" (216). Elinor Coleman left after her freshman year; McCarthy confesses she had never revealed her own identity. "Shouldn't I have mentioned my Jewish grandmother?" she asks (217). Then, with her usual candor, she remembers she never even considered it. Further, she avoided having her Tower friends come to Seattle to meet her Preston, née Morganstern, grandmother, whose aquiline nose would surely have "spilled the beans" about convent-bred Mary's secret.

Later in life the mature McCarthy used her "double" life for the most transcendent of teaching devices. She made her ambivalence work for her as an instructive tool in a brace of cautionary tales. The two essays "Artists in Uniform" and "Settling the Colonel's Hash," written within the space of a single year, offer evidence that she took her politics personally and then objectified them to teach a valuable lesson to herself as well as to her students, to whom the second essay was addressed.

The first essay tells the story of a conversation McCarthy had in 1953 with a colonel in a club car on a train westbound for St. Louis. Secure behind the "map of Ireland" writ large on her features, she engages in an argument with the colonel, who is spewing violent anti-Semitism, and chastises him from the impeccable safety of her maiden surname and tip-tilted nose. The colonel was not stupid and made some attempt to justify his antipathy, causing McCarthy to reflect that "anti-Semitic statements were generally delivered in an atmosphere of profundity" (68), and woven from a variety of arguable and inarguable evidence. At the end, she tells the colonel that her married name is Broadwater, leaving him to conclude that it is Brodwater, a Jewish equivalent to names such as Goldwater. She does not correct the colonel's misapprehension, even when she sees the glimmer of understanding reflected in his smirk. She has it both ways; her "dirty" little secret—her Jewish blood and gentile husband—is unrevealed.

Less than a year later, McCarthy wrote the essay "Settling the Colonel's Hash," a commentary on "Artists in Uniform," beginning with the premise that the whole point of the story is that it really happened to her, and that she had received a lot of mail from students who had read it and teachers who had taught it. She uses the essay as an illustration of the use of symbols to make a point, in this case the "hash" she had settled, the hash the colonel was actually eating in the club car, and the hash of his clever arguments in defense of his anti-Semitism, as well as the hash she made of obscuring the truth of her identity. She had gotten away with murder owing to her duplicity. Even the title of the first essay, "Artists in Uniform," is analyzed for its symbolic content. But the chief value of the "autopsy" in the second essay is the postmortem examination of her prior craven behavior, her failure to reveal the truth, which, to her prosecutorial temperament, is more manipulative and wicked than a downright lie.

The two essays, taken together, make a package of biography, political analysis, and instruction without peer, reminiscent of John Berryman's "The Imaginary Jew," another ingenious application of personal experience in the service of high morality, while the writer remains guiltless of "smelling of the lamp." Further, when all the evidence is in, McCarthy is forced to come to the soul-searching conclusion of complicity arising from ambivalence. She discovered that while she "was willing to have Jewish blood, she was not willing to show it"; that she cheated herself by "having her cake and eating it"; and that "it is dangerous to be drawn into discussions of the Jews with anti-Semites: you delude yourself that you are spreading light, but you are really sinking into muck" ("Settling the Colonel's Hash" 239). What Mary McCarthy has done in these two essays, without sinking into the heresy of the didactic, is to present a summary of the ambivalence that haunted her throughout her life in a seamless amalgam of the formal and familiar essay with the conjoined goal of confession and instruction.

McCarthy is Jew and gentile, sometimes alternately and at others simultaneously. In her essay "The Hue and Cry" she is the gentile defending her Jewish mentor Hannah Arendt against the charges of anti-Semitism from the ranks. At Vassar she is the guilt-ridden "underground" Jew hiding her secret from her friends' impeccable gentile credentials. She is in and out, central and marginal, always scrupulously honest about her own deceptions and "passing." The uses of her ambivalence are finally prismatic, offering her an angle of vision denied to others whose insight is limited to one single perspective.

WORKS CITED

Brightman, Carol. *Writing Dangerously: Mary McCarthy and Her World*. New York: Clarkson Potter, 1992.

McCarthy, Mary. "Artists in Uniform." *On the Contrary*. 55–74.

———. *Birds of America*. New York: Harcourt, 1965.

———. *Cast a Cold Eye*. 1950. New York: Harcourt, 1972.

———. "The Friend of the Family." *Cast a Cold Eye*. 43–84.

———. *How I Grew*. New York: Harcourt, 1987.

———. "The Hue and Cry." *The Writing on the Wall*. 54–71.

———. *Intellectual Memoirs: New York 1936–1938*. New York: Harcourt, 1992.

———. *Memories of a Catholic Girlhood*. New York: Harcourt, 1957.

———. *On the Contrary*. 1946. New York: Farrar, 1962.

———. "Settling the Colonel's Hash." *On the Contrary*. 225–41.

———. *The Writing on the Wall and Other Literary Essays*. New York: Harcourt, 1970.

III

Mind and Body

13

The Stink of Father Zossima: The Medical Fact in Mary McCarthy's Fiction

Perri Klass

In her 1960 essay "The Fact in Fiction," Mary McCarthy argued that the hallmark of the novel as a literary form is "a deep love of fact, of the empiric element in experience" (251). She pointed to the tendency of novelists to include even informative material somewhat extraneous to the plot, suggesting that this "boiler plate" indicated the journalistic roots of the novel. What distinguishes a novel from a fable is the absence of the supernatural, of miracles; what further marks the novel is the presence of facts which tie it to the real world. "We not only make believe we believe a novel, but we do substantially believe it, as being continuous with real life, made of the same stuff, and the presence of fact in fiction, of dates and times and distances, is a kind of reassurance—a guarantee of credibility" (263).

If Mary McCarthy was not always successful as a novelist, she was always both interested and interesting, always engaged with each novel as an important endeavor and with the question of the form itself. As a critic and as a practitioner, she made it clear that her heart was with this fact-laden genre. In "The Fact in Fiction," she protested somewhat ingenuously that "I do not mean 'Novel good, fable bad,' merely 'Novel novel; fable fable' " (253). On the other hand, when she was speaking without the attempted evenhandedness of the literary taxonomist, she wrote in "A Tin Butterfly" about her hatred of *Uncle Remus,* the one book that her anti-intellectual guardian, Uncle Myers, read aloud to Mary and her siblings over and over again: "It seemed to me that this reduction of human life to the level of talking animals and this corruption of language to dialect gave my uncle some very personal relish. . . . to this day I cannot read anything in dialect or any fable without some degree of repugnance" (*Memories of a Catholic Girlhood* 65). As a novelist, McCarthy was obsessed with factual accuracy, as illustrated, for example, by a letter she wrote to William Jovanovich during the time she was writing *Cannibals and Missionaries*; McCarthy had just obtained a floor plan of an Air France 747, and had to do extensive rewriting to correct for the realities of the smoking/no-smoking division and the placement of the serving pantries. " 'I have this fanatical obsession with accuracy. The events in my books may be improbable or lightly fantastic, but the characters have to take real airplanes that can be found on a schedule: the schedule in force in January 1975' " (Gelderman 329).

The novelist, then, in McCarthy's terms, writes out of a fascination with fact, but also works under an obligation to fact; fact limits the plot of the novel, in the sense that miraculous events cannot occur. "You remember how in *The Brothers Karamazov* when Father Zossima dies, his faction expects a miracle: that his body will stay sweet and fresh because he died 'in the odor of sanctity.' But instead, he begins to stink. The stink of Father Zossima is the natural, generic smell of the novel" ("Fact" 252). In a broader sense, the natural generic smell of the novel comes from the hard truth of human mortality, the fleshiness and fleshliness of life. In fable, characters can escape this truth; bodies can do things that bodies cannot do (fly, change shape), and need not do the things that bodies really do (die, stay dead). In a novel, human beings must die if they are killed, by illness or by accident, and after they die, must begin to decay and stink.

Although McCarthy's fiction does abide by these rules, her approach to medical events, to the corporeal frailities and vulnerabilities of her fictional characters, suggests an intriguing balance on the border of fact. Medical events and medical problems, intimations of mortality as details of plot, are consistently revealed to be deceptions, inventions, illusions, and outright lies. These most organic details are almost always fictions within fictions, not facts within fictions.

McCarthy's own early life, of course, was shaped by a dramatic medical fact: the death of both her parents in the 1918 influenza epidemic. This turn in the fortunes of her childhood has a clear and even microbiologically identifiable cause; a tragic turn of plot which is explained not by character or individual choice, but by virology. McCarthy herself recovered from influenza and went on to enjoy excellent health. In fact, in *Memories of a Catholic Girlhood*, she gave some credit to her aunt's extremely unpleasant methods of child rearing, replete with castor oil and root vegetables: "I have a perfect digestion and very good health; I suppose I owe it to Aunt Margaret. It is true that we children were sick a great deal before we came to her; and no doubt she hardened us with her prunes and parsnips and no pillow and five-mile hikes" (85). In 1938, when she was admitted as a psychiatric patient to New York Hospital, she received that perfect score (a zero) on the basal metabolism test which in fiction she gave to Kay Petersen in *The Group*, evidence of physiologic energy balance (Brightman 176).

That was a peculiar contact with the medical world, that 1938 hospital admission in which McCarthy was committed for psychiatric observation by her husband, Edmund Wilson, following a violent drunken quarrel. McCarthy lied about the bruises on her face and arms and ended up accepting the idea of a "rest" as therapeutic; Wilson pointed out that thanks to her insurance coverage, the psychiatric ward would be cheaper than a hotel stay. As the marks of a beating became injuries self-induced in insanity, as marital tension was redefined as psychosis, and institutionalization was treated as a welcome rest, medical reality turned into deception and self-deception, strategy and counterstrategy in a problematic marriage—and the whole incident, ultimately, into anecdote and fiction in *The Group*.

The strategic deployment of false medical facts is a recurring theme in McCarthy's fiction, far more frequent and more striking than any attention to real illness or mortality. In the 1951 novel, *The Groves of Academe*, Professor Henry Mulcahy's campaign to avoid being fired for incompetence rests on two assertions: first, that he is actually a member of the Communist Party, a victim of a witch-hunt being fired for his politics, and second, that his wife has a serious medical condition, and may die if she finds out that he has lost his job. He thus fights back by claiming extreme vulnerability, for himself on political and ethical grounds (if he really is a member of the party, he has committed perjury by claiming not to be), and for his wife on medical grounds. Both of these are false premises; he is not (and has never been) a communist, and his wife has no serious medical complaint. The stories have in common the plausibility of outrageousness; who would claim something as ostensibly damaging as Communist Party membership if it weren't true, who would assign his wife a mortal illness if she in fact were perfectly healthy?

Mulcahy's wife's health is first mentioned in the opening pages of the novel as part of one of McCarthy's catalogues of character attributes. "His wife's women's complaint" is sandwiched between his children's damp bottoms and his own sandy eyes in the list of features which mark his family out on the campus as lower middle class, unattractive but mesmerizingly "genuine" to other members of the progressive Jocelyn College community (14).

As Mulcahy crafts his defense, or rather, his counterattack on the college president who has fired him, he formulates his wife's illness in greater detail, making it from a vague "women's complaint" into a multisystem disease which assumes convenient life-threatening properties reminiscent of literary illnesses in nineteenth-century fiction. When he first describes the problem to Domna Rejnev, his colleague and ally, it is "a heart and kidney condition brought about by Stephen's birth. . . . There's low blood pressure too and a secondary anemia" (44). Later on, he adds a retroverted uterus. And, most important, whenever he brings up the illness, he underscores the message: "Nothing that she won't recover from, given freedom from worry" (44). His wife has been left weakened and almost destroyed by the physiologic upheaval of childbirth—as he has been left weakened and vulnerable after his supposed political travails.

And despite the medically unconvincing nature of this "syndrome" (as a physician, I cannot resist pointing out, for example, that pregnancy-related kidney problems usually involve high blood pressure, not low, and that a woman with a retroverted uterus has most likely always had a retroverted uterus; it can make pregnancy more difficult, but is hardly likely to threaten her life postpartum), despite the peculiarly old-fashioned air of a disease which will be fatal if the patient is worried and completely curable if she is left in peace, Mulcahy's academic colleagues find the story of Cathy's illness completely convincing. The only character in the book who reacts to the story with any kind of common sense is Mulcahy's nemesis, the college president, always identified as the nonintellectual in the cast. "The President's face wore a look that vacillated between amusement and curiosity. 'You take this very hard, Domna,' he said, wonderingly. 'I scarcely think Cathy's heart condition can warrant such drastic attitudes. I myself have a slight heart condition,' he warned her with mock severity. 'Shall I complain that at this moment you're endangering my life?' " (158). Domna Rejnev herself repeatedly asks the question, what would Tolstoy think, and the fact is that this illness belongs in a novel by Tolstoy or one of his contemporaries; it has the ring of the grim portents offered up over nineteenth-century characters, the predictions that bad news, or childbirth, or being moved, will mean death. Mulcahy himself, as he embroiders the details of his wife's illness, is aware that the phrase he rehearses, "I will not answer for the consequences," is so familiar from movies that he cannot in fact remember whether he has ever heard it said by one of his wife's doctors.

McCarthy's narrative perspective in this novel is largely inside Mulcahy, an untrustworthy narrator if ever there was one. She speaks with Mulcahy's voice and sees with his eyes, and in her essay "Characters in Fiction," she comments that in *The Groves of Academe*, along with other modern novels, the reader "finds himself puzzled by the very vocal consciousness he has entered: is it good or bad, impartial or biased?" (282). (She goes on to chafe against the restrictions that this impersonation, this authorial act of ventriloquism, imposes on the writer: "There are moments when one would like to drop the pretense of being Mulcahy and go on with the business of the novel" [287].) The novel's narrative voice quivers with Mulcahy's own awareness on the border of the lies he is telling, which grow quickly in his mind from convenient and even amusing strategies to furious challenges thrown out at the world which so notably fails to give him his due. He sets out to convince Domna Rejnev of "the imminent danger to Cathy, a danger which, only a few moments before, he had been so fuzzy-minded as to regard as merely hypothetical but which, now that he had faced up to it, should make everything else secondary" (*Groves* 41). This awareness, within the text and therefore within Mulcahy, that he has gone in a matter of a few moments from hypothetical to imminent, is couched in the self-serving mental phrasings of Mulcahy's very vocal consciousness; he has "faced up to it" rather than invented the danger, he was previously "fuzzy-minded" rather than realistic.

Mulcahy himself, then, as he invents the story, comes immediately to believe as well. Not necessarily to believe that it actually *is* true, but to believe that the world owes him deference and special consideration because it *could be* true, just as it could be true that he had once been a communist. He makes the jump immediately from seizing on the strategic promise of his wife's illness to feeling outrage and indignation at the callous way in which the college president is willing to put her life at risk. "And yet there were many, he thought vindictively, on this 'liberal' campus who would suppose that Cathy's condition was something cooked up by himself to ward off being dismissed without so much as a thank-you, many . . . who would want a thorough medical report signed by an 'impartial' physician, in fact a coroner's inquest certifying the cause of death, before they would believe the simple clinical truth, just as, he presumed, they would have to see a Communist Party membership-card (produced by an F.B.I. agent) made out to Henry Mulcahy, before they would be willing to admit that his dismissal was a part of a campaign of organized terror in the universities against men of independent mind" (41–42). In fact, of course, he would be no more able to produce that thorough medical report than he would be able to show a Communist Party membership card, but he has transformed his complete lack of evidence, his own outright fabrications, into a sense of withering scorn directed at anyone so cynical as to refuse to believe those fabrications.

The parallel political and medical perils that Mulcahy conjures in order to impel his colleagues' support and sympathy are very much the stuff of which McCarthy believes novels should be made. In Communist Party membership,

Mulcahy is claiming involvement with the great historical currents of his time (and McCarthy's); in his wife's potentially mortal illness, he is invoking the tragedy of the body's frailty and the biological boundaries of life. *A man with a communist past, a woman whose health has been destroyed by childbearing.* But in *The Groves of Academe,* McCarthy declines the gambit. Neither politics nor illness will actually serve as a source of suspense or even as a turn in the plot, because both are invented by the central character. The untangling of the plot rests on his attempts to get other characters to believe his stories, or to act as if they do; the stories are invented to direct the plot of his own story. If the stink of Father Zossima is the right and proper smell of the novel, then this is something else, this odor of self-serving mendacity which almost seems to deny the characters the right to their own corporeal reality. They have no roots in body or body politic, Henry and Cathy; both are inventions and elaborations of the self-serving and scheming imagination which is also the novels' very vocal consciousness.

In *A Charmed Life,* on the other hand, the parameters of bodily reality lead into a different complexity of deception. The medical facts of fertility and conception (if you have intercourse, you can get pregnant; if you have intercourse with more than one man during a single cycle, you will not know for sure who the father is) dictate the course of the plot: when the protagonist, Martha Sinnott, finds herself pregnant, her immediate concern is to date her last menstrual period and thereby establish whether her single act of adultery with her ex-husband, Miles Murphy, could possibly have been responsible. "She was trying to remember when the Coes' play-reading had been. On a Friday, she felt certain, and she had started menstruating on a Monday. But was it the Monday before or the Monday after?" (254). It is probably safe to assume that an author who made sure that her novel jibed with the Air France floor plan took similar special care with the timing of her main character's menstrual cycle, synchronizing the timing of the infidelity and all the events before and after it so that nothing in the text would contradict the possibility that Miles Murphy might be responsible for the pregnancy. The timeline of the novel is thus determined by the hormonal ebb and flow of the main character, a fact in fiction if ever there was.

But the pregnancy itself is the result of deception, in the sense that Martha Sinnott has "deceived" her husband, and also possibly the occasion for more deception, as she tries to decide whether to abort this fetus or whether to go on and have the baby without telling her husband that it may not be his. Childbirth is again linked to sexual deception in *The Company She Keeps,* this time to the infidelity of the husband, Jim Barnett in "Portrait of the Intellectual as a Yale Man," who first kisses the heroine, Meg Sargent, on the occasion of his wife's maternity hospitalization: "Young husbands were supposed to go slightly on the loose when their wives were in the hospital having babies; it was the Yale thing, the manly thing, to do" (198). Similarly, the doctor Martha Sinnott consults in *A Charmed Life* advises her that having the baby and lying to her husband is the normal womanly course, what she is *supposed* to do. " 'Your case isn't as unusual as you seem to think. It happens to lots of women, respectable women too. A few drinks; husband's away. . . . *You* know. They go ahead and have the baby and everybody's happy' " (266).

The doctor reassures Martha Sinnott with the statistical probability that the baby is her husband's, though he admits that it is impossible to be completely certain, and advises her to proceed with the pregnancy: " 'Your husband will never know, unless you tell him. This other man won't know. No psychological complications' " (266). Martha's own sense of obligation to the truth thus becomes both overintellectual (" 'You think too much; that's the trouble with you,' " the doctor tells her [267]) and dangerous. Her unwillingness to live a lie and deceive her husband for the remainder of their life together is what may lead her to interrupt the pregnancy and put her own life at risk in a dangerous and illegal abortion. Medicine, in the person of the doctor, and biological reality, in the form of the pregnancy, are thus arrayed on the side of falsehood. Wives routinely present their husbands with babies conceived in adultery; husbands routinely commit adultery when their wives are in the hospital having babies. And everybody's happy, and it's the manly thing to do. Human reproduction, as basic a "fact" as death, is the occasion for deception and lifelong lies.

In *Cannibals and Missionaries* death itself becomes the occasion for deception. Here is a novel in which the plot truly *is* driven by politics, by people risking their own lives and those of others for their politics—in other words, by terrorists. And here is a novel in which a character, in fact, an elderly holy man, probably the closest McCarthy ever came to writing a Father Zossima, does die, and after death does begin to decay, to the point that his body attracts buzzards, scavengers drawn to dead flesh. And yet, the death of the Bishop, rendered as it is in strict accordance with medical fact, is transformed into a lie by the terrorists who have been holding him among their hostages, and the dead body itself is altered to falsify the medical evidence.

The Bishop's stroke, in itself a very strongly medical turn of plot for McCarthy, is described with her usual exactitude and multiplicity of detail: "There was a feebler motion of the head and a facial sign like a wink. One eye was wide open and staring" (172). The other hostages bring their widely varying degrees of medical expertise to bear on the problem, suggesting everything from adrenalin to bloodletting. When the Bishop is given an injection, McCarthy provides the name of the drug, Papaverine, its pharmaceutical function, a vasodilator, and the humiliating reality of the injection: "Thanks to Denise's butter-fingers, there had been no avoiding a glimpse of his private parts" (273).

The Bishop dies quietly during the night after his stroke, and the next morning the terrorists, lead by Jeroen, riddle his dead body with bullets from a submachine gun. This is their response to Washington's refusal to meet their demands; they will announce that a hostage has been executed, and use the Bishop's dead body to demonstrate their determination. This is an almost metafictional assumption of control by the terrorists and their guns; they are "killing," as an act of will, a man who has already died by the frailty of his own circulatory system. The scent of the blood that leaks out of the Bishop's body and attracts the carrion birds is not the true stink of a decaying holy man, but rather the false corruption of bloodletting by submachine gun of a body already dead. A related deception takes place in *A Charmed Life*, when Warren's mother dies and Jena, his wife, decides not to tell him. As the terrorists take over the Bishop's onstage death and turn it to their own ends, Jean takes over the offstage death of her mother-in-law, concealing it from her husband for her own reasons: she doesn't want Warren to cancel the play reading they have scheduled. "But since the old lady was gone, what could be the harm of letting him have the play-reading before he found out?" (160). The "real" old lady becomes much more amenable to fiction and sleight of hand than the play and the playacting, which are fixed and important realities to Jean. This same practical well-as-long-as-he's-dead-anyway attitude informs the willingness of the terrorists in *Cannibals and Missionaries* to use the Bishop in their much more dangerous play on the world stage. Jean suppresses a death to save a dramatic reading; Jeroen fakes an execution to make a death more dramatic to the watching world.

The other hostages, saved at least temporarily from the danger of execution thanks to this strategem, debate whether medical science will in fact be able to establish the truth of the Bishop's death. " 'And the fact that we can sit here debating when we witnessed the whole thing shows what a free-for-all the pathologists'll have with the autopsy. Hell, there are likely to be *two* autopsies, one here and one when they get him home' " (285). Once again, medical fact has become the stuff of deception, here to such an extent that forensic investigations within the text may not be able to determine what has really happened to the character. Once again, the deception takes on a certain ambiguity; if it works, and the terrorists' desecration of the old man's body is accepted as an execution, the other hostages are safe.

In addition to medical deception as political deception, *Cannibals and Missionaries* interweaves the questions of medical verisimilitude and artistic verisimilitude. In a truly remarkable scene, the authentication of a Vermeer, delivered in capitulation to the terrorists' demands, is juxtaposed with the faking of an illness by Victor, the hostage who is actually a CIA agent. As the expert from the Rijksmuseum examines the painting with a magnifying glass, Victor fakes an elevated temperature by hiding a cake of soap in his armpit. In fact, the art expert is nervous at having to pronounce on the authenticity of a painting when surrounded by armed terrorists and without having recourse to lab tests. "No wonder he was so uneasy; physical fear would be heightened by professional fear arising from lack of practice. It was probably years since he had arrived at an independent judgment of a work of art" (334). Sophie, another one of the hostages, draws the specific medical analogy: " 'Like doctors today. . . . They're afraid to diagnose a case of chicken pox unless they can send samples to the laboratory' " (334).

And so the expert dallies and worries over the painting; he is determined " 'to live up to the highest professional standard' " (334). And immediately juxtaposed with that painstaking determination to sort out real from fake is the conspirators' anxiety about the success of Victor's deception: 'Can't you light a fire under him? Christ, how long can a man's body maintain an artificially induced 103° temperature?' " (334). As the painting is successfully authenticated, the illness is successfully fabricated; Victor is flown out by helicopter before Jeroen and his comrades discover that in fact he is a CIA agent. His false illness protects his false identity, and he is saved by the helicopter which is carrying away the art expert. The painting is real; the fever is fake. The man with the false identity, escaping by means of a faked fever, is flown to safety in the helicopter which brought in the genuine Vermeer, as well as the expert who authenticated it. In a novel which is much concerned with the relative worth of people and paintings, this suggests not any facile scale of value (even a false and unappealing human being like Victor is worth more than a genuine and beautiful painting), but rather the intense and complex shifting natures of artistic value, political reality, and human life.

The terrorists are taken in by a faked illness, even as they go to elaborate lengths to make sure that they are not taken in by a faked painting. The faked illness saves the "real" life of a character who will surely be executed if his CIA identity becomes known. The authentication of the Vermeer painting, on the other hand, leads directly to its destruction. As with Henry Mulcahy, it could be argued, and even as with Meg Sinnott's fetus, deception is a prerequisite for survival. McCarthy, an author obsessed with truth telling and fact, suggests in her fiction that deceptions and the alteration of facts are the stuff of human lives and the plots of novels.

Mulcahy fabricates a life-threatening illness for his wife. Victor fakes a temperature. These are illnesses as whole-cloth inventions, stories within a story. The Bishop's death, however, and Martha Sinnott's pregnancy are real biological events, which McCarthy makes into sources of deceit and misunderstanding. This is also what she does with Kay's black eye in *The Group*, and with the cuts that John and Martha Sinnott sustain on their hands in the opening pages of *A Charmed Life*. Kay's black eye, inflicted by her husband, is presumed to be self-induced and taken as possible evidence of her insanity when she is hospitalized; paradoxically, the Sinnotts' cuts, both sustained in innocent household activities (John trying to raise a stuck window, Martha cutting an onion), on the other hand, may be seen by their community as evidence that they have been fighting with each other. The battle wounds of domesticity, however acquired, are subject to misinterpretation.

And when Priss Hartshorn Crockett in *The Group* attempts to breast-feed her newborn son, everything that should be most biologically "natural" and honest feels strange and artificial. She is nursing for all the "right" medical reasons; the arguments her pediatrician husband lists would be the same arguments used to advance breast-feeding today. The baby will get his mother's immunities, he will be protected from colds. All demonstrably true, then as now. When someone puts forward the question of whether breast-fed babies have warmer psychological relationships with their mothers, Priss's husband the pediatrician waves it aside: psychology is not a science. " 'Let's stick to measurable facts. Demonstrable facts' " (241). The citation and celebration of these medical "facts" in the fiction of *The Group* underline the larger fact of human biology; after Priss gives birth, her body produces milk to nourish the baby. (And, by the way, Priss really does have a retroverted uterus, which has made it difficult to carry a pregnancy to term.) A human is a human is a mortal is a mammal; this is a novel and therefore bound by our boundaries.

And yet, what Priss feels as she tries to fulfill this basic biological role is that she is doing something false and unnatural. When it is suggested that she may start a breast-feeding trend among pregnant Vassar alumnae, she thinks bitterly that she is "a party to a gross deception—one of those frauds on the public that the government Bureau of Standards was always out to uncover" (251). The fraud is that Stephen cries for hours every day; the price of nursing him on a rigid schedule seems to be that though he is gaining weight, he is always hungry. (And in fact, as a 1990s pediatrician, or even a 1990s mother, reading this chapter, I am impressed by how complicated and terrifying the pediatric establishment of the 1930s had managed to make breast-feeding, what with swabbing the nipples with alcohol so the baby rejects them and weighing the infant before and after every feeding so that the mother is fixated on ounce-by-ounce weight gains.)

At first Priss formulates the "fraud" as one she is perpetrating on other unsuspecting women who may try to follow her example. As the chapter goes on, though, she discerns a larger deception, one that has been practiced on her and on her baby. When her classmate, Libby, calls to ask her if she will write an article about breast-feeding, and Priss refuses, saying it would be in poor taste, Libby reminds her that " 'it's the most natural thing in the world. In Italy, the women do it in public' " (260). And Priss finally, angrily, responds, " 'and if it's so natural, why are you so excited about putting it in a magazine? You think it's unnatural, that's why' " (260). Priss has been aware that the story of her "achievement" may lead other women to try breast-feeding. She refuses to formalize that story, to make herself chief shill for the "fraud" rather than merely a party to it. She will not narrate her own story as an example for others, though the reasons she gives Libby at first are based on etiquette rather than honesty: it would look like her husband was trying to advertise, it would be in bad taste. But there is something more fundamentally wrong with her "experiment" in breast-feeding and the attention she is getting for it. It is her argument with Libby which leads her to her final conclusion: "She was doing 'the most natural thing in the world,' suckling her young, and for some peculiar reason it was completely unnatural, strained, and false, like a posed photograph" (261).

The atmosphere of rueful biological comedy that pervades this chapter, the sense of twisting your physical reality to suit what is expected of you, is reminiscent of the scene in *Memories of a Catholic Girlhood* when the twelve-year-old Mary McCarthy bleeds onto the convent sheets from a small cut on her leg, and the nuns insist on assuming that in fact she has started to menstruate and needs sympathetic explanations and monthly issues of sanitary towels. The young Mary tries to explain, but all her true statements are attributed to ignorance of the facts of life, or fear of puberty. Eventually, she gives in and accepts the situation. McCarthy notes a parallel between this false menarche and her lie that she had regained her faith after losing it (and losing her faith was initially itself a lie, which became the truth, and led to the necessary lie about gaining it back). "I had to pretend to have become a woman, just as, not long before, I had had to pretend to get my faith back—for the sake of peace. . . . For fear of being found out by the lay sisters downstairs in the laundry . . . I reopened the cut on my leg, so as to draw a little blood to stain the napkins, which were issued me regularly, not only on this occasion, but every twenty-eight days thereafter" (134). Her sense of apology and embarrassment that she is not undergoing the biological change expected of her suggests the same irony as her description of poor Priss Hartshorn, gamely struggling to do the "most natural thing in the world," but feeling all the time that it is completely unnatural, an exercise in fraudulence and deceit. Both the young Mary McCarthy, in her memoir, and the fictional Priss are somehow peculiarly at odds with what is natural, with their own biological identities, with their very hormones and bodily fluids. One feels compelled to perpetrate a fraudulent sexual maturation, and the other, completing the "work" of reproduction by suckling her young, feels that she is party to a fraud. What will come naturally in time must be anticipated and faked, what should be natural feels most unnatural.

Birds of America, as a novel of ideas, is much concerned with the place of humans in the world of nature. At the close of the novel, the hero, Peter Levi, is bitten by a swan in Paris, a bizarre and somewhat over-the-top turn of plot which feels rather unusual for McCarthy's fiction. In fact, Peter's mother, Rosamund, comments on how unlikely an event this is: " 'You were bitten by a black swan. Just like a person in a myth' " (340). He develops swellings in his armpits which remind him of the buboes described in Boccaccio's *Decameron* (a work cited in "The Fact in Fiction" as the seed of the novel; McCarthy points to the factual matter it contains on the subject of the Black Death, including "the tumors or buboes in the groin or armpits, some the size of a common apple, some of an egg, some larger, some smaller" ["Fact"] 254). Actually, Peter's delirium is not only unrelated to bubonic plague, but is not even caused by any interesting swan salivary organism. His delirium and the danger to his life result from the administration of penicillin for the infected wound; he is allergic to penicillin and has what would be called in medical terms a life-threatening anaphylactic reaction. It is the American Hospital, not the black swan, which nearly kills Peter; the ultimate medical deceit of harm in the guise of help is practiced upon him. Once again McCarthy raises the specters of remarkable and dramatic medical events, swan injuries and buboes, and once again she declines the gambit. The life-threatening event is strictly iatrogenic—a result of the treatment, not the disease. Even here, at the end of the novel, as McCarthy invokes a somewhat apocalyptic tone, as the bombs begin to fall on Vietnam, as Kant appears to proclaim the death of nature, the physical frailties of the human body give rise to irony and error.

McCarthy's use of medical facts and medical events in her fiction suggests both her strengths and her weaknesses as a novelist. Among her strengths is her steadfast refusal to be conned, that famous "cold eye" she casts on her characters, on their motives, on their self-consciousness and self-deceptions—even on their sense of themselves as characters. This same refusal to buy in to her characters' enthusiasms, however, can sometimes be confining, even paralyzing to her novels, draining them of a certain amount of emotional punch and resonance. At her best (notably in *Birds of America*, *The Group*, and at least parts of *Cannibals and Missionaries* and *The Company She Keeps*), her narrative voice finds a higher poetry in the catalogues of facts and details she uses with such precision, and her characters achieve a certain sympathetic apotheosis of self-consciousness.

She turns this same cold eye on their medical problems, on the frailties of the flesh, and on the often humiliating details of human biology. Nothing is as it seems; illnesses are invented or magnified for ignoble ends, pregnancy is compromised, breast-feeding is unnatural. Her characters interpret and to some extent even invent their own medical stories. Her plots are rarely driven by medical turns of event; two of the few important deaths which take place on stage in her fiction are poised between accident and suicide (Kay in *The Group*, Martha in *A Charmed Life*), and have nothing to do with illness. These characters rush forward to meet their own mortality, falling or driving into death, betrayed not by their bodies but by blind curves, drunk drivers, low windowsills. When a character does die of a medical illness, his death is taken over by other characters, rewritten with submachine gun bullets into a different plot altogether.

McCarthy's fiction follows strictly the rules she set forth in "The Fact in Fiction," keeping close continuity with real life in all matters, great and small. However, her approach to that overwhelming fact of human mortality suggests a complex and somewhat ambivalent relationship to the limitations of the body which must also be the limitations of the novel. Her fiction is haunted not only by the stink of Father Zossima, but also by the smell of self-interest and deceit, even around the bodily functions, even around birth and death. When it comes to this absolute boundary of the body and its ills, McCarthy's characters often lie—to themselves and to others. This dishonesty about the body is often related to dishonesty *of* the body—that is, to sexual deception, but also parallels political and even artistic deceptions and frauds. In this way, human duplicity itself becomes a fact and a fact of life, as real as the reality of corporeal disintegration.

And there is also, finally, an ironic transcendence. McCarthy's characters manipulate and reinterpret their own health, and the health of others, playing games with maternity, paternity, mortal illness, the timing and the cause of death. Their motives are often less than laudable, but they are, in a certain sense, struggling against the boundaries and limitations of their lives, and even of life itself. They do not and cannot escape these human limits, but they are not completely subject to them. What is achieved is not the "escape" of the supernatural, the transcendence of human limitations which properly belongs to fable, but instead a transcendence constructed of deceitfulness and self-interest, revealed through the self-conscious detail and the cool-voiced skepticism that are McCarthy's trademarks as a writer, the facts of her fiction.

WORKS CITED

Brightman, Carol. *Writing Dangerously: Mary McCarthy and Her World*. New York: Clarkson Potter, 1992.
Gelderman, Carol. *Mary McCarthy: A Life*. New York: St. Martin's, 1988.
McCarthy, Mary. *Birds of America.*. New York: Harcourt, 1971.
———. *Cannibals and Missionaries*. New York: Harcourt, 1979.
———. "Characters in Fiction." *On the Contrary*. New York: Farrar, 1961. 271–92.
———. *A Charmed Life*. 1955. San Diego: Harvest/Harcourt, 1992.
———. *The Company She Keeps*. 1942. New York: Harcourt, 1967.
———. "The Fact in Fiction." On the Contrary. 249–70.
———. *The Group*. 1963. New York: Avon, 1980.
———. *The Groves of Academe*. 1952. New York: Signet, 1963.
———. *Memories of a Catholic Girlhood*. New York: Harcourt, 1957.

14

Frigid Women, Frozen Dinners: The Bio-Politics of "Tyranny of the Orgasm"

Priscilla Perkins

In their 1947 volume of popular psychology, called *Modern Woman, the Lost Sex*, authors Ferdinand Lundberg and Marynia Farnham argue that the advent of mechanized production during the industrial revolution eventually led women, who saw many of their most important domestic duties usurped by machines, to despise their own reproductive capabilities. Women's new hatred of their roles as mothers led them to agitate for gender equality, the price of which was widespread sexual dysfunction and neurosis. Western culture, the authors repeat at many points in their study, has been punished for the dissatisfaction of women with social phenomena like communism, alcoholism, and even modern art (41); if women were happier, men would be happier, and none of these manifestations of neurosis would exist. Until women understand that they need sexual satisfaction in order to be healthy, and that they can achieve "true" orgasms only within the context of reproductively oriented, married intercourse, neurosis will rule the lives of both women and men (271). Since the time of the industrial revolution, Western history has shown that the psychological disorders of individuals spread to the culture at large. Everyone suffers, they warn, when women avoid their inescapable biological destinies.

In "Tyranny of the Orgasm," Mary McCarthy's review of this profoundly ahistorical psychohistory, McCarthy's response focuses, in part, on Lundberg's and Farnham's notion that the competition between women and machines is what ultimately led to the catastrophic "epidemic" of female frigidity. McCarthy turns the authors' claims inside out: rather than conceding that industry is a cause and symptom of female neurosis, she argues that Farnham and Lundberg are able to construct the neurotic only because they are already enslaved to a standardized, even mechanized, idea of normality. It is not, she suggests, that women have had to compete against machines; according to the American psychomedical establishment, women *are* machines, and men are, in her words, their "tenders." If their husbands cannot sexually calibrate them to function contentedly as housewives and mothers, then the women are condemned, to quote McCarthy, to "the junkyard of society, like an airplane grounded by the Federal Aviation Authority" (162).

This chapter will examine McCarthy's comparison of female bodies and airplanes as an unusually self-conscious postwar instance of what critic Mark Seltzer, describing the period before World War I, has called the "perverse *accouchements*" of the American "body-machine complex" (38). Seltzer sees the "body-machine complex" reflected most vividly in naturalist representations of antibiological reproduction involving new transportation and agricultural technologies: steamships expelling armies of men in Jack London's novels and tractors "impregnating" the earth with wheat in Frank Norris's are only two privileged ways of imaging the social anxiety brought on by the clash between modes of production and reproduction.[1]

I will argue that, in the socially turbulent period after World War II, old anxieties about the relationships between people and machines, between the "natural" and the "cultural," surfaced in debates about the proper disposition of the white, middle-class, American female body. One hotly contested question was whether women should be allowed to occupy paid positions in factories once their husbands and brothers had returned from the war. How, wondered many, should the newly unemployed female worker occupy her time and her mind? What kind of social danger might the figure of the educated, experienced woman present in a culture that was retooling its military industries for consumer production? What would women in this position want?

It is within the context of overwhelming economic and social displacement that McCarthy's, not to mention Farnham's and Lundberg's, invocations of femininity and machine culture make sense. But such discussions were not limited to the pages of psychology texts or intellectual journals like *The New Leader*, which originally published McCarthy's review of *Modern Woman, the Lost Sex*. The terms of such debates are recognizable in texts which appear to come out of completely different discursive spaces, as, for example, the pages of a magazine like *Popular Mechanics*, which in April 1947 (the same month as McCarthy's review) ran an article on frozen-food technology called "Dinners without Drudgery." My goal in yoking such disparate texts together is to use McCarthy's own imagery in order to offer some more satisfying answers to the question which still troubles her at the end of her book review: what is the social meaning of so-called female frigidity? For the purposes of this chapter, I might put her question another way: what does the *frozen* signify in interfaces between female bodies and machines, or between nature and culture?

When she writes that "mass production methods (statistics) yield an average woman who is tested by a bureau of standards that expects uniform 'perform-ance' " (162), McCarthy exhibits keen insight into a phenomenon which Michel Foucault would explore in more detail almost thirty years later: normative psychology, with its emphasis on the average, works to *produce* "individuals" by pulling them out of family and community contexts for the purpose of scientific evaluation. The judgments of experts are sometimes enough to marginalize those "individuals" who fall at either extreme of a psychologist's scale; with the right kind of test, members of a feared or disliked minority can be made to appear abnormal and further separated from their families and communities. In Foucault's terms, psychology is a disciplinary technology which produces persons who fit the particular ideological require-ments of a given society.

Throughout her review, McCarthy's discomfort with Farnham's and Lund-berg's antifeminism is palpable. At the beginning of the text, for instance, she notes that Marynia Farnham, the female author of the book, is a doctor; later, she relates the duo's contention that women should avoid higher education in favor of childbearing, "except," she writes rather tartly, "in very special in-stances, such as that of the female doctor" (161). Taken as a whole, however, McCarthy's review is not primarily an argument for women's rights to eco-nomic and sexual self-determination; instead, McCarthy is concerned with the ways that normative psychology dictates appropriate gender roles for both women and men. If she is to produce the proper quota of orgasms and children, woman-as-machine depends upon a particular construction of manhood for her maintenance. McCarthy sees that the ideally constructed male, "the husband with the psychiatric know-how," is every bit as oppressed by his role as his wife is. "His whole life," she writes,

must be a character reference open to the investigation of experts. The "fully masculine male" must marry, make money, work regularly and prolifically, sustain an erection for the "normal" length of time, somewhere under half an hour. He must enjoy good health, show no feminine traits of character and have "a masterful ego-structure" (163).

She resents the power that psychomedical professionals—particularly those whose work is consumed by a huge lay audience—have to mold both individual self-perception and domestic relationships.

The magazine *Popular Mechanics* is itself an instance of the power of the "body-machine complex" to produce a particular kind of man, and to prescribe that man's various relationships both to machinery and to women. The magazine's articles show, on the one hand, how machinery can be made to mediate in relationships between men and women: the "good" husband, it claims, is always building gadgets and furnishings that make the domestic environment more efficient for housewives and more comfortable for families. The magazine's writers also use gendered language in order to demonstrate the kind of control the ideally constructed man should exercise over his machines and, by analogy, over "his" woman. Everywhere, cars, airplanes, cameras, and tools are called "she"; men are urged to respect technology, but not to fear it, because it was made for their use. In photographs and drawings, ecstatic-looking women in gingham scarves hold paint cans and pass wrenches to husbands on ladders and under sinks.

Popular Mechanics advertisements offer the most poignant evidence of the pressure postwar men received to be the "fully masculine male." An overwhelming number of ads in the April 1947 issue are for either bodybuilding programs or correspondence courses in engineering, car repair, or radio operation. The images of men in the various ads are nearly identical, except that the models are clothed in the latter category; most of the ads promise that their programs will enable men to impress women and earn the respect of other men. Within the context of *Popular Mechanics*'s emphasis on what anthropologist David Gilmore has termed male "performative excellence," it is not surprising that the author of "Dinners without Drudgery" carefully notes that the inventor of quick-frozen dinners, William Maxson, is a 260-pound engineer who graduated from Annapolis. Educational credentials and physical size are assumed to be equally important to readers of *Popular Mechanics*.

According to the article, frozen-food technology was first developed for the military, but was being adapted to make both housewives and airlines into more efficient servants of their varying constituents. On land or in the air, the gender politics of frozen food are worth examining, because they highlight the fascinating conflation that was being made between women and machines in the postwar era. *Popular Mechanics* shows uniformed stewardesses popping frozen dinners into quick-heating convection ovens located, appropriately enough, at the tail end of Boeing's new Stratocruiser planes. In this version of the "body-machine complex," new technology, designed by men, helps female workers turn airplanes into something resembling giant mothers that can warm and feed up to 200 passengers before expelling them to unfamiliar places. On the ground, frozen dinners are marketed toward housewives—not men or paid female laborers—who wish to save food storage space and time that would otherwise be spent on cooking and dish washing.

Somewhat surprisingly, considering the subsequent discursive treatment of so-called TV dinners, the author of "Dinners without Drudgery" never suggests that frozen foods might be used by women to alleviate the guilt that they were expected to feel about their commitments outside of the home. As far as the reader of this article can tell, stewardesses are the only American women who have business outside the home, and they are identified with the now motherly airplanes in which they work. The message of *Popular Mechanics* is that frozen foods can help to turn potentially menacing technological spaces into comforting pseudodomestic ones, but they also threaten, as Farnham and Lundberg are quick to point out, to destroy the psychological sanctity of spaces which have long been designated as domestic. "Women might observe and ponder the significance," they write, "of the alacrity with which men have seized upon the food-preparing functions and institutionalized them in the form of restaurants, delicatessens and preserving and packaging plants" (366). According to these authors, processed foods are only the latest in a chain of "advancements" which free women from "the 'tyranny' of pots and pans," only to leave them sexually frigid and hopelessly neurotic. In the postwar discourses I have been describing, the "frozen" serves as a problematically mobile marker between what is supposed to be "natural"—women's roles as reproducers and caretakers—and the man-made, "cultural" realm of technology.

For McCarthy, the privileged example of the blurry line between the natural and the cultural involves the figure of the "frigid" woman herself. Here, as before, McCarthy works to subvert the psychologists' claims by redefining the terms of their argument. In the example I offered at the beginning of this chapter, McCarthy shows that the problem is not "women versus machines," but "women *as* machines." In the instance I am about to describe, she is less equipped to wrest definitional power away from the experts because she relies on their own research for the argument she wishes to make. In doing so, she reveals how difficult it is, even for a strongly oppositional voice, to critique a totalizing and socially powerful discourse like normative psychology. Whether she likes it or not, she finds that her own subjectivity is circumscribed and defined by the discourse she is attacking.

McCarthy disputes Farnham's and Lundberg's claim that the female orgasm is the "natural" reward to those women who obey the biological imperative to reproduce and nurture children within the institution of heterosexual marriage. Using (biologically dubious) evidence from A. C. Kinsey's research of the mid-1940s (work which also informs the arguments of *Modern Woman, the Lost Sex*), she contends that, though the orgasm is "natural" in men and other male animals, it is a behavior that human females originally *learned* from men, one that can be forgotten, and, presumably, retaught. Other female animals, she says, do not experience orgasm; among women, such behavior is decidedly cultural.

She concludes, understandably, that the "frigid" woman is the pathologized creation of those psychomedical professionals who refuse to consider the material and social causes for female sexual dissatisfaction. But by switching the terms of the old woman:nature/man:culture dichotomy so that man is identified with "nature" and woman with "culture," McCarthy is unable to escape from the ideological equivalence between women and machines. According to the model she suggests, women do not *have* to have orgasms in order to be "true" women, but, except for lesbians, those who enjoy or wish for orgasms are still, in some sense, beholden to men. Though she tries to release men from the oppressive role established for them by the psychologists and replace it with an emphasis on reciprocity and shared passion, the new role she creates is itself problematic because it forces men into the false and disempowering position that has been traditionally reserved for women. This does not seem to be McCarthy's goal. Finally, though McCarthy's conclusion does make a space for women on the "cultural" side of the sexual equation, it is not a space that allows women to be active definers of their own sensations. Instead of "making culture," they are still "made by culture." McCarthy's solution to the "problem" of female orgasm does not give women, either frigid or fervent, a way out of the body-machine complex.

NOTE

1. In his definition of the "biopolitical," Mark Seltzer quotes from Jacques Donzelot's *The Policing of Families*:

Taking as its field of analysis a politics of the body and of the social body, such an analytic identifies a network of practices located "between the empty gesture of the voluntary and the inscrutable efficiency of the involuntary," and reexamines "the endless cleavage between politics and psychology" by focusing on the constitution of the subject as the subject of power (Seltzer 41; Donzelot 6).

WORKS CITED

Donzelot, Jacques. *The Policing of Families*. With a foreword by Gilles Deleuze. Translated by Robert Hurley. New York: Pantheon Books, 1979.

Gilmore, David. *Manhood in the Making.* New Haven, Conn.: Yale University Press, 1990.

Hamilton, Andrew. "Dinners without Drudgery." *Popular Mechanics.* April 1947: 174.

Lundberg, Ferdinand, and Marynia Farnham. *Modern Woman, the Lost Sex.* New York: Harper, 1947.

McCarthy, Mary. "Tyranny of the Orgasm." Review of *Modern Woman, the Lost Sex,* by Ferdinand Lundberg and Marynia Farnham. *The New Leader.* April 5, 1947: 10. Reprinted in *The Humanist in the Bathtub.* New York: NAL, 1964.

Seltzer, Mark. *Bodies and Machines.* New York: Routledge, 1992.

15

Damn My Stream of Consciousness

Katie Roiphe

Gertrude was as all knowing as Time. All clichés, slogans, fashions, turns of speech, details of dress, disguises of affection, tunnels or by-passes of ideology . . . lived in Gertrude. If one of Gertrude's heroines, running to snatch from the lips of her little daughter a half-emptied bottle of furniture polish, fell and tore her skirt, Gertrude knew the name of the dress maker who made the skirt—and it was the right name for a woman of that class at that date; she knew the brand of the furniture polish.

—Randall Jarrell, *Pictures from an Institution*

With his famous caricature of Mary McCarthy, Randall Jarrell picks up on McCarthy's attempt to capture a social milieu through its details. The Gertrude of his vivid comic portrait is more concerned with brand names and social signs than the plight of the child or the anxiety of the mother. In mocking McCarthy's romance with the right details, Jarrell suggests that her cerebral mode of writing obscures the human or emotional dimension of literature. Jarrell has captured something of the frozen precision of McCarthy's prose, her insistence on the social rather than the internal, on aspect rather than development. In his review of *The Company She Keeps* in *The New Yorker*, Clifton Fadiman was responding to the same tendency when he dismissed the novel's protagonist, Meg Sargent, as a "characterless" character (73).

With its wit, its phrasemaking, its concern with the social world, the satiric style that dominates McCarthy's first novel, *The Company She Keeps*, does resist the demands of psychological depth, the introspective thrust of Freudian concerns, the idea of characters fleshed out. It is the style she is best known for. Filled with an enduring sarcasm, with what McCarthy refers to as "invisible quotation marks," her stylized prose judges and appraises (Grumbach 203). She draws on the magazine voice cultivated by Dorothy Parker and other writers of the 1920s and 1930s: that of the sophisticated arbiter of taste.

McCarthy often conveys character through long social inventories; she sees in the minutiae of the kind of cigarette holder a woman held, or the kind of earrings she wore, the intricacies of the class she was from and the class she was aspiring to. Her characters are drawn with fine attention to mannerisms of speech and dress, to the nuances of their relation to the social world, the books they might carry and why, the parties they would go to, the ways in which they might think about the parties they would go to, their evaluation of their own position in society, and their calculations about the positions of those they love or admire. These are the main delineations in McCarthy's character sketches.

McCarthy's carefully crafted satire is composed of descriptions that signal and wink to those in the know. She assumes an intimate familiarity with cultural signposts. We are supposed to know, for example, the social meaning of a Brooks Brothers shirt, or of Yale, or the Village, or tennis. McCarthy's satiric style, then, emerges from what could be called an aesthetics of clique. She is, as Jarrell suggests, concerned with a kind of social anatomy, a dissection of character, that involves not soul, not psyche exactly, but a complex network of social motivations.

McCarthy puts it another way: like Meg Sargent, her fiction is endowed with a "sense of artistic decorum that like a hoity-toity wife was constantly showing poor biography to the door" (*Company* 264). McCarthy's comic idiom defies the Freudian thrust of character analysis and what she calls "poor biography." She is more interested in art and artifice, in the way people present themselves, than in childhood traumas and subconscious motivations.

Given all of this, is the image of Mary McCarthy's shallow comic voice skimming the surface of experience really fair? Or has Randall Jarrell left something out? His Gertrude doesn't do justice to McCarthy's attempt to capture, pin down, and analyze human emotions and motivations. With his talk of furniture polish and brand names, he does not take McCarthy's forays into psychoanalysis into account. After all, Meg Sargent, the "characterless" character, does spend an entire chapter on a psychiatrist's couch. McCarthy does not confine her narrative to the realm of invisible quotation marks, she does not choose, as she could have, to strip her text of Freudian underpinnings and flashes of childhood memories.

Of course, she was writing at a time when people were more concerned with psychoanalysis than we are today. Freudian ideas were so pervasive it was hard to be specifically aware of their influence. Freudian interpretation moved through the highest intellectual circles, to movies, pop psychology, and mass literature. It permeated American culture. In opposition, many writers of the 1940s and 1950s expressed contempt not only for the crushing reductionism of popular Freudian thought but also for the more sophisticated schematic probing of Freudian critics. Even so, for writers like Mary McCarthy Freud was still a force to be reckoned with. She was, after all, writing for an audience alert to psychoanalytic cues, an audience accustomed to thinking in terms of conscious and subconscious repression and symbols. With a readership so aware of psychoanalytic readings, a cigar could no longer be just a cigar. Although Mary McCarthy once dismissed Freudianism as "an absurd set of myths," she was not unconcerned with Freudian interpretation (Gelderman 80).

Instead of allowing the language of psychoanalysis to break through her satiric certainty, however, McCarthy incorporates it into her comic mechanism. She does not allow poor biography to get in the way of artistic decorum. In the last chapter of *The Company She Keeps* ("Ghostly Father, I Confess") the therapeutic session consists more of witty sparring than the baring of subconscious feelings. Meg's intellectual familiarity with Freudian thought gives her the distance to smile and tease. Engaged in a sort of chess game of personal revelation, she stays one move ahead of her psychiatrist. She anticipates Freudian interpretation as she starts telling him a dream about matriculating at a school called Eggshell College. "I must have dreamed that just to please you," she says to the analyst with a teasing smile. "It's custom-made. The womb fantasy" (240). Later, she preempts his discussion of the castration complex by bringing it up before he gets a chance to (257).

When Meg Sargent launches her social commentary, her judgments and opinions, the psychiatrist refuses to accept them as detached observations of the external world. In retaliation, she satirizes his resistance to her wit in a parody of transference:

She would spend half a session trying to show him, say, that a man they both knew was a ridiculous character, that a movie they had both seen was cheap. And it would be hopeless, absolutely hopeless, for he *was* that man, he *was* that movie, he was the outing cabin, the Popular Front, the League of American Writers, the *Nation*, the *Liberal*, the *New Republic*, . . . Colonial wallpaper, money in the bank and two cocktails (or was it one?) before dinner (250–251).

Her humor is so effective, her satire so sharp, that Meg Sargent undermines the psychoanalytic process even as she lies on the couch. In the competition for interpretation, the push and pull for control over the narrative that characterizes Meg's relation to the psychiatrist, such a vivid comic perspective gives the victory to her.

In another display of knowledge, Meg Sargent mocks the idea of stream of consciousness: "Damn my stream of consciousness, her mind said, why must it keep harping on this embarrassing topic?" (251). By comically deflating the idea of stream of consciousness—the central concept that assimilates psycho-analysis into literature—she argues against the idea of a story drifting along a stream of unconscious associations. With her flippant joke on the Freudian version of storytelling she asserts her own control over the narrative.

Mary McCarthy often follows Meg Sargent's lead. She uses excessive literal references to Freudian thought to block its usefulness. In *Birds of America*, Peter, the young protagonist, explicitly addresses the question of oedipal tensions: "He had known for a long time about the Oedipus Complex; his stepfather used to tease with 'And how is young Oedipus?' But he did not think that, on balance, he would like to sleep with his mother" (11). By making the oedipal tensions so literal, and therefore so absurd, McCarthy diffuses their power. With her casual reference to the Freudian interpretation of events, certainly an interpretation that presents itself in a book centered around a mother-son relationship, McCarthy defies its seriousness. Through her deadpan excess of Freud, she blocks this particular entrance into the book. She successfully anticipates and preempts the Freudian reading by making it into a caricature of itself.

Like Meg Sargent, McCarthy seems to compete with Freudian interpreta-tion for control of her narrative. In McCarthy's fictional universe, psychoanaly-sis represents a loss of composure and power. The characters most closely associated with it are usually weak, emasculated men like Warren in *A Charmed Life* and Gus in *The Group*. They are both paralyzed and ineffectual. McCarthy connects psychoanalysis to their moral limpness and their inability to assert control over their own destinies. Warren's analyst actually tells him that moral values are just rationalizations. Gus can't leave his wife because his analyst won't let him. He breaks off his affair with Polly because it is an obstacle to his analysis. With images of such extreme dependence McCarthy expresses the idea that by surrendering interpretation one surrenders control over one's life. The submerged implication is that this kind of introspection is itself paralyzing. It is the stuff of satire, not of wisdom.

McCarthy's struggle against psychoanalysis takes its most literal form in "The Appalachian Mountain Revolution" (*Hounds*). The arrival of psychiatrists marks the disturbance and ultimately the destruction of a secluded summer spot. The psychiatrists arrive, as their black and orange license plates reveal, from New York City, and the conflict is staged between these loud, vulgar psychiatrists and the tasteful, reserved young matrons. The story has a clear allegorical dimension: the psychiatrists have altered the scenery, particularly the significantly named "Mirror Lake." McCarthy scatters hints of the larger cultural plot throughout her story: "The young mothers could not help but feel forlornly that they were witnessing the end of an epoch" (163). They were right to feel this way, as the story reveals. The psychiatrists have imposed themselves and there is no escape. It *is* the end of an epoch for these matrons, for their pond will be destroyed by beavers, the magical counterparts of the psychiatrists.

When the psychiatrists arrive at the beautiful lake one of them notes with satisfaction, "It's like a picture," a telling comment that reveals how indirect his access to nature really is (161). They come laden with rubber tires and radios, sun tan oil and the *New York Times*, unable just to enjoy the beach without the mediation of civilization. As one of the young matrons complains later to her husband, "They're against Nature" (167).

The psychiatrists have changed the rules. While the young matrons communicate with subtle looks and gestures, the psychiatrists shout through "the megaphone of their hands" and speak in "blaring, self-commendatory tones" (163). They are impossible to ignore. Before the psychiatrists came the lines were invisible and understood. And it is their crude demand for explicitness that threatens the peace of the community. McCarthy explains that "their profession had made them overbearing . . . they methodically pulped every experience like an orange juice extractor" (169). With their arrival Mirror Lake has been violated. The private beach is no longer private.

WORKS CITED

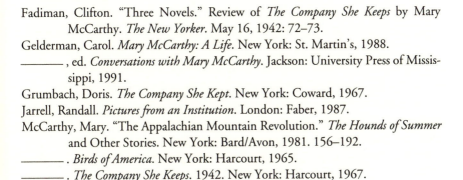

Fadiman, Clifton. "Three Novels." Review of *The Company She Keeps* by Mary McCarthy. *The New Yorker*. May 16, 1942: 72–73.

Gelderman, Carol. *Mary McCarthy: A Life*. New York: St. Martin's, 1988.

————, ed. *Conversations with Mary McCarthy*. Jackson: University Press of Mississippi, 1991.

Grumbach, Doris. *The Company She Kept*. New York: Coward, 1967.

Jarrell, Randall. *Pictures from an Institution*. London: Faber, 1987.

McCarthy, Mary. "The Appalachian Mountain Revolution." *The Hounds of Summer and Other Stories*. New York: Bard/Avon, 1981. 156–192.

————. *Birds of America*. New York: Harcourt, 1965.

————. *The Company She Keeps*. 1942. New York: Harcourt, 1967.

IV

Facts in Fiction

16

A Single Truth, but Tell It Sharp

Mary Ann Caws

Tell all the truth but tell it slant.

—Emily Dickinson

Telling it slant wasn't Mary McCarthy's way with things. Especially not with truth, which mattered to her more than anything, as she constantly said. Her truth, which she conceived of as single, seemed to be for her quite simply coincident with truth itself. For those of us who believe in multiple truths, a part of the problem in our relation to her writing may lie here. By "problem" I mean what may most interest us, explaining our fascination, immeasurably increased by her sharpness of tongue, eye, and mind. That sharpness compels our admiration, even as it invites our discomfort.

Her truth, angled as it is sharp, is meant to coincide with her being. "I think I'm really not interested in the quest for the self anymore. . . . what you feel when you're older, I think, is that . . . you really must *make* the self" (Interview 28). Although she claims never to have written a "developmental novel in which a self . . . is forged" (28–29), her entire body of writing speaks as such a novel.

Did McCarthy, in the 1960s, believe in the "solidity of truth"? "Yes," she says, "I believe there is a truth, and that it's knowable" (29). Her work wants to be about knowing it. Nothing obsessed her more. As she circles around her own seeing and speaking, or not seeing and not speaking, the truth, she draws the reader into the same obsession. The wonderfully peculiar fascination she manifests for the cover-up or the lie is finally, in my reading, turned to the positive, to what I think of as the generosity of her occasional lie.

To outline my subject and my position, I will state openly and without apology which texts in her immense body of work I most admire and refer to most often. Among her essays on literature, I gravitate toward "General Macbeth," "On *Madame Bovary*," "On Rereading a Favorite Book," and "The Fact in Fiction." In her fiction, I particularly love the very early "The Weeds," for reasons I will give. In her travel or art writing, I take to parts of *Venice Observed*, although I would argue with her about Tintoretto, which only proves her point that he is the literary person's favorite. But every page of *The Stones of Florence* is for me a masterpiece of informal, close dealing with a city and its art. Here, as elsewhere, I believe that what she sees as truth itself controls her taste. Among her personal and autobiographical essays on living and writing, my main concern, I take to *On the Contrary*, and I greatly appreciate *Memories of a Catholic Girlhood, How I Grew*, and the autofiction called *The Company She Keeps*. I put in last and honored place the infinitely moving elegy "Saying Good-bye to Hannah," about Hannah Arendt, her friend and, in a sense, mentor. In that loving and haunted piece there appears a small and all the more telling example of what I call "cognitive courage."

COGNITIVE COURAGE

In Mary McCarthy's work and life, I don't see a lot of self-deception; she was fearless about discomfort, hers and the reader's too. She says repeatedly how much she learns about herself through writing: we see her doing just that, which is why I take her work as a whole to be, or at least to resemble, a developmental novel. She takes the grave step of creating a protagonist—purportedly fictional, but clearly autobiographical—very like herself and yet frequently dislikeable. She discusses this strategy in her surprising story "Artists in Uniform" of 1953 and its subsequent risky reflection, "Settling the Colonel's Hash" of 1954. This odd couple of texts provides a clear if complicated example of her involvement in the topic of self-discovery and truth.

McCarthy is good in trains, a classic setting for self-discovery: see "The Man in the Brooks Brothers Shirt," but especially "Artists in Uniform." The protagonist, called Mary McCarthy, is identified by others on the train as a sculptress because, she imagines, of the two tones of green in her skirt and blouse and her pink earrings, a costume which in fact, she tells us, had been assembled with care at an expensive shop. Yet to one observer, a talkative colonel, this was "simply a uniform that blazoned a caste and allegiance just as plainly as the colonel's khaki and eagles," (57). Unable to retain her own sense of self under this labeling, she gazes down at her outfit: "My contrasting greens seemed to be growing more and more lurid and taking on an almost menacing light, like leaves just before a storm that lift their bright undersides as the air becomes darker" (57).

Indeed, the air will darken. A discussion begins about politics at Harvard; sure of her truth on this point, she states it and, feeling a certain smugness at having set her interlocutors right, she reopens her book. Then, upon the colonel's proffering some anti-Semitic remarks, she leaves the compartment, worried all the same that her departure will be ascribed to her (unstated) Jewishness and equally annoyed by her companions and herself: "I am in fact a quarter Jewish, and though I did not 'hate' the idea of being taken for a Jew, I did not precisely like it, particularly under those circumstances" (61). I wanted them to know, she continues, that it was my principles that were offended and not myself. "To let them conjecture that I had left because I was Jewish would imply that only a Jew could be affronted by an anti-Semitic outburst; a terrible idea" (61). We can hear her conscience turning over, in anguish, and it goes on, as she explains to the colonel that she cannot have lunch with him, because of his sentiments. " 'Oh come now,' he repeated, with a look of amusement. 'You're not Jewish, are you?' 'No,' I said quickly. 'Well then . . .' said the colonel. 'But I might have been,' I stammered. 'You had no way of knowing. You oughtn't to talk like that.' I recognized, too late, that I was strangely reducing the whole matter to a question of etiquette" (63–64). She thinks of her Jewish grandmother, whom she has not mentioned (nor will she, in this conversation), disputes with him, notices that their walking together isolates them "like a pair of lovers," and finally lunches with him after all, joined as they are by their Irish names, as she herself has signaled: "I'm Irish, just like you, Colonel" (64). The complicity deepens, as she does not mean it to: " 'I'm not 'for' them,' I protested. . . . This word, *them*, with a sort of slurring circle drawn round it, was beginning to sound ugly to me. Automatically, in arguing with him, I seemed to have slipped into the colonel's style of thought" (65–66).

Something stealthy hovers over them, "over the dark table." "I was stubbornly sitting on the fact of my Jewish grandmother like a hen on a golden egg" (69). Later, when the train pulls out, she waves back at him, unable to stop herself, and even gives him "the corner of a smile" (73). He finds out her married name—Broadwater—assumes it is Jewish, and, she laments, "The victory was his" (74). (Much of McCarthy's writing is couched in game terms: victory, concession, losing, defeat, failure.)

How to retrieve a victory? Reflecting on this account in "Settling the Colonel's Hash"—a talk given in February 1954 to writers at the Breadloaf School in Middlebury, Vermont—she tells how she had to insist to the readers who had written her to inquire about the "symbols" of the hash the colonel had eaten and her sandwich, and further details, that "Artists in Uniform" was not fiction, but absolutely true, and that the symbols were not chosen, but natural ones: "our provisional, *ad hoc* symbols of ourselves" (230). She had not wanted to be identified, she says, by her clothes or anything else as "a member of a peculiar minority—an artist or a Jew; but brute fate and the colonel kept resolutely cramming me into both those uncomfortable pigeonholes" (230). She wanted to be seen as transcending categories, as universal, "to be anybody and therefore everybody" (230). But here comes the odd and brave statement: "I wanted to embarrass myself and, if possible, the reader too" (227). And that she does.

She had tried to force the colonel, whom she assumed to be a Catholic, as she no longer was, into religious tolerance. "But the colonel, it turned out, did not believe in God, either, and I lost. And since, in a sense, I had been cheating all along in this game we were playing, I had to concede the colonel a sort of moral victory in the end; I let him think that my husband was Jewish and that that 'explained' everything satisfactorily" (238). Her honesty here lies in her openly recounting her semi-lies and total concealments. But she draws a moral: "You cannot be a universal unless you accept the fact that you are a singular, that is, a Jew or an artist or what-have-you. What the colonel and I were discussing, and at the same time illustrating and enacting, was the definition of a human being. I was trying to be something better than a human being; I was trying to be the voice of pure reason; and pride went before a fall" (239). Her confession continues, elucidating in a sort of *explication de texte*, an unfolding of her own text, the meaning of the experience, which she had not grasped during it.

This very development of both conscience and consciousness is what her writing brings about. That realization, quieter elsewhere, is startling in "Settling the Colonel's Hash." She reflects on the incident and its meaning, rewriting it as she retells it:

[W]hen I went back over the experience, in order to write it, out came these meanings, protruding at me, as it were, from the details of the occasion. I put in the green dress and my mortification over it because they were part of the truth, just as it had occurred, but I did not see how they were related to the general question of anti-Semitism and my grandmother until they *showed* me their relation in the course of writing. . . . A story that you do not learn something from while you are writing it, that does not illuminate something for you, is dead, finished before you started it (240).

Elsewhere, the truth about her Jewish grandmother is forgotten, then remembered, like a secret she is embarrassed at having forgotten, when she sees an entire ballroom with herself as the only gentile present. "It was as though I had forgotten the flock of Morgensterns in my family tree; out of sight, out of mind. . . . By senior year this had changed. Doubtless the rise of Hitler had something to do with it. By senior year I was well aware of having a Jewish grandmother and aware of it—let me be blunt—as something to hide" (*How I Grew* 217). Would she, Mary, have denied it outright, if questioned? But she never was. Over fifty years later she felt that lack of being tried as its own punishment.

This excessive rumination and reiteration are, I believe, what marks cognitive courage. It is brave enough to depict a protagonist with your own name who conceals something she probably should have revealed; it is doubly brave to elaborate upon the embarrassment potential, weaving it by implication into a network of denial and self-questioning, with no answer possible. This process also embarrasses—as it is meant to—the reader.

Meg Sargent in *The Company She Keeps* is at once understandable, admirable, and deliberately problematic. In the bizarre and layered tale "Ghostly Father, I Confess," which has, like many McCarthy stories and memoirs, an intensely Catholic resonance, Meg, in reaction against her psychiatrist's kindly neutrality, sketches for him a cruel portrait of himself.

[Y]ou see about six plays a year. Your wife makes a list of the things that are really worth while, and you check them off one by one. You get the tickets well in advance, and you generally take another couple with you. You never go on the spur of the moment. . . . You like the movies, and you never miss one that the *New Yorker* recommends. . . . Your wife has a three-quarter-length silver-fox coat and several very dear girl friends. You take excellent care of your health. You have small feet and are proud of it, and this is your only foible (252–53).

Everyone is squirming here, for him and for her.

Her dislikeable female protagonists are mirrored by her remembered dislikeable self, transcending even her unquestioned gift for self-ironization. Take her reflection, in *Memories of a Catholic Girlhood*, on her own meanness toward one:

[S]upercilious fat girl, the petted daughter of a rich meat packer, with heavy rings on her fingers and a real fur coat, who was my principal rival for honors in the classroom. . . . [W]as it my fault if she blubbered when I applied, perfectly accurately, a term I had heard mothers whisper—*nouveau riche*? Wasn't it *true*, I argued, when I was rebuked by Madame Barclay, our mistress of studies, and wasn't fat Beryl always boasting of her money and curling her baby lip at girls whose mothers had to work? It wasn't kind of me, replied Madame Barclay, but I did not think it kind of her when she passed me over for Beryl in casting the class play. Everyone could see that I was much the better actress, and the leading role of haughty Lady Spindle was precisely suited to my style (108–9).

Imagine my satisfaction, she goes on, dreadfully and endearingly, when Pork Barrel forgets her lines: "I supplied them, to my neighbors, in a vindictive whisper, till somebody told me to hush" (109).

McCarthy is determined to refuse the facile play for sympathy—that "whole pathos of the changeling, the orphan, the stepchild. . . . I reject all those tableaux of estrangement" (*The Company She Keeps* 263). Her amused and amusing insistence on her awfulness permits us to identify with her. She fictionalizes the facts and draws us into the facts as well as the fictions; fortunately, the meaning can remain elusive: "Luckily, I am writing a memoir and not a work of fiction, and therefore I do not have to account for my grandmother's unpleasing character" (*Memories of a Catholic Girlhood* 33). No, but she can certainly depict her: "An ugly, severe old woman with a monstrous balcony of a bosom, she officiated over certain set topics in a colorless singsong, . . . my crooked little fingers and how they meant I was a liar; a miracle-working bone; the importance of regular bowel movements; the wickedness of Protestants; the conversion of my mother to Catholicism; and the assertion that my Protestant grandmother must certainly dye her hair" (32). As for that Protestant grandmother, she wasn't. A slip of the pen, perhaps.

Always she is conscious of her narrative as it takes shape in fiction or memoir and, simultaneously, resonates in her: "I have noticed this trait in myself," she will interrupt in an aside to the reader (*Memories of a Catholic Girlhood* 43). Such sudden breaks are salutary shocks; the dynamic dialogue between the writer recalling the past experience and the present telling nourishes the relationship between reader and writer. In "Characters in Fiction" McCarthy comments on Proust and his *Recherche*: "It is Marcel himself, not just the reader, who is trying to find out what actually took place before the book started, and this quest for certainty is itself a hero's goal" (291).

Mary McCarthy's quest is as much about conscience as about certainty; that single truth she aims at is complicated by the mind's own relation to itself. She is concerned about a letter criticizing the landscape near Vassar, when she remembers being rapturous over it: "This is alarming, above all to one who has set out to write her autobiography. It raises the awful question of whether there can be multiple truths or just one. About truth I have always been monotheistic. It has been an article of faith with me, going back to college days, that there is a truth and that it is knowable. Thus Vassar either repelled me . . . or it didn't" (*How I Grew* 199). Should she blame this inconsistency on a lapse of time? a variance of mood? Although it cannot possibly matter so much to the reader as to the writer, her intense concern about what is fact and what is fiction begins early, and never ends.

Working on her last novel, she writes to Hannah Arendt that as a person she learns, but her fictions ("i.e., one's creative side") remain constrained by "those confining boundaries . . . set by my life-experience." We may indeed find a certain sameness in her fictive creations and those autofictions—but is that not also part of this would-be single truth? "One *is* one's life," she concludes (335). And yet, her writing is full of self-acknowledged rearrangements; how exactly is this about truth? It is less about truth to the event than to perception. Even if you saw things completely straight, you couldn't relate them that way and retain any audience. In one of my favorite passages of *Memories of a Catholic Girlhood*, she explains what she does with the truth, habitually: "There are some semi-fictional touches here . . . I arranged actual events so as to make 'a good story' out of them. It is hard to overcome this temptation if you are in the habit of writing fiction, one does it almost automatically" (164–65). So the single truth does have its modifications. We are, I think, vastly relieved. We didn't want to inhabit a monolithic universe.

SEEING AND SAYING

McCarthy's eye is as sharp as her tongue and ear and mind. Her *Stones of Florence*, linking the city's personality to age-old traditions, to the gossip about the painters, is particularly strong on Paolo Uccello, Piero della Francesca, and Leonardo, three geniuses whom she treats as such. You sense the clear mind behind her vivid preference of Florence over Venice, which has to do yet again, I think, with her strong moral convictions about truth. Space and depth are grave matters for the Florentines, analytic like McCarthy herself. "For the Venetians, trompe l'oeil, which they learned from the Florentine pioneers, was a game—a game they continued to play for centuries, never tiring of the deception of feigned marble, feigned brocade, fictive doors and windows, false vistas. Their city of masks was itself a painted toyland, a gay counterfeit of 'real life.' " For the Florentines, instead, "civic halls, churches, and dwellings were too real for games of make-believe" (108).

Indeed, nowhere in her writing is her seeing at fault. From the dance in those ghastly *Groves of Academe*, where everything is "silky, shining, glossy, transfigured, and yet everyday and serviceable, like a spool of mercerized cotton or a pair of transparent nylons reinforced at heel and toe" (21) to the meticulous transcriptions of the editors' offices at little magazines, it is all infinitely recognizable. We know she likes things sharp, likes her fictions full of fact, rounded with details. Her "The Fact in Fiction" reminds us that in *Anna Karenina* we can learn how to make strawberry jam. In "Characters in Fiction" we are reminded that Tolstoy's Pierre seems real, stands out in sharp relief precisely because he is "fat and awkward and wears a funny-looking green civilian hat as a sign of his irreducible innocent stoutness" (289). She sees and notes what we all see and forget to note, or sometimes even miss: Vronsky's bald spot, Prince Andrei's small white hands.

But my goodness, what singular views she did have on what she called the "art novel," all fuzzy and unfactual. Of course, it makes sense from where she stands, but to me McCarthy's ideas about Henry James and Virginia Woolf seem off target. From *To the Lighthouse* she claims to remember only Mr. Ramsay—neither Mrs. Ramsay nor, of all people, Lily Briscoe (*On the Contrary* 277). The irony is that Woolf's essays have the same sort of punch as McCarthy's best ones, Woolf's eye and tongue the same painfully sharp powers; but McCarthy doesn't deal with the essays.

As for James, she says in *Ideas and the Novel*: "He did not broaden a way for his successors but closed nearly every exit as with hermetic sealing tape. . . . He etherealized the novel and perhaps etherized it as well" (5–6). "Before leaving James hoist—if I am right—by his own petard, I want to ask whether his exclusion of ideas in the sense of mental concepts was connected or not with the exclusion of common factuality" (13). It is his exclusion of facts she reacts against, consistently from her point of view. No persons there, she says, and no moral teaching: "There all is allusion and murmurous, indistinct evocation of objects and vistas, in comparison with which Whistler's 'Nocturne' is a sharp-edged photograph" (9).

McCarthy's pointed disdains can be seen as delightful, or even funny: they include those art novelists and painters loved by literary types, professors of literature, and Simone de Beauvoir. The latter represents more than herself: someone to spar with. (To Hannah Arendt on December 22, 1964: "I think I've been longing to get into a fight with someone—France or Sartre or Simone. It is the same thing.") In a sense, it is. She is a good fighter, believing truth to be on her side. We fuzzy literary types may even find some appeal in her most outrageous convictions; she's certainly no wimp.

GOOD CLOTHES AND LATINATE LANGUAGE

Mary McCarthy writes to her third husband, Bowden Broadwater, "I am in favor of nice suits, flowers, and furniture. Why not? That is what all the quattrocento painters were in favor of, after all." Her sense of self-parody was matched by that devastating honesty. It was, she thought, her love of gardening, pretty clothes, and cooking that put her at odds with her notion of feminism. In "The Weeds" the heroine contemplates taking, for the sake of independence, a menial job, leaving behind "Bonwit Teller, Mark Cross, hat by John-Frederics, fragrance by Schiaparelli" (17).

Her affections are often matched, keenly, to her sartorial appreciation. The man in the Brooks Brothers shirt, with his pale gray hair, wears gray trousers to match, as his brown eyes somehow match his voice, giving "the effect, already striking, of his having been put together by a good tailor" (*The Company She Keeps* 89). Meg, like McCarthy, notices everything about him and also about the surroundings: how the highballs are gold in the glasses, the way the little breakfast after their lovemaking is like a feast.

She and her heroines are full of self-knowledge. In "The Man in the Brooks Brothers Suit" the man tells Meg that he can talk easily to her: " 'I know,' she said, full of gentle omniscience. (This was her best side, and she knew it. But did that spoil it, keep it from being good?)" (98). She is nothing if not self-conscious about her gifts: "It was these quick darts and turns, these flashing inconsistencies that gave her the peculiar, sweet-sour, highly volatile charm that was her *specialité de la maison*" (99). Sweet-sour, that's exactly the way this writing feels.

Mary and her heroines are also full of knowing; they love thought and the language that enhances it. At college "I fell in love with Caesar. . . . just, laconic, severe, magnanimous, detached. . . . the very grammar was beatified for me by the objective temperament that ordered it. . . , [I] liked the spirit of justice and scientific inquiry that reigned over the *Commentaries*, the geographer's curiosity and the Roman adaptiveness" (*Memories of a Catholic Girlhood* 154–55). These are McCarthy's own attributes. Her stories frequently end with a Latin aphorism, as if that would tie them up surely, truly. Her consciousness of language, as of its power, is clear: "[L]anguage is a consciousness-raiser. The problem there is that the power of using and understanding language, like all power, carries responsibilities with it. You consent to having it or you don't. And most people today would rather not have it" (*Occasional Prose* 98–99). Language is to be taken seriously, and she does so, even from the couch in *Memories of a Catholic Girlhood*, where she corrects her psychoanalyst's vocabulary: " 'It gave you a basic conplaisancy,' a psychoanalyst once told me. (I think he meant 'complacency')" (13). And later, Meg Sargent will be proud of her doctor for asking one good question: "Perhaps he was not so stupid as she feared" (*The Company She Keeps* 257).

Martha Sinnott in *A Charmed Life* has this kind of sharpness. Miles pronounces Latin in a way that displeases her: he pronounces "*Reginam*" with a soft "g." " '*Reginam*,' murmured Martha to the vicomte, with a grimace, making the g hard. 'I hate that soft, squelchy church Latin; after all, it's *Tacitus* he's quoting.' " The vicomte furls his lower lip, like a little flag, and shows himself inferior: " 'A matter of taste,' he said, 'Who knows how the Romans pronounced?' 'We *do* know,' whispered Martha" (171).

To be found wanting by Mary McCarthy, as a character or as a real person, happened to many. This is part of the discomfort created by such high and unforgiving intelligence.

GARDENS AND THE GENEROSITY OF THE LIE

My great admiration for Mary McCarthy's story "The Weeds" comes from the way it deals with the uncomfortable subject of the lie and leaves the interpretation open-ended. The story, as I read it, is about pardoning, sparing, and the compromise it might seem more heroic not to make. It is about the growing and dying of people in relation to a garden. When the wife contemplates leaving her husband, the petunias she is growing inside for her garden hold her back: "Suddenly they would flash into her mind, white, ruffled, with yellow throats . . . her heart would contract with love and despair as she saw that she could not leave them—she was in bondage unless they should die" (5). The entire cycle comes to her mind: the wheel of birth, reproduction, and death; the death of the garden and the return of the gardener; the transmittal of responsibility; and the final lie, for what endures is "the creative, constructive principle which, in its restless anticipation of change, built structures of semi-permanency—a series of overnight cabins that in their extension formed, not precisely a city, but at least a road, a *via vitae*" (36–37). That is what this story is also about: those brave structures.

Let me quote a few lines from the end, in their combination of supreme irony and quiet truth. Here is a pause marked between a statement, untrue, and a response, equally untrue—but humanly right. The wife has returned and abandons everything, including the garden, which is almost dead, but which the husband takes over. Looking at her with tenderness, he speaks of his loss, of how he misses "those yellow things you used to have on the coffee table." (How superb a finding, that "things"!) His wife sees through his eyes, a rather smeary vision, confused, unspecific by contrast with her own lucid sight, but nevertheless she recognizes a vision:

[A]nd the sense of his loss, his large, vague loss, overwhelmed and engulfed her.

She pressed his hand lightly, murmuring, "Yes, I remember," and then let his fingers drop. He regained her hand, however, and squeezed it. She felt, as once before in the fields, that he was on the verge of some fine avowal. She herself, only now, had made the great leap from pity to sympathy. . . . "I've always loved your flowers," he said, his voice blurred and high with emotion. "You know that" (40–41).

She feels his heartfelt insincerity, sees the myth developing, hears the tears in his voice, suspects her pity had been wasted, and that he has got her where he wants her, and knows, all the same, that

the lie was a necessity to him, a cardinal article of faith. . . . And in a final thrust of rejection, she yielded, conceding him everything—flowers, facts, truth. Let him put them into his authorized version; she had failed them, and would do so again and again. With him, they would see service.

She tightened her grasp on his hand.

"Yes," she said mistily, "I know."

The lie came easier, after all, than she would have thought (42).

Now I am reading this masterpiece of irony and sadness as part of what I want to call the generosity of McCarthy's potential lie. All the more generous, given her strength of feeling about truth. For I think the story is about a courageous untruth, precisely in order to build one of those cabins on the *via vitae*, although I am not sure that Mary McCarthy or many other readers read it that way.

There are other cases of the generous lie in her writing, and here it is that I find some of the greatest warmth. For example, at school, she feels it her duty to break the rules, but then speaks a final untruth, which she perceives as a favor being asked of her after she is caught coming back from a prohibited meeting with a boy. She later lunches with the supervisor she has spared through her lie, a teacher with whom she had shared her love of Caesar, and brings the book they had enjoyed together. But it doesn't work, and she feels a failure. "Filled with guilt, boredom, and a sense of helpless treachery to this mysterious individual who seemed to be wanting something I did not know how to give, I became confused and left my Caesar on the luncheon table." As for the teacher, "She went her terse way, back to Canada and Empire" (*Memories of a Catholic Girlhood* 161–63).

This lie is totally different from the social one mocked in *The Company She Keeps* when Meg Sargent "learned to suppress the unpleasant, unnecessary truths: why let an author know that you do not like his book, why spoil a party by getting into an argument, why not tell your friend that her ugly house is pretty?" (277). That kind of lie doesn't take courage and isn't particularly about generosity, as are the ones I value.

The final generosity is in a confession, such a tiny and massive one, found in the beautiful eulogy "Saying Good-bye to Hannah." I am thinking of Mary McCarthy's avowal of her affection through a gesture which was refused, a refusal which she has the gallantry of spirit to understand. The anecdote is about privacy. From staying often with Hannah Arendt, Mary knew she liked anchovy paste for breakfast, and so purchased a small tube of it when Hannah came to stay with her. "What is that?" asks Hannah. And then Mary sees, with the sharpness not of her eyes but of her soul: "She did not wish to be *known*, in that curiously finite and, as it were, reductive way. And I had done it to show her I knew her—a sign of love, though not always—thereby proving that in the last analysis I did not know her at all" (*Occasional Prose* 42). To me this confession of a deep failure of knowledge—of exactly the thing McCarthy most prides herself on—is very moving. I believe that admiring the particular in someone often requires the greatest generosity, and I know that Mary is here at her best.

ENDURING

I have wanted to be as direct as Mary McCarthy was, to show how she saw, and cared about, and amassed so much behind her knowledge that her telling—of the truth or the sidesteps it takes—is full. As her life was full. What she says of Hannah Arendt, we might recognize in her: "A sort of typical awe-struck modesty before the world's abundance and intense particularity" (38).

As for the story of her own life, she asks herself, and us, in a moment of discouragement, "Why should I care that I have lived my life as a person and writer in vain? . . . Most of our lives are in vain. At best, we give pleasure to some" (MacDowell Medal acceptance speech). I want to say to her, in closing, that the sharpness of her eye and of her writing endures, beyond the normal and common, in the ways it helps us see and think and write. And I would like to say, too, that her life and the forthrightness of her writing weren't at all in vain; I say that to Mary now.

WORKS CITED

Dickinson, Emily. *The Complete Poems of Emily Dickinson*. Boston: Little, Brown, 1960. Poem 1129.

McCarthy, Mary. "Artists in Uniform." *On the Contrary*. New York: Farrar, 1961. 55–74.

——. *Cast a Cold Eye*. New York: Harcourt, 1950, 1972.

——. "Characters in Fiction." *On the Contrary*. New York: Farrar, 1961. 271–92.

——. *A Charmed Life*. New York: Harcourt, 1955.

——. *The Company She Keeps*. New York: Simon, 1942. Reprint, New York: Harcourt, 1967.

——. "The Fact in Fiction." *On the Contrary*. New York: Farrar, 1961. 249–70.

——. "General Macbeth." *Mary McCarthy's Theatre Chronicles 1937–1962*. New York: Farrar, 1963. 235–48. Also collected in *The Writing on the Wall and Other Literary Essays*. New York: Harcourt, 1970. 3–14.

——. "Ghostly Father, I Confess." *The Company She Keeps*. New York: Harcourt, 1942. 249–304.

——. *The Groves of Academe*. New York: Harcourt, 1952.

——. *How I Grew*. San Diego: Harcourt, 1987.

——. *Ideas and the Novel*. New York: Harcourt, 1980.

——. *Intellectual Memoirs: New York 1936–1938*. New York: Harcourt, 1992.

——. Interview with Elisabeth Niebuhr. Gelderman, Carol, ed. *Conversations with Mary McCarthy*. Jackson: University Press of Mississippi, 1991. 3–29. Also collected in *Writers at Work*, 2nd series. New York: Viking, 1963.

——. Letter to Bowden Broadwater. September 14, 1957. Quoted in Carol Brightman, *Writing Dangerously: Mary McCarthy and Her World*. New York: Clarkson Potter, 1992. 389.

——. Letter to Hannah Arendt. February 17, 1975. Brightman, Carol, ed. *Between Friends: The Correspondence of Hannah Arendt and Mary McCarthy, 1949–1975*. New York: Harcourt, 1995. 373.

——. MacDowell Medal acceptance speech (August 26, 1984). Quoted from the *New York Times*, August 27, 1984: C-14. Gelderman, Carol, ed. *Conversations with Mary McCarthy*. Jackson: University Press of Mississippi, 1991. 250–52.

——. "The Man in the Brooks Brothers Shirt." *The Company She Keeps*. New York: Harcourt, 1942. 81–134.

——. *Memories of a Catholic Girlhood*. New York: Harcourt, 1957.

——. *Occasional Prose*. New York: Harcourt, 1985.

——. "On *Madame Bovary*." *The Writing on the Wall and Other Literary Essays*. New York: Harcourt, 1970. 72–94.

——. "On Rereading a Favorite Book." *Occasional Prose*. New York: Harcourt, 1985. 179–86.

——. *On the Contrary*. New York: Farrar, 1961.

———. "Saying Good-bye to Hannah." *Occasional Prose*. New York: Harcourt, 1985. 35–42.

———. "Settling the Colonel's Hash." *On the Contrary*. New York: Farrar, 1961. 225–41.

———. *The Stones of Florence*. 1959. New York: Harvest/Harcourt, 1963.

———. *Venice Observed*. 1956. New York: Harvest/Harcourt, 1963.

———. "The Weeds." *Cast a Cold Eye*. 1950. New York: Harcourt, 1972.

———. *The Writing on the Wall and Other Literary Essays*. New York: Harcourt, 1970.

17

Mary McCarthy
as a Fictional Character

Thomas Mallon

In 1991 I published a novel called *Aurora 7*, and from the start it was my intention to base one of that book's characters, a fifty-year-old novelist named Elizabeth Wheatley, on Mary McCarthy. Mary has been an important person for me—an object of youthful admiration, then a critical subject, and eventually a friend. Her place in my life has been large and complicated, and I didn't quite know how she would fare as Elizabeth, who disembarks from the *Leonardo da Vinci* on page 35 of *Aurora 7*. The novel is set entirely on May 24, 1962, the day of Scott Carpenter's space flight, and at 9:00 A.M. Elizabeth is wondering how she will spend the rest of the day.

Perhaps she'll walk all the way home; and maybe, since she'll be walking east on 44th Street, she'll go in the back entrance of the *New Yorker* offices and stop up to see her editor. He'll be pleased when she tells him that at breakfast yesterday she saw a passenger, a rather nice-looking young man, reading *The Committee*, her out-of-print satire about the very literary jury that had once awarded her its prize. . . . What she will spend no part of the day doing is watching this spaceman. Elizabeth's romantic streak, the wide soft spot in her left-wing politics, will permit her to be enthusiastic over, say, an Elizabethan explorer, but as a lover of scratch cakes, natural fibers and manual typewriters she finds herself unable to care about a sterile man in a sterile can being applauded at this moment by every one of her Catholic Rotarian cousins in Wisconsin (Mallon 35).

I realized early on in this book that something odd was happening. Not only was Mary, as Elizabeth, turning into a comic character, reduced to her edges and foibles; she was becoming the *only* comic character in the novel. I recalled an answer Mary herself had given in 1961 to an interviewer from the *Paris Review*:

Something happens in my writing—I don't mean it to—a sort of distortion, a sort of writing on the bias, seeing things with a sort of swerve and swoop. *A Charmed Life*, for instance. You know, at the beginning I make a sort of inventory of all the town characters, just telling who they are. Now I did this with the intention of describing, well, this nice, ordinary, old-fashioned New England town. But it ended up differently. Something is distorted, the description takes on a sort of extravagance—I don't know exactly how it happens. I know I don't mean it to happen (Interview 310–11).

I didn't mean to do to her what she had done to dozens of characters, not only in *A Charmed Life* but in most of her novels. Yet, it turned out that way, and my caricature of Mary McCarthy ended up joining a whole gallery of caricatures that have appeared in fiction over the last half century.

Delmore Schwartz refracted what he knew of her into a number of stories, among them an unpublished manuscript called "The Complete Adventuress," whose margin he actually labeled "Mary & Philip (1937)." This small sketch of McCarthy's affair with Philip Rahv puts an emphasis on the ridiculous:

To their friends who composed a curious circle in which those who were engaged in left-wing politics mixed with those from the theatre and the concert-hall, the infatuation Helena felt and expressed for Stanislaus was such as to make it difficult for one to keep a straight face, for Stanislaus might have remarked merely that the day had been a cold one for early October and Helena then felt compelled to declare that Stanislaus had a consciousness of the external world which disregarded nothing (Atlas 99).

In a *Paris Review* story called "Ciao," published in 1961 but set in 1947, McCarthy's third husband, Bowden Broadwater, also gave us a comical glimpse of her as the "dear wife" or "d.w." of the arch, unemployed narrator. While unfailingly good-mannered throughout this short tale, the "d.w." does give some suggestion of being a time bomb. " 'Darling,' she murmurs at the breakfast table, 'may I have the second section now, please?' " (44). After she gets it, in her voice reminiscent of the "morning dew, very fresh" (45), she scolds the husband, gently but unnervingly: " 'But, darling,' she said, 'you *can't* have looked very carefully.' She extended the Classified with several items neatly checked for me" (48). When the d.w. straightens up the sitting room, she does so with zealous precision, "three plumps per pillow" (49). Counting the plumps, and being aware of the number's comic value, is exactly in keeping with McCarthy's own methods in fiction; and if the reader of "Ciao," even with all the details about the real-life McCarthy-Broadwater apartment by the Third Avenue El, retains any doubt about the d.w.'s identity, there are her "pretty eyes [that] sparkled like green shampoo shaken well" (42).

For a glimpse (again comic) of McCarthy at her height, two decades and one husband later, one can open James Jones's novel *The Merry Month of May*, set during the Paris *événements* of 1968, and find her as the American writer Magdalen McCaw, married to an OECD official. The narrator worries about a man who decides to bring his mistress instead of his wife to one of Maggie's cocktail parties. "Maybe he thought Maggie and George, Maggie being such a famous American lady writer, were Bohemians—which only shows how little he knew Maggie . . . with her hair skinned back, and her toothy smile, which I have always found innocent and charming, though many others have called it sharklike" (163–64).

The McCarthy smile—described by Randall Jarrell as "the smile of a suspended, autonomous intelligence . . . [belonging] to nothing, not even itself" (99)—figures with such frequency and prominence in memoirs and fiction that it is almost a separate character. Jarrell's portrait of McCarthy as Gertrude Johnson in *Pictures from an Institution* (he denied the basis to McCarthy but more or less admitted it to Rahv) is the most extended fictional depiction we have of her, as a novelist who comes to a small, progressive liberal arts college ostensibly to teach, but actually to gather material. Gertrude is tone-deaf, speaks French so badly "that anyone could understand every word of it" (233), finds the childish behavior of children to be "almost affectation on their part" (193), and, of course, smiles: "It was like a skull, like a stone-marten scarf . . . torn animals were removed at sunset from that smile" (65).

Above all, as a novelist, Gertrude is preoccupied by the facts. In perhaps the book's most famous passage, we are told,

If one of Gertrude's heroines, running to snatch from the lips of her little daughter a half-emptied bottle of furniture-polish, fell and tore her skirt, Gertrude knew the name of the dressmaker who had made the skirt—and it was the right one for a woman of that class, at that date; she knew the brand of the furniture-polish that the little girl had swallowed; she knew, even, the particular exclamation that such a woman, tearing her skirt at such a moment, would have uttered. . . . But how the child felt as it seized and drank the polish, how the mother felt as she caught the child to her breast—about such things as these, which have neither brand nor date, Gertrude was less knowing; would have said impatiently, "Everybody knows *that!*" (133).

Pictures from an Institution is really no more a novel than McCarthy's own satire *The Oasis*, and if, in Gertrude, Jarrell permits McCarthy more than her usual cameo, the portrait is still less character than caricature. Why, one must finally ask, is the McCarthy fictionalized by all these men almost never permitted more than a few quick comic turns before she's given the hook? In my own novel, Elizabeth Wheatley ends up as a sort of benevolent *dea ex machina*, but there's no soul in the machine. Is it that high seriousness, which McCarthy had, morally and artistically, is inherently comic, and allows for no other sort of fictional treatment? Surely not: think again about Delmore Schwartz, and what Saul Bellow was able to do with him in *Humboldt's Gift*. Were any of the portraits I've quoted motivated by revenge? Certainly not in my case: Mary had never been anything but generous to me. And, even with the others, the results are too likeable to have served such a purpose. Simple fascination seems the most likely motive. But why did it always produce comedy?

For one hint of an answer we should go to McCarthy herself, specifically her essay "Characters in Fiction," where she takes exception to the old Forsterian view that comic characters are "flat":

A comic character, contrary to accepted belief, is likely to be more complicated and enigmatic than a hero or a heroine, fuller of surprises and turnabouts; Mr. Micawber, for instance, can find the most unexpected ways of being himself . . . we really, I believe, admire the comic characters *more* than we do the hero or the heroine, because of their obstinate power to do-it-again, combined with a total lack of self-consciousness or shame (288–89).

Even so, in no case can novelists *go inside* comic characters. To Forster's way of thinking that's because they have no interior to reach; by McCarthy's reckoning, it would be more from fear of disrupting what she calls "the principle of eternity or inertia represented by the comic" (289).

McCarthy, the rare noncommunist, nonreligious modern writer who believed that the world contained a knowable truth, did not set any special value upon a second, private life, for her characters or herself. "I grew ashamed to write little observations about [the North Vietnamese] in my notebook," she says in "Hanoi," "for you ought not to be two people, one downstairs, listening and nodding, and the other scribbling in your room." Her Catholic upbringing had left her with "the idea that it was necessary to be the same person at all times and places" (316). If there *was* such a thing as an inner life, she wanted to see it join the outer one, like one spacecraft coming up to dock with another.

I think that when novelists considered McCarthy as raw material, the task ahead appeared a bit too much like picking up uranium with their bare hands. Writers who knew her were scared of her, less because she herself was so formidable than because she had a way of making you feel weak, ethically and otherwise. Gertrude "had great expectations for humanity" (*Pictures from an Institution* 169), says Jarrell's narrator, and if she "was a sketch for a statue of

Honesty putting its foot in its mouth" (45), nonetheless, "After a few minutes with Gertrude you wanted to be good all day every day" (45). I would bet I'm not the only person who used to emerge feeling like that from an encounter with Mary.

She had startling gaps in self-awareness, perhaps even more than most people. (Twenty years ago, for instance, she wrote me that when she was writing her essay "The Fact in Fiction," it didn't occur to her that her own books were full of facts.) But more than anyone I have known, she attempted to be honest, sometimes even in the smallest bits of what other people would call social behavior. What I think really made novelists so uncomfortable, once they started to write about her—and made them settle for nervous laughter—was this radical candor, this lack of respect (even interest) she had in that so-called interior life. This was a unique, probably impossible, kind of honesty, and I don't think any novelist, myself included, has ever felt up to portraying it.

WORKS CITED

Atlas, James. *Delmore Schwartz: The Life of an American*. New York: Farrar, 1977.

Broadwater, Bowden, "Ciao." *Paris Review*. Winter 1961: 41–51.

Gelderman, Carol. *Mary McCarthy: A Life*. New York: St. Martin's, 1988.

Jarrell, Randall. *Pictures from an Institution*. 1954. Chicago: University of Chicago Press, 1986.

Jones, James. *The Merry Month of May*. New York: Delacorte, 1971.

McCarthy, Mary. "Characters in Fiction." *On the Contrary*. New York: Farrar, 1962. 271–92.

———. "The Fact in Fiction." *On the Contrary*. New York: Farrar, 1962. 249–70.

———. "Hanoi." *The Seventeenth Degree*. New York: Harcourt, 1974. 170–322.

———. Interview with Elisabeth Niebuhr. *Writers at Work*. 2nd series. New York: Viking, 1963. Reprinted in Gelderman, Carol, ed., *Conversations with Mary McCarthy*. Jackson: University Press of Mississippi, 1991.

———. Letter to Thomas Mallon. March 23, 1973. Mary McCarthy Papers, Vassar College Library.

———. *The Oasis*. New York: Random House, 1949.

———. *On the Contrary*. New York: Farrar, 1962.

———. *The Seventeenth Degree*. New York: Harcourt, 1974.

Mallon, Thomas. *Aurora 7*. New York: Ticknor, 1991.

18

The Minotaur as Mentor: Edmund Wilson's Role in the Career of Mary McCarthy

Avis Hewitt

Examining the problematic nature of the relationship between Mary McCarthy and her second husband, Edmund Wilson, to whom she was married from 1938 to 1945, reveals inordinate parallels in their literary ambitions and accomplishments that could have predisposed them to a marriage of unusual rapport and pleasure in common interests. Yet when Richard Costa asked Wilson about marital satisfaction between Wilson and his third wife, Wilson replied that the experience had been "hideous" (129). For her part, McCarthy told Carol Brightman in an interview for *The Nation* that Wilson was "a terrible bully and a tyrant and paranoid . . . a minotaur" (615), and she spends considerable attention in her posthumously published 1992 *Intellectual Memoirs* trying to answer for herself—at a distance of over fifty years—why she married him. Finally she concludes that she is "fooling [her]self" still about her motives with Wilson, at age seventy-seven, when she "should be old enough to know better" (99).

In order for *us* "to know better," we need to acknowledge her several fictional portraits of the "minotaur" who took up with her when she was the theater critic for *Partisan Review* and saw her established as a successful writer of fiction before they parted. From "Ghostly Father, I Confess," a 1942 analysis of childhood traumas reenacted by antagonizing a smug and sanctimonious husband, to "The Weeds," a 1944 short story about her futile attempt to leave a similarly domineering husband, McCarthy's protagonists repeatedly encounter Wilson-like antagonists and recite the litanies of their character flaws as though well trained by Catholic girlhood. This process culminates in *A Charmed Life* (1955) when the overbearing and erudite Miles Murphy, "soured, boiled as an owl a good deal of the time, bored to desperation except when he was working" (70), becomes the object of Martha Sinnott's quarrel with her past. Her motive in stationing herself near him after they had each gone on to new marriages was "to compete with him again" (78).

McCarthy's fictional fixation on Edmund Wilson, using him not only as antagonist in these three narratives but as a part of the composite male villain in *The Group* and as background presence in *Birds of America*, indicates a tie worth examining. When *Intellectual Memoirs* was published in May 1992, McCarthy's ambivalence about Wilson after half a century caused Jean Strouse to speculate that while McCarthy was in no way an Eliza Doolittle to Wilson's Henry Higgins, she does seem to have singled him out as an expedient attachment because he "was simply the most powerful man in her world" (17). McCarthy confesses in *Memoirs* that "[a]pparently [she] liked him much more than [she] remembered" and is surprised in reviewing her 1937 letters to him at the "note of tenderness and teasing," at "the intimacy and friendliness of [her] tone" (99). McCarthy's attitude toward Wilson at twenty-seven—and for the next fifty years—was evidently disdainful and antagonistic, yet she constructed for herself a career that resembled his so closely that we must assume she took him for her role model unawares.

Having been the bright and eager "teacher-pleaser" since Forest Ridge Convent School, McCarthy surely saw life with Wilson as the environment that would best facilitate her development as a *littérateur*. If, as Wilson pointed out to McCarthy, "[Philip] Rahv doesn't *do* anything for you" (103), this chapter will demonstrate that Wilson *did* do something for her, that his initial encouragement and his later function as her nemesis were both powerfully positive forces in her literary career. His brutish violence toward her and her resentful disenchantment with him were both likely caused by a budding professional rivalry. If Wilson was the brooding minotaur, then McCarthy was not the sacrificial virgin but the clever Ariadne who gained access to the inner chambers of the Wilson labyrinth and emerged in literary triumph.

McCarthy's most detailed study of who and what Edmund Wilson was to her is her 1955 novel *A Charmed Life*. In both her marriage to Wilson and in that book, she found, as she told Elisabeth Niebuhr in her 1962 "Writers at Work" interview for *Paris Review*, "something wrong" in the construction (86). She had intended, when she set it in an isolated artist/intellectual community in New England which she calls New Leeds, to write a novel that showed the "haunted" or "fairy tale" quality of the place, to reveal it as "pregnant with catastrophe" while delineating realistic characters (86). McCarthy doubted the effectiveness of what she had written. She suspected that the mix of supernatural with natural had made it a failure artistically. In the novel that most pointedly of all her works shows her protagonist struggling with doubt in the throes of a moral dilemma, we can find the autobiographical touchstones that connect it to the most conflicted era of her own adult life.

In a letter to her friend Nicola Chiaromonte in the late 1960s, she confessed that she found it a novel that she did not "much like at this distance in time" (Gelderman 190). As Carol Gelderman points out, not a single 1955 reviewer saw the work correctly according to authorial intent (190). McCarthy had told Niebuhr the theme: "The novel is supposed to be about doubt. All the characters in different ways represent doubt" (86). Does the fact that McCarthy came to disdain the book mean that she had not succeeded in her purposes or that she had succeeded too uncomfortably well?

The central moral dilemma of *A Charmed Life* finds the protagonist, Martha Sinnott, pregnant by a former husband whom she apparently disdains. Given Martha's mind-set, no alternative is a saving one. A sense of self-possession should allow her to take the child she has wanted, the play she has written, and the life she has thereby redeemed into her own hands and savor them. Instead, self-abnegation haunts Sinnott, telling her she cannot have because she does not deserve two separate joys. While readers can applaud the moral exactitude that informs Martha's decisions, they shudder that she can reach a state of grace only through death. Her scruples reject an existence based on bovine, sensuous pleasures, but what Elaine Showalter refers to as McCarthy's "veritable chorus of female self-hatred" emerges once again to deprive her of fullness of life. McCarthy admitted that this story deals with doubt. What she could not admit, from a male-identified perspective, is the underlying issue of doubt which the novel examines: the doubt that females can claim successfully both personal and professional autonomy.

In her portrayal of Martha, McCarthy demonstrates not only that breaking with a mentor—when the relationship is complicated by sexuality—becomes the exorcising of a demon, but also that choosing a fate becomes the extremity of either self-denial or self-indulgence. McCarthy doubts that her protagonist can find the saving path of self-possession. What doubts does Martha Sinnott (Irving Stock sees her last name suggesting "the McCarthy heroine's usual vain wish" [30]) represent through the life she leads and the choices she makes? If not one reviewer saw the point McCarthy thought she had been illustrating, then something unidentified must have fallen through the gaps between the flesh-and-blood author at her manual typewriter and the implied author who believes in what she thinks she is presenting us. Perhaps the doubt was Mary McCarthy's, but the implied author was too smart, too clever at games and dramatics to let it be exposed consciously.

The central truth about *A Charmed Life* is that the segment of McCarthy's life that it depicts involves her wresting herself free from the shadow of Edmund Wilson. She was free of him legally as her second husband in October 1945, after having left him on a summer night in 1944 when he made fun of her and came to blows with her as she carried out two heavy pails of garbage from a party they had just given. McCarthy wrote her brother Kevin in 1979 that she had left Wilson out of "desperation," that she had "no other man in the picture" at the time. "The only husband I left for incompatibility was Edmund" (Gelderman 109).

In her typical roman à clef style, McCarthy "populated" *A Charmed Life* with characters from her own history. Edmund Wilson becomes Miles Murphy, the novel's overpowering antagonist. Bowden Broadwater, who became McCarthy's third husband in December 1946, is second husband John Sinnott in the novel. The essential characteristics of the two men are carried over intact from biography to fiction, and the essential point of the plot carries over just as readily, too. Why does a woman move back with her new husband to a small, rarified community where she had lived with her former husband when that former husband and his new wife still live there? The answer is apparent in any western novel or film: she has a score to settle. She has come back for a showdown.

Mary McCarthy was always a savvy survivor even though she was not always willing to explore her own motives. She is on record as not wanting to marry Wilson, as never even having loved him. In *Intellectual Memoirs* she is surprised at the end of her life to notice how fondly disposed she had once been toward him. She admits in *Intellectual Memoirs* that in reading over her letters to Wilson, she had anticipated neither the friendly, intimate tone nor the tenderness and teasing they evidence (99):

Apparently I liked him much more than I remember, more than I ever would again. What I hear in the letter is not love, though—I never loved Wilson—but sympathy, affection, friendship. Later I grew to think of him as a monster; the minotaur (100).

And indeed Wilson seems to have been a minotaur. He went through many wives and numerous mistresses (wielding his "club" as readers of his 1946 *Memoirs of Hecate County* hear him term his sexual organ) with the same appetite that his rotund figure and his recurring bouts of drunkenness indicate he went through food and liquor. But these deviations from temperance are easily forgiven Wilson by literary historians because he had one voracious appetite that superseded all the rest: "the amazing range of [his] interests and of his knowledge" (Muste 1505). His journals are "highly impressive" because the index reveals the multiplicity of "people Wilson knew, the books he read, the ideas he considered," and he was never casual in his interests: "If something attracted his attention, he studied it, read about it, and if possible, examined it first hand" (1505).

The description of Miles Murphy toward the beginning of *A Charmed Life* indicates that "he had a brilliant mind . . . educated by the Jesuits . . . on to Heidelberg, and the Sorbonne and the London School of Economics" (26). Miles has even studied with Jung at Zurich and has excelled in a variety of fields—as a playwright, a boxer "who used to work out with Hemingway," a magazine editor, a psychologist, "a practicing mystic," an amateur analyst, and an adventure story writer (27). This stands in stark contrast to the dilettantism of most inhabitants of New Leeds, but it is an apt parallel to Edmund Wilson.

His career, like McCarthy's, spanned more than fifty years—the 1920s to the 1970s. He began as a reporter and literary journalist and went on to write literary, art, and social criticism; he wrote on popular culture, on "the lively arts," on history—both modern and ancient; he did travel books, fiction, poetry, and drama (Castronovo 305). John Muste calls Wilson "unquestionably the United States' best known and most respected critic and its only genuine man of letters" (1503).

This range and its particular specialties bear an eerie resemblance to the career McCarthy carved and the freelancing, wide-ranging role she sought in American letters. *Newsweek* named her in 1963 our "only real woman of letters" (Hanscom 83). The true thematic scheme at work in *A Charmed Life* demonstrates the birth struggle of the McCarthy-identified protagonist to free herself from the tutelage and tentacles of the intellectual giant responsible for her literary gestation. The underlying tone of the book conveys the screams and struggles of a sailor's descent into a maelstrom, and we readers, unable to affect the outcome, call from the shore, "Why did you sail into those waters?" Martha Sinnott's answer is that she is "afraid of being afraid" (13) and therefore must sail straight into the deepest, fiercest part of her ocean. Sinnott deems "the hardest course" to be "the right one," sees that equation as "an almost invariable law" (213). Her rule is that if "her nature shrank from the task, if it hid piteously and cried for mercy, that was a sign that she was in the presence of the ethical" (213).

The ethical within the immediate context of the quote refers to the abortion she has decided she must require of herself. She has been trying to have a baby—her covert operation in coming to New Leeds—though the overt one, according to her husband John, is for her to finish writing her play. Now after one erring evening with Miles, she cannot be sure of her child's paternity. By engaging sexually with Miles, she has acted out the ultimate relocking of horns between two madly ambitious career *littérateurs*. Miles/Wilson has made fertile the intellect, the literary output, and finally the womb of the Martha/ McCarthy protagonist. To bear his seed attaches her to him permanently. And it is her attachment to Miles—psychically and professionally—that causes Martha's inner turmoil throughout the book. Moments before her death, Martha Sinnott, driving home from her neighbors with the money for the abortion in her purse, realizes that "she could trust herself" because "she was no longer afraid of herself" and sees her newfound trust and courage as "the reward of [her] fearsome decision" to exorcise Miles from her life through the abortion (252).

Such a passage, when transferred to an autobiographical context, shows McCarthy painfully dominated by Wilson's presence in her life. But to say he overwhelmed her at times is not to say that she did not seek out what he had to offer—to her female ego and to her career. She acknowledges in *Intellectual Memoirs* that she "may seem hard on Wilson . . . ungrateful . . . for what he did . . . to push [her] into 'creativity' " during their first months of marriage (104). She admits that "[i]f he had not shut the door firmly on the little room he had shepherded [her] into," she would "not be the 'Mary McCarthy' " that we read today. Yet the realization does not evoke particular gratitude in her (104).

Jean Strouse, in the *New York Times Book Review*, disdains "the grandiosity of that pronouncement" (17) because McCarthy is no Eliza Doolittle, and it seems "disingenuous" that she should construe herself as such—"given the ferocity and grandeur of her public life" (17). Perhaps McCarthy thinks so too and is chagrined to argue that she "agreed to marry [Wilson] as [her] punishment for having gone to bed with him" (101), after readers have heard her "three men in twenty-four hours" boast a few pages back; she then rationalizes that "modern girls" do not think in terms of "sin" but that *this* modern girl was "compelled" into marriage somehow—"if that was what [Wilson] wanted" (101).

She confesses that she "could not accept [having] slept with this fat, puffing man for no reason, simply because [she] was drunk" (101). Then she probes memory for deeper attractions—he was an older man with a patrician background: "Wilson . . . was upper class. That was all there was to it" (105). McCarthy delighted in what marriage to Wilson offered: "the intellectual attraction . . . a shared classical education . . . to read Juvenal together" (102–3). She also romanticized a future that would include "the whole world of nature" with horseback riding, trout fishing, and looking for wild flowers in the woods—Wilson knew their names—around his country home, Trees, in Stamford, Connecticut (96–102). Additionally, Wilson promised her children (105). Philip Rahv of *Partisan Review*, with whom she was currently living, could not afford a divorce from his wife and would not have wanted children had he been free (105). But beyond these inducements is the singular truth on which *A Charmed Life* is based: Wilson promised her achievement. McCarthy recognized that to marry him would "do something" for her, for her "literary gift" (103). Wilson had argued, "Rahv doesn't do anything for you," meaning Rahv was "slothfully content to have [her] do those theatre columns," which, according to Wilson, "were not up to [her] real measure" (103).

That McCarthy needed some new avenues of literary adventuring seems obvious in biographic retrospect. She had worked for *Parisian Review*, *The Nation*, *The New Republic*, and the offices of Covici-Friede as editor and reviewer. Her association with Rahv and the other leftists of that magazine would keep her, if it continued, as heavily involved in social and political issues as in literary ones. Evidently Mary McCarthy did not have quite those priorities and was searching—not necessarily consciously—for a way to see herself from where she was to where she needed to be. Jean Strouse admits McCarthy very likely needed a strong man to help and encourage her to begin to write fiction (17). McCarthy at twenty-six was a little adrift, and Wilson was obviously strongly attracted. It is a period in his life, however, about which he is strangely silent in his four-volume, four-decade journals.

Nevertheless, McCarthy would get what she needed to do what she had to do—the discipline, the encouragement, and the literary immersion that life with Wilson provided. Here self-knowledge eludes her because although she "readily admits to vanity, cruelty, selfishness, betrayal, competitiveness, [and] showing off," she hesitates to admit to "ambition" (Strouse 17).

She also hesitates to admit that Miles Murphy represents Edmund Wilson. She warns readers that the novel's antagonist "must not be taken for a disguised portrait of Wilson," but concedes that Martha resembles *her* pretty closely. She confesses that she "tried to change [Martha] and failed" and that when she wrote *A Charmed Life*, she was "fooling [her]self about Martha's motives" and that she is "still fooling [her]self today, when [she] should be old enough to know better, about what drove [her] into Wilson's study that long-ago night" (99).

McCarthy comments in the 1962 Paris interview that "the girl [Martha] . . . has to put up a real stake—and she does put up a real stake—at that moment she becomes mortal" (Gelderman, *Conversations* 23). The real stake of *A Charmed Life* keeps the McCarthy protagonist "in the presence of the ethical" (213). The reader, however, can hardly be content with the limited artistry that an isolated sexual encounter and the ethical crisis that arises from it demonstrate if the story lacks significance otherwise. But the story signifies strikingly. McCarthy's remaining conflicted about this novel and the Edmund Wilson chapter of her life indicates how much of her sense of self as female and as literary artist lies "buried" in it. *A Charmed Life* is another version of McCarthy's *Bildungsroman*.

McCarthy could be as carelessly snobbish with her readership as with the characters she "wrote up." She expected to change some minor features of Wilson and have both her own circle, the intelligentsia, and her wider audience accept her denial of the Miles/Wilson identification without further question. Because Wilson had brown eyes and Miles green, because Wilson was not a smoker and Miles was, because Wilson was shorter with a crest of brown hair and Miles was taller with a crest of red hair, the issue should be settled. Although both man and character are known for their bulging eyes and bulging bellies and for living erudite lives in an autocratic manner while perpetually keeping a lustful eye out for appealing women, McCarthy assumes that by having Miles light up, she can keep the two forever distinct among her readership. McCarthy did make *this* concession in a letter to Arthur Schlesinger, Jr.: Miles is "not really meant to be Edmund. . . . To the extent that Edmund is a boor and a four-flusher"; however, she recognizes that "Miles is a kind of joke extrapolation of him—minus the talent, minus the pathos" (Gelderman 187). McCarthy also admits to using "certain episodes, altered from my married life with E., as the raw material to create [Miles]" and to having "drawn on [her] own feelings quite directly, in the chapter where Martha remembers her marriage"; but it is"all changed around—not for purposes of disguise, but to make a new whole" (187).

Readers may agree, upon seeing the evidence, that both the underlying purpose and the ultimate benefit of the McCarthy-Wilson alliance were literary. McCarthy has six reasons why she engaged with Wilson, but seems to find none of them satisfactory. Why did *he* undertake to engage with *her*? David Castronovo reports that the literary giant found aspects of the marriage "hideous" and "nightmarish" and the cause of much "economic and psychological strain" (308). But for him also the match offered compensations.

One of the benefits to American letters of the Wilson-McCarthy marriage is *his* productivity during those seven years: six books on literature and politics. By closeting himself in his study all day every day, Wilson benefited from the stability at the center of the storm. And if he was a tyrant, he was also a tireless supporter of McCarthy's talent. In fact, a hallmark of his whole career was boosting young writers with promise. With McCarthy that meant hiring a nurse for Reuel, who was born on Christmas Day 1938 after their February

10 wedding, so that she could spend at least part of each day writing. They had little money during most of their marriage. Wilson's two "fatal" extravagances were liquor and taxis—the latter he took frequently from Stamford to Manhattan, a ninety-minute trip. Yet Wilson took temporary work to tide them over. For example, he taught University of Chicago summer classes in 1939 while McCarthy took the baby to Seattle to show her grandmother. Until he was given the book editorship of *The New Yorker* in 1943, both had only sporadic incomes.

McCarthy, who though an antifeminist always delighted in pointing out Wilson's chauvinisms, recalls having to fight for—but also having won—her own checking account. She did not like asking Wilson "for a nickel to make a telephone call" (*Intellectual Memoirs* 106), but Wilson recalls that "his wife wanted to buy a fur coat when he was down to his last dollar" (96) during the summer he taught in Chicago. Because he expected her to give large and frequent parties, she developed extraordinary culinary skills and was, from that period forward, renowned for her outstanding talents as a hostess. Both benefited in unexpected ways from the ordeal that the marriage evidently proved to be.

On the other hand, we should not doubt that the Wilson-McCarthy marriage hurt the heart of each of them—McCarthy's perhaps more because hers was seventeen years younger and more innocent. We know the illusions with which she entered it. She remembers that "he gave the appearance of a man of quiet habits with an interest in books, pictures, and music," that he was "well-known as a literary critic," and that she had "admired his work" even before they met (Gelderman 90). Her attraction stemmed in part from his having "held out great promise of a quiet settled life and the rearing of a large family" during their courtship (90). What similar vague longings in Wilson were conjured up by his association with McCarthy—in addition to the obvious ones stimulated by her youth, loveliness, and fine mind—he did not record. The fact that he was, by more accounts than just her own, horribly brutal with her and possessive of her shows a frustration and dysfunction more extensive than anything seen in his admittedly irascible nature either before or after that period in his life.

Forty-six years later, McCarthy told Carol Brightman in a 1984 interview for *The Nation*, when asked about the trouble she had had with Edmund Wilson, that Wilson had been "hard to oppose because he was so stubborn and so mean and violent when drinking" (615), but went on to recount their conflict over banking in matter-of-fact terms: "I took a stand and Edmund gave in and I had my own bank account and that was the end of it" (615). Someplace between the hysterics of the pregnant twenty-six-year-old and the pronouncements of the complacent seventy-two-year-old, some crucial lived experience has slipped into the gap. Brightman pushed McCarthy closer to the point: "Did you have competition problems?" McCarthy defended her second husband: "No, [Wilson] was excellent on that score. . . . in terms of work he was marvelous" (614). Then, anticipating the acknowledgement in *Intellectual Memoirs*, she notes for the record that "[h]e made me write. I would never have written fiction, I think, if it hadn't been for him" (614). McCarthy's complication was that she was maritally and procreatively entangled with her mentor. To authenticate herself as a *littérateur*, she had to extricate herself from that entanglement.

WORKS CITED

Brightman, Carol. "Mary, Still Contrary." *The Nation*. May 19, 1984: 611–18.

————. *Writing Dangerously: Mary McCarthy and Her World*. New York: Clarkson Potter, 1992.

Castronovo, David. "Edmund Wilson." *Dictionary of Literary Biography: Modern American Critics, 1920–1955*. Ann Arbor, Mich.: Gale-Bruccoli, 1988. 304–15.

Costa, Richard. *Edmund Wilson: Our Neighbor from Talcottville*. Syracuse, N.Y.: Syracuse University Press, 1980.

Gelderman, Carol. *Mary McCarthy: A Life*. New York: St. Martin's, 1988.

————, ed. *Conversations with Mary McCarthy*. Jackson: University Press of Mississippi, 1991. 3–29.

————. *Mary McCarthy: A Life*. New York: St. Martin's, 1988.

Hanscom, Larry. "Contrary Mary: Vassar '33." *Newsweek*. September 2, 1963: 80–83.

McCarthy, Mary. *A Charmed Life*. New York: Harcourt, 1955.

————. *Intellectual Memoirs: New York 1936–1938*. New York: Harcourt, 1992.

Muste, John. "The Thirties, the Forties, and the Fifties." Magill, Frank, ed. *Masterplots II, Nonfiction Series*. Englewood Cliffs, N.J.: Salem, 1989. 1500–1506.

Stock, Irving. *Mary McCarthy*. Minneapolis: University of Minnesota Press, 1968.

Strouse, Jean. "Making the Facts Obey." *New York Times Book Review*. May 24, 1992: 1, 16–17.

V

Biography and Reminiscence

19

My Secret Sharer

Carol Brightman

Hypocrite lecteur—mon semblable—mon frère

—Charles Baudelaire

We always write for someone, and whether that person knows it or not *we* know. Or think we know. "I want this to be the kind of book I like to read," I wrote Mary McCarthy in January 1985, when the proposal for *Writing Dangerously*, then called "Mary McCarthy, an American Heretic," was making the rounds of publishers; "namely, one that reconstructs the historical ground out of which chance and choice conspire to fashion a life, and a life's work." I was staking my claim; but even then I wonder if it wasn't Mary McCarthy herself whom I was casting as my silent reader. And if so, what did I have to tell her?

"Chance and choice"—these were her themes. Like an alternating current, one chases the other through nearly all her memoirs, with chance generally disposing of choice, especially when a political or romantic allegiance is under investigation. But they were my themes too, though it had been years since I had copied out Yeats's "Solomon and the Witch" in a notebook:

Chance being at one with Choice at last,
All that the brigand apple brought
And this foul world were dead at last (ll, 15–17).

Had I remembered my romance with Sheba and her Solomon, I am sure I would have been unable to write that sentence to Mary. Memory would have interfered with invention. And yet invention, as we know from McCarthy's fiction, as well as from her memoirs, is more often than not rooted in contingency: in what actually happened that is still happening. Memory is the demiurge, the subordinate deity, who invokes the Muse.

Mary McCarthy knew I was going to write about her whether she cooperated or not. "I can't stop you, and I wouldn't want to try," she told me early on in our transatlantic conversations, thereby opening the gate to the next question, which was when and where we would meet for the first interview. Ultimately, she gave me access to her private papers, to her friends and family, and to her life story, fashioned and refashioned in over a dozen interviews, without retaining the right to review my manuscript. A biographer's dream, it was a shrewd move on McCarthy's part, for it allowed me to write for myself, and thus, in a sense, to write for her.

I was free to explore the themes that had drawn me to her: not just in 1985, but in 1960 at Vassar, when I was "losing my faith" and read *Memories of a Catholic Girlhood*; and in 1963, when I added her to a master's thesis on two women writers (Simone de Beauvoir and Anaïs Nin) who had begun to bore me; and in 1967, when we met in the antiwar movement; and again in 1980, when I wondered whatever had happened to Mary McCarthy and interviewed her in Castine, Maine.

I wasn't thinking about these prior connections when I began rereading her work and writing a book proposal in 1985. Later I saw that in choosing to write a biography about Mary McCarthy I had embraced the literary side of my own experience—which had oscillated between politics and literature, with politics generally taking command. Probably this give and take in McCarthy's career is what drew me to her, though in time it was her literary sensibility—her rigorous attention to the emotive power of language to focus the mind on the riddles of experience—that moved me more than her political engagements. As for the latter, with the exception of her travels to both South and North Vietnam and the deeply discerning character studies that resulted, McCarthy's political instincts, I think, were not always reliable.

In any event, it was Mary McCarthy who interested me: not my historical ground, but hers; and hers precisely because her generation's zeitgeist departed so dramatically from my own. How to describe the latter? Writing ten years after I began the biography, and three years after its publication, I am still struck by the torpor that hangs over American intellectual life, as if some spirit of inquiry and adventure that enlivens the writing of the 1920s, 1930s, 1940s, and 1960s lies, like "the thing" in that old movie from the 1950s, encased in a block of ice. And only a blowtorch of history—another Crash, Holocaust, Hiroshima, or Vietnam—will succeed in bringing it to life. "Shit happens" remains our sad fin de siècle lullaby.

One misses critical voices like McCarthy's, Hannah Arendt's, Dwight Macdonald's, or Edmund Wilson's, for that matter, writers who read the world's events as carefully as any text, and saw themselves as participant-observers in history's dramas. In place of their broad-ranging criticism, we have perfected the art of lamentation, and a kind of highbrow gossip about literary personalities that remains largely indifferent to literature. A few critics, whose entertainment value is high—Camille Paglia on the Right, Alex Cockburn on the Left—are licensed to kill. Most are content to amuse themselves, rooting among the ephemera of culture (I'm speaking of North America) until such time as "World-history," as Hannah Arendt and her husband Heinrich Blücher used to call the tug of calamity, intervenes.

Mary McCarthy's life and times, I hoped, would offer a perch from which the complicated legacy of the last great age of ideas could be explored afresh. The "dissenter's dissenter," as I called her, McCarthy had critical faculties that remained intact long after those of many of her contemporaries had dried up. Thus, she might provide us with a literary life that stood in stark and useful contrast to the prevailing infatuation, especially among women, with writing as an instrument of personal salvation. Her biography would have to reconstruct a larger world than the conventional "life" centered on the nursery, the bedroom, and the rue Morgue; and yet it had to reimagine that incredible childhood, whose crises remained the wellsprings of her talent.

Such a biography would not be what Janet Malcolm later called "the medium through which the remaining secrets of the famous dead are taken from them and dumped out in full view of the world" (86). But even as I tried to acquaint Mary in 1985 with "the kind of book I like to read," I knew I would soon be wading into the rapids of a complicated sex life, and stirring up old feuds. To ignore Mary McCarthy's capacity to inspire fear and loathing among certain people who had known her would be to scant the ground that nourished her.

The dilemma was how to reconcile the inclusion of potentially damaging material with the perception I was fast developing, especially as our interviews progressed, that the project I had embarked upon was at bottom a collaborative one. In July 1988, when I was struggling to find the through-line of a difficult chapter on wartime New York—"War Babies," it's called in *Writing Dangerously*—the temptation to confide in my subject was irresistible. Who else, after all, would be as interested in getting it right?

"I am writing about so many things, engaged with so many ideas, personalities, events, that it is a struggle just to keep track of them," I wrote Mary in

1988 from the attic room I rented over the Riverview Market in Pemaquid, Maine. Nor did I want to say what had already been said, or leave a doubtful interpretation unchallenged, which is why I was also reviewing secondary sources. "It's like holding the reins to a half-dozen braces of horses, each one of which must be given its lead to move forward, and all somehow held together." "When I solve the problem, which is usually one of interpretation," I added, trotting the metaphor back to the barn, "the solution often turns out to be something quite simple (something a pony could pull)."

Shamelessly, I wanted Mary to know "that my difficulty [was] only the other side of my ambition." In case she hadn't noticed, my book was "a full-blown cultural history," one in which her performance was "the touchstone to understanding the work of many others," while I was also "trying to answer some important questions of my own." The occasion for these lofty sentiments was the publication of Carol Gelderman's *Mary McCarthy: A Life*, the "authorized" biography, which, while I had long expected it, suddenly seemed to blow my cover. I could no longer hide my "larger" agenda behind the biogapher's screen, since one had just been written. I had to show Mary (or was it myself?) that what I was doing was different, that while "the book I am writing has much, much more of you in it than the Gelderman biography," it was also very much the story of a generation.

Such letters are way stations in the pilgrim's progress. They require no response, even when the plaintiff assures her subject that she feels "good about the book," which is one that—what chutzpah!—she "can even imagine [her] reading with pleasure." By then the manuscript included the kind of material that led Carolyn Heilbrun, writing in the *Women's Review of Books*, to find in it "a nasty woman of vaulting ambition, capable neither of compassion nor of revealing the hidden wound that made compassion forever impossible." (Others, closer to Mary, found the same life "celebrated" in the book, "warts and all [as] she would wish" [FitzGerald].)

In October 1989, when Mary lay dying of lung cancer in New York Hospital, and I went to see her, it was with the draft of an unfinished chapter about her friendship with Hannah Arendt tucked under my arm. How foolish of me, how impossibly arrogant, I thought later. Of course I didn't understand that she was dying until I entered the intensive care unit and saw the bright blue breathing tube jutting from her mouth. She couldn't speak but could only respond to visitors with her eyes and hands. I never mentioned my bundle. When I returned the next day, it was with a manila folder in which I had inscribed the alphabet in press-type, so that she could point to letters, form words; but she was beyond words.

It wasn't vanity that made me think a dying woman would be interested in what I had to say about her life, though there is nobody blinder than a biographer or autobiographer in the rapture of creation. Nor was I seeking reassurance. I had been writing to Mary McCarthy all along. She was my secret sharer. That in the normal course of events she wouldn't read the book until it was published is what made it possible for me to imagine her as my reader in the first place. I didn't have to please her. She didn't have to correct me (though she would have caught a good many errors, had she lived to review names and dates). All she had to do was be there when I finished.

Of course, there is an alternate ending to the tale, which remains open. Like Eliot's Prufrock, "I am no prophet—and here's no great matter." Anyway, Mary lives and the book speaks. "I am Lazarus," it says,

".... come from the dead,
Come back to tell you all, I shall tell you all—"

Whereupon Prufrock wonders, and so might we, what

If one, settling a pillow or throwing off a shawl,
And turning toward the window, should say:
    "That is not it at all,
    That is not what I meant, at all" (ll 94–95, 107–10).

WORKS CITED

Brightman, Carol. Letter to Mary McCarthy. January 31, 1985. Mary McCarthy Papers, Vassar College Library.

————. Letter to Mary McCarthy. July 28, 1988. Mary McCarthy Papers, Vassar College Library.

————. "Memorandum on my conversation with Mary McCarthy." February 22, 1985. Carol Brightman's personal papers.

————. *Writing Dangerously: Mary McCarthy and Her World.* New York: Clarkson Potter, 1992. San Diego: Harcourt/Harvest, 1994.

Eliot, T. S. "The Love Song of J. Alfred Prufrock." *Collected Poems 1909–1962.* New York: Harcourt, 1963.

Fitzgerald, Frances. Letter to Carol Southern. October 3, 1992. Carol Brightman's personal papers.

Gelderman, Carol. *Mary McCarthy: A Life.* New York: St. Martin's, 1988.

Heilbrun, Carolyn. "A Man's Woman." Review of *Writing Dangerously* by Carol Brightman. *Women's Review of Books* X, 4. January 1993. 17–18.

Malcolm, Janet. "Annals of Biography: The Silent Woman." *New Yorker.* August 23 and 30, 1993. 84–159.

Yeats, William Butler. "Solomon and the Witch." *The Collected Poems of W. B. Yeats.* New York: Macmillan, 1961.

20

Just the Facts, Ma'am, and Nothing but the Facts: A Biographer's Reminiscence

Carol Gelderman

"Just the Facts, Ma'am, and Nothing but the Facts" is an odd title for me to have chosen for this reminiscence. If I'm not mistaken, these words were repeatedly spoken by a detective in the long-running television series, *Dragnet*, not one episode of which I ever watched. Still, the words, which must have been the trademark of the program for me to be able to so readily conjure them up, make me think of Mary McCarthy. After all, McCarthy and facts are conjoined like salt and pepper, love and marriage (as the late 1950s popular song had it), and hide and seek. No writer I can think of is or was as concerned with facts as McCarthy. I like what Jean Strouse said in a 1992 essay in the *New York Times Book Review*. She said that Mary McCarthy believed in fact the way some people believe in God (1).

All of McCarthy's fiction embodies what was to her the very definition of the novel: "its concern with the actual world, the world of fact, of the verifiable, of figures, even, and statistics" ("The Fact in Fiction" 250). And so too in her three memoirs she strove for the greatest possible factual and emotional accuracy. *Memories of a Catholic Girlhood* (1957), her finest achievement, displays all her best literary qualities—polish, acerbic wit, sparkle, candor, and at times exuberant hilarity—plus a depth of feeling Dwight Macdonald found absent in her fiction.

If it's true that when we grow old we are still ourselves, only more so, then Mary McCarthy provides corroborating evidence in her recent memoirs, *How I Grew* and *Intellectual Memoirs*. Her requisite "heavy dosage of fact," "this fetishism of fact," to use her own words, had gotten out of hand. Her once vivid and original voice becomes fact-sodden in both books. Describing a studio apartment on Beekman Place in *Intellectual Memoirs*, she writes, "Instead of [bed]spreads, we have covers made of dark brown sateen (Nathalie Swan's idea, or was it Margaret Miller's?)" (12). And, "It may have been that day that I first saw Martha Gelhorn—blond and pretty, talking about Spain. Or was it Martha Dodd, daughter of the former ambassador to Spain? (73).

As a hopeful future McCarthy biographer in 1980, I soon discovered her facts-obsession applied to others' writings as well, and, during the eight years I worked on telling her life story, especially to mine. When McCarthy had agreed to cooperate with me, she never asked to see what I would write before publication, but when I had finished what turned out to be an early draft, I mailed it to her asking her to check it for fact. In a letter I'd sent ahead of the manuscript announcing its imminent arrival, I worriedly added a postscript informing her that she had been misspelling her grandmother's name Morgenstern as Morg*a*nstern for the past half century. My "audacity" led to an epistolary exchange that characterized the next two and a half years.

Your P.S. is a bit disquieting. I don't know who Elizabeth Greenebaum is (an editor at McGraw-Hill?), but she can hardly be an expert on how my grandmother's name is spelled. Normally, I agree, it's spelled "Morgenstern" in German, but something happened to the "e" in the United States in the case of quite a few Jews, not just my grandmother's family. I suppose it was a kind of Americanization; maybe they got "Morgan" from the House of Morgan. . . . Anyway that's how it was. You refer to "the De Young," but I don't know what that is. (MM to CG, July 7, 1984)

"Forgive me," I answered.

I assumed you knew Elizabeth Greenebaum. She is your cousin, Elkan Morgenstern's third child, born in 1910. The DeYoung Museum is the San Francisco museum where a portrait of Rabbi Elkan Morgenstern, your great, great grandfather, hangs. The portrait was painted by Charles Nahl, and was the 1922 gift of Mrs. Ray M. Nelson, Samuel Morgenstern's daughter. Abraham Morgenstern, your great grandfather, worked for Samuel Morgenstern, an accountant whose office was located in San Francisco on the SE corner of Front and Broadway. Therese and Abraham Morgenstern died in 1884 and are buried in the Jewish cemetery. Anyway, Elizabeth Morgenstern Greenebaum says her name is spelled with an "e." So too does your uncle, Frank Preston. The name on the portrait of your great, great grandfather is spelled with an "e." So, I really think that is the correct spelling. (If you want to speak to Mrs.

Greenebaum, her number is 213-BR9-2150. Of course your uncle could settle this too.) Finally, I did research on the Morgensterns at the California Historical Society, the Western Jewish History Center at the Judah I. Magnes Museum, at the Washington State Jewish Historical Society, at the Society of California Pioneers, and in the Genealogical Division of the San Francisco Public Library. Nowhere is there a spelling of Morgenstern with an "a." (CG to MM, July 13, 1984)

Keep in mind that McCarthy had not yet received my manuscript. When she did, she read it immediately and responded, in a letter to me, with absolute horror (one of her favorite words) and much justification. Since my present discussion focuses on facts, I'll concentrate on her criticisms of my fidelity to them and omit other complaints about my style, grammar, and general lack of grasp of the intellectual life.

A lively correspondence between us began and continued, seemingly interminably. She objected to and I defended nearly every fact. Her letters simmered with heated allegations like "This manuscript is a hydra; chop off one mistake of fact and a hundred spring up to replace it" (November 17, 1984); "I don't know what it is that impels you to misquote me at every opportunity and embroider quite crudely simple statements of mine with products of your own imagination" (March 18, 1988); "It would interest me clinically to know the cause of such self-confident error" (ibid.) A few samples from two early letters, McCarthy's to me on November 17, 1984, and mine to her on January 4, 1985, illustrate the cross fire that characterized the next several years.

MM: You infer the habits of Bocca di Magra [Italian fishing village] from "The Hounds of Summer" [McCarthy short story]. But a piece of fiction can't be treated as a literal transcription of reality. You can't rely on "The Hounds of Summer" for the daily program at Bocca di Magra. "The Hounds of Summer" tries to give a poetic account of life there.

CG: I have not inferred the habits of Bocca di Magra from "The Hounds of Summer," and I would never treat a piece of fiction as a literal transcription of reality. I have used quotes from the story that accurately describe the village, a village I visited in 1982. The facts about the daily program at Bocca di Magra come from letters, principally yours to Carmen Angleton [McCarthy friend] and to William Jovanovich [McCarthy's publisher], and Nicola Chiaromonte's [Italian intellectual] to Dwight MacDonald [American intellectual]. Even so, I eliminated the gathering and eating of mussels since you objected to that last summer.

MM: You rely all too credulously on your sources, some of which—for example, Rosamond Bernier [copublisher, with her first husband, of McCarthy's *Venice Observed*] and Uncle Harry [Harry McCarthy], are less trustworthy than others. And in any case, memory is fallible, especially where other peoples' lives are concerned. My own letters, I see, are fallible. If I wrote Nikki Mariano [Bernard Berenson's secretary and companion] that Jim and I went to Geneva, I must have mixed it up strangely with Berne, where in fact we did go, and saw the bears.

CG: You say I rely too credulously on sources, and you specifically cite Rosamond Bernier and your Uncle Harry as untrustworthy. I altered Rosamond Bernier's comments to conform to your recollection of what happened in Venice and in New York. The only information from Uncle Harry is that you filled your mother's perfume bottles with ink and that Kevin [McCarthy's brother] started a fire shortly before entraining for Minneapolis, and that your father was uncomfortable with even the least reprimand given to you children. The facts concerning the money each family expended to take care of you and your brothers came from Louis's notebooks [an uncle], diaries, cancelled checks, and letters to and from the Prestons [maternal grandparents]. Yes, you did write Nikki Mariano that you and Jim went to Geneva. I changed that to Zurich according to what you told me this summer. In this letter, you say it is Berne. Berne it shall be.

MM: Your pressing an assumption too hard is what makes me still take violent exception to your use of the Elizabeth Daniels interview [This was an interview McCarthy gratuitously sent to me.] I wasn't at all my most clear-headed that morning evidently. It is true that the words you quote about Miss Kitchel were spoken by me, but I must have been thinking of my first year at Vassar, in which case they would have been right. She was the saving grace then. Yet, as the rest of the Daniels interview clearly demonstrates, I valued Helen Sandison as highly as or maybe more highly in the end than Anna Kitchel. You could not know that since you knew neither of those people nor me as a girl, but you wanted to *appear* to know.

CG: I don't know what assumption I pressed too hard from Elizabeth Daniels's interview. I merely quoted you; moreover, I think I make it clear that Miss Sandison was as valuable to you, probably more so, than Miss Kitchel. Even so, I have deleted the following: "favorite teacher" on page 82 and "the best thing I ever got out of Vassar was Kitchel" on 105.

MM: One of the more odious sentences, to my taste, is "The Wilsons [Edmund Wilson, McCarthy's second husband; Elena Wilson, his fourth wife] breathed a temporary sigh of relief." The right to enter into the feelings of others is something that must be earned, and not by eager suppositions as you put yourself in what you think is their place.

CG: "The Wilsons breathed a temporary sigh of relief" is not an example of my entering into the feelings of others, but a statement from Adelaide Walker [close neighbor and friend of the Wilsons']. If I were guessing about someone's feelings, I would say so. In any case, I've dispensed with any mention of the Wilsons' feelings at the time, feelings Adelaide Walker described in detail during my interview with her on 91st Street.

MM: You tell me that I *said* in a letter that Bowden [MM's third husband] was translating *I Vicere.* Maybe I said so, but he wasn't. I hoped he would.

CG: You said Bowden was translating *I Vicere* in a letter to Bernard Berenson 9/17/58. I've gotten rid of this sentence, since you say you meant that you hoped he would.

After thirty months of comparable correspondence and in desperation, I asked if she would or would not let me quote from her letters and books in the biography, which was obviously going to be published whether she liked it or not. She wrote back that "since the milk was already spilt, let's hope for the best," and the stewing about facts abruptly ended.

After McCarthy and I had agreed on what the facts were, I was free to mold them into a story. Her last words to me on my first meeting with her in Castine, Maine, in 1980 were about how much she admired Boswell's *Life of Johnson.* Choosing to ignore her Shakespearean standards, I focused on the why of her admiration; that is, Boswell presented the facts and let the facts speak for themselves. Fortunately I had expressed a similar philosophy of biography writing in the preface of the biography of Henry Ford I had written, which McCarthy read and on the basis of which she had agreed to cooperate with me in the writing of her own life. Believing the accuracy consisted in presenting facts and letting them stand for reality in retrospect seems rather naive on both our parts. After all, what are facts? "The moment one begins to investigate the truth of the simplest facts which one has accepted as true," wrote Leonard Woolf in his autobiography, "it is as though one had stepped off a firm narrow path into a bog or quicksand—every step one takes one sinks deeper into the bog of uncertainty." Magazines are filled with charges and countercharges of journalists, historians, and biographers obsessed with the elusiveness not only of truth but of facts. The Caro-Blumenthal exchange is an illustration. When Robert Caro, well known for factual probity, came out with *Means of Ascent,* volume two of his multivolumed biography of Lyndon Johnson, Sydney Blumenthal (and others of similar intellectual standing) conceded that Caro got the facts right, but argued that he got the story wrong. Blumenthal wrote a cover article for the *New Republic* expressing this view, and Caro responded in a lengthy afterword to the paperback of his biography. Blumenthal rebutted in a long letter in the *New York Times Book Review.* Caro plans to get the last word in the preface to volume three.

Any responsible biographer tries to let the facts speak for themselves, but in arranging these facts to create a narrative, he imposes on them his unique sensibility. And herein lies the trouble. Even an ardent admirer is intrusive, introducing an alien point of view necessarily different from that mixture of self-recrimination and self-justification that the biographee has made the subject of his/her lifelong conversation with him/herself. Moreover, as the *New Yorker* nonfiction writer Janet Malcolm observed, "Narratives called biographies pale and shrink in the face of the disorderly actuality that is life" (158). Fiction is biography's direct opposite in this: a good fiction writer will give us truth under the guise of an entertaining story. A biographer turns letters, journals, historical records, and the memories of others into a new kind of fiction called biography. No wonder Oscar Wilde said that all great men have disciples and Judas is the biographer, James Joyce that the biographer is a biografiend, and Germaine Greer that biography is rape, an unpardonable crime against selfhood.

Maybe readers can't always know the whole truth, but they can know whose partial truth to believe, a confidence based on the biographer's voice. Even though the biographer has been as relentless as Flaubert in keeping himself invisible, his voice, always discernible, elicits trust or mistrust. A reader has got to feel that the author is fair, that he or she is not living in a fairy-tale world and is not going to pose stark demons and heroes. He is going to see complexity, texture; his voice is calm and reasonable. Nevertheless, it is abundantly clear that, as Elizabeth Hardwick wrote in a generous and affectionate introduction to *Intellectual Memoirs*, Mary McCarthy did not distinguish between truth and her truth. Nor did I in making illusionary efforts to impose narrative order on the multifarious and contradictory stuff of life.

WORKS CITED

Blumenthal, Sydney. "The Epic Errors of Robert Caro." *New Republic.* June 4, 1990: 29–36.

Caro, Robert. *Means of Ascent: The Years of Lyndon Johnson.* New York: Knopf, 1990.
———. *Means of Ascent: The Years of Lyndon Johnson.* 1990. New York: Random House, 1991.

Dragnet. NBC weekly series: December 16, 1951, to September 6, 1959; January 12, 1967, to September 10, 1970. Terrance, Vincent, ed. *The Complete Encyclopedia of Television Programs 1947–1978.* Volume 1. New York: A. S. Barnes, 1979.

Gelderman, Carol. *Henry Ford, the Wayward Capitalist.* New York: Dial, 1981.
———. Letters to Mary McCarthy, 1980–1989. Collection of C. G.

Malcolm, Janet. "Annals of Biography: The Silent Woman." *New Yorker.* August 23 and 30, 1993: 84–159.

McCarthy, Mary. "The Fact in Fiction." *On the Contrary.* New York: Farrar, 1961. 249–70.

————. "The Hounds of Summer." *The Hounds of Summer and Other Stories*. New York: Bard/Avon, 1981. 193–240.

————. *How I Grew*. New York: Harcourt, 1987.

————. *Intellectual Memoirs: New York 1936–1938*. New York: Harcourt, 1992.

————. Letters to Carol Gelderman, 1980–1989. Collection of C. G.

————. *Memories of a Catholic Girlhood*. New York: Harcourt, 1957.

Strouse, Jean. "Making the Facts Obey." *New York Times Book Review*. May 24, 1992: 1, 16–17.

Woolf, Leonard. *Downhill All the Way: An Autobiography of the Years 1919–1939*. London: Hogarth, 1970.

21

No Stone Unturned: Contracts and Nymphets

Frances Kiernan

On August 11, 1993, I spotted an item of particular interest in the Book Notes section of the *New York Times*: the New York Public Library had acquired the papers of the publisher Farrar, Straus and Giroux. Suddenly the library had in its possession untold boxes of letters from, and about, Farrar, Straus authors—letters dating from 1946 to 1980 and ranging from the "quotidian" to the "poignant." To give some idea of the treasures lurking in these boxes, the *Times* quoted from a "funny" note Clifford Odets had written, acknowledging receipt of *Sights and Spectacles*, a spanking new collection of Mary McCarthy's theater criticism. Odets, who had little reason to love McCarthy or her theater criticism, wrote back, "I shall learn from this book how to become a better citizen, human being and playwright" (Lyall).

It looked like a windfall. Unfortunately, when I called Lisa Browar, the library's assistant director for rare books and manuscripts, I learned that the Farrar, Straus papers were not as yet catalogued. Indeed, there was some question as to whether the collection was ready to be open to the public. She warned me not to expect much. In the end, I was able to get my hands on one yellowing manila Mary McCarthy folder. That was it. The folder held the correspondence attending the purchase of *Sights and Spectacles* and appeared to be devoted almost entirely to contract negotiations and subsidiary rights.

As a biographer I have learned to approach Mary McCarthy with respect, amusement, and affection. Three times she wrote directly about her life—first in one eloquent memoir and then in two volumes of autobiography. Always I am struck by her desire to get at the truth of what happened, her passion to get things right. I can only admire her persistence in an enterprise that she herself saw as being fraught with peril. I do not feel that it is my task to try and catch her out. If I have any task, it is to place events in context and provide a different perspective—and, perhaps, to provide some entertainment.

Only a fool would try to tell Mary McCarthy's story as she told it. In 1990, when I started, I was going to show her as a working writer, through the eyes of her family and her editors, her fellow writers and her close friends. It was my plan to put together an oral history, interlaced with my own commentary and quoting liberally from her work. Writers often tend to be solitary or reclusive, but for a great part of her life Mary McCarthy had been a public figure. At one point she had been an international celebrity. Given all that, I felt an oral history would suit her fine.

An oral history would also suit *me* fine. For a great part of my life I had worked as an editor of short stories. As I saw it, a good oral history—with its reliance on voice, point of view, and narrative tension—was not unlike a good piece of fiction. In any case, to go out with a tape recorder and knock on strange doors seemed more inviting than spending long hours shut away in my study or in the stacks of some library.

Unfortunately, for a biographer there is no escaping the library. When someone's memory fails in an interview, a bit of gossip, a dinner menu, or a snippet of conversation can do the trick. For such details you can't rely totally on secondary sources. Like it or not, you have to go to letters and diaries and any document you can unearth. As it turns out, a diary or letter may be of value for its own sake—even a letter devoted to the negotiation of a contract. Although a letter may be shaped with a specific purpose or audience in mind, it has the virtue of being unencumbered by hindsight. Back forty years ago, let's say, things may have looked very different from the way they look today.

In a letter dated October 22, 1954, Mary McCarthy announced to Roger Straus that at last she was sending him her proposed outline for *Sights and Spectacles.* "I should have written sooner," she writes, "but complications intervened: moving, finishing a block of a novel, illness, guests." That fall, Mary McCarthy was approaching a turning point in her career and in her marriage. With her third husband Bowden Broadwater she was living in a rented house in Newport, finishing a novel set in a small New England village, and trying to earn some extra money. Bowden Broadwater was having difficulty finding full-time work. She, on the other hand, was taking on more projects than she could comfortably handle, desperate to make up for the year she had wasted trying to find backers for a new magazine called *Critic*.

Although they were renting in Newport, the Broadwaters had a house of their own in Wellfleet, a small village near the eastern tip of Cape Cod very much like the village in her novel. Purchased two years earlier, that house was beginning to look like a mistake. Not only had it used up most of their capital but it had landed McCarthy smack in the middle of the very circle in which a decade earlier she had fought publicly and bitterly with Edmund Wilson, her second husband. A world-famous essayist and critic, Wilson continued to live in their old house in Wellfleet with his new wife, Elena. The "monster" or "minotaur," as the Broadwaters sometimes called him, was a presence to be reckoned with. While relations with Wilson were much improved, and even cordial, living down the road from him could sometimes be awkward. Like any small village, Wellfleet derived much of its daily entertainment from a heavy dose of gossip and a liberal dash of troublemaking. In any case, once the weather turned cold, the Broadwaters had no choice but to leave: their Wellfleet house was not winterized.

At that point in her life Mary McCarthy had not made much money from her writing. Her fame was nothing like Edmund Wilson's, but she had produced an impressive body of work. For two decades her criticism and essays had been appearing in well-respected magazines and literary quarterlies. With its sexual candor, her first book, *The Company She Keeps*, had come closest to reaching a wide audience. Harcourt Brace, which two years earlier had brought out *The Groves of Academe* and *Cast a Cold Eye*, held an option on the novel she was writing—a novel called *A Charmed Life*, which would be long remembered for a scene in which the heroine, a newly remarried young playwright, is raped on her own horsehair Empire sofa by her overbearing former husband.

In her October 22 letter to Roger Straus, McCarthy speaks breezily of her plans for a collection culled from the best of her old *Partisan Review* theater pieces. "The model, I think, should be Edmund's *Classics and Commercials*, which was not a complete record either," she writes. But very quickly she adds, "The title—mine, I mean (*Sights and Spectacles*),—I thought of a few years ago, before his came out, but perhaps it's too much like it. If so, I can think of something new and not alliterative."

The "Edmund" is of course Edmund Wilson, who casts a shadow that stretches far beyond Wellfleet. McCarthy is torn between accepting and ignoring it. Indeed, she has mixed feelings about the theater pieces as well: "I'm delighted that you're interested," she writes Straus. "I think it will make a nice book. The Chronicles were awfully popular, almost depressingly so to me, since people still keep asking me, 'When are you going to do those theatre pieces again?' when I'd prefer an inquiry about my new novel."

In the fall of 1954, a good many publishers would have been happy to bring out a novel by Mary McCarthy. But publishers back then were no more enthusiastic about collections of essays than they are now. Roger Straus was an exception. In soliciting the theater pieces he was no doubt hoping to one day get hold of her fiction. Straus was known for his small advances, but at this point in McCarthy's life *any* advance, no matter how small, was welcome. She and Straus had never been close, but they had many friends in common. For this deal McCarthy did not use her agent. Rather than trust to his staff, Straus handled the negotiations himself.

In a letter dated November 12, with her contract in hand, McCarthy questions Straus's royalty scale, asks for anthology and digest rights and for approval of all translations, and then turns to the subject of her $500 advance. "I'd like to have it in toto, now, when and if the contract is signed," she writes. She then goes on to explain precisely why this is both necessary and reasonable. "I'm not a collector of advances on daydreams, as any of our friends can tell you." More important, "the sum isn't very large (I'm not complaining about that) but it's larger to me than it is to you."

In his very next letter, dated three days later, Roger Straus gives McCarthy virtually everything she wants. Under the circumstances, Straus's response is hardly astonishing. What *is* astonishing—certainly to anyone who has worked in book publishing in the last decade—is the penultimate paragraph of Straus's letter, written in response to the final paragraph of McCarthy's. Without missing a beat, Straus and McCarthy have put aside their contract negotiations to embark on a serious, if mildly flirtatious, literary discussion.

Of pressing concern to both Straus and McCarthy was the manuscript of Vladimir Nabokov's new novel *Lolita*, which was slowly making the rounds among a select group of concerned readers. In 1954 there were no Xerox machines and no multiple submissions. Publishing was a leisurely business. Not only Roger Straus but Edmund Wilson and his wife Elena had read *Lolita*. McCarthy herself had managed to read three-quarters of it during a brief stay in New York, before passing it on to her former lover Philip Rahv, one of the two founding editors of *Partisan Review*.

Today, thanks to *The Nabokov-Wilson Letters*, just about everyone knows that Edmund Wilson, hitherto a great supporter of Nabokov's fiction, had no use for *Lolita*. Wilson, who was anything but a puritan, found the subject matter offensive. Nasty subjects "may make fine books; but I don't feel you have got away with this," he declared with the authority of a critic who had

had a book of his own banned by the courts. For good measure, he included an excerpt from a letter he had received from his former wife—a letter in which McCarthy said, among other things, "I thought the writing was terribly sloppy all through, perhaps worse in the second volume. It was full of what teachers call haziness, and all Vladimir's hollowest jokes and puns" (288–89).

Though never having had a chance to finish reading the manuscript, McCarthy had not hesitated to offer an opinion. However, she *did* venture to say that she liked *Lolita* better than Wilson did. Still, that was not saying much. Perhaps to offset her harsh words, Wilson included with his letter an enthusiastic note from the French-born Elena, who not only liked the book but found it touching. Of course Elena could not claim to be a professional writer or critic. She merely brought a different perspective to the manuscript: "She has seen America from the foreigner's point of view and understands how it looks to your hero" (287).

For more than one reader familiar with the Nabokov-Wilson letters, McCarthy's cool response to *Lolita* has gone a long way toward explaining her subsequent readiness to proclaim Nabokov's next novel, *Pale Fire*, a masterpiece. Whether you choose to credit her enthusiasm to guilt or ambition or a simple overreaction, it often feels willed. Certainly, such pleasure as she takes in the book seems to derive from successfully ferreting out and tracking down each and every clue in an impossibly difficult paper chase.

But, to be fair, tracking down clues and figuring things out was one of McCarthy's greatest joys in life. That, finally, is what makes her so cross with *Lolita*: hard as she tries, she is unable to figure out what Nabokov is up to. In her letter of November 12, 1954, she writes Roger Straus, who may be her publisher but who carries none of the weight with her that Wilson does, that she cannot go along with his view of the book: "The second volume didn't bore me; I liked the motels and the awful American scene and the desolation of the whole business. What troubled me was that I didn't understand the latter part; it seemed to be turning into some sort of myth or allegory, but what it was I couldn't make out."

To know what to make of a manuscript that defies all expectations is no easy matter. A book in manuscript has yet to acquire the authority it will possess once it is set in type. To Roger Straus, McCarthy ventures to suggest that Nabokov *may* be on to something—something puzzling and disturbing but perfectly acceptable not only to French-born Elena Wilson but to Russian-born Philip Rahv, who is actually thinking of publishing part of it in *Partisan Review*. "What I do feel sure of is that anybody who published it would be prosecuted. He makes nympholepsy or whatever it is too seductive, like an actual temptation. Is Philip going to dare it?"

Roger Straus, who is on the advisory board of *Partisan Review* and who likes *Lolita* little better than Wilson does, never quite answers her question. "I agree with you that nobody will dare touch this, leaving out its literary merits or demerits," he writes, thereby putting the matter to rest once and for all. But in his own way Straus, too, acknowledges *Lolita's* strange power. "It is the damnedest book, and as I walk down Madison Avenue I can now see a nymphet or a juvenile nymphet or an overage nymphet at least three blocks away."

The following year, another publisher not only dared to touch *Lolita* but had the courage to bring it out with much fanfare, making Vladimir Nabokov both rich and famous. That same year, Mary McCarthy enraged all but the most thick-skinned residents of Wellfleet with her new novel, *A Charmed Life*, making any future summers there unthinkable. In the end Roger Straus never succeeded in getting hold of McCarthy's fiction. For the moment the title *Sights and Spectacles* stayed put.

However, in 1963, when *Sights and Spectacles* was reissued with a few changes and additions, it was called *Mary McCarthy's Theatre Chronicles*. By then McCarthy had reason to feel more at ease with her old theater pieces. She also had reason to want to shuck any suspicion of a debt to Edmund Wilson. She was living happily with Jim West, her fourth husband, in Paris. Frequently she was referred to as the first lady of American letters. Her much anticipated novel *The Group* was finally finished and promised to cause the same kind of scandal and excitement that *Lolita* had.

Thanks to the enormous success of *The Group*, McCarthy never again had to ask for an advance "in toto." All the same, whenever it suited her, she persisted in taking time off from a business letter to write about the things that mattered to her. To her publisher or editor, to her lawyer or fellow executor, she wrote on subjects ranging from literature and politics to her latest debilitating illness. Up until her last stay in the hospital she continued to call things as she saw them. As a letter writer she was indefatigable. And as a working biographer I can only be grateful.

WORKS CITED

Lyall, Sarah. "Book Notes." *New York Times*. August 11, 1993: C-17.
McCarthy, Mary. *Cast a Cold Eye*. 1950. New York: Harcourt, 1972.
————. *A Charmed Life*. New York: Harcourt, 1955.
————. *The Company She Keeps*. 1942. New York: Harcourt, 1967.
————. *The Group*. New York: Harcourt, 1963.
————. *The Groves of Academe*. New York: Harcourt, 1952.

————. Letters to Roger Straus. October 22, 1954; November 12, 1954. Farrar, Straus and Giroux Collection, New York Public Library.

————. *Mary McCarthy's Theatre Chronicles 1937–1962*. New York: Farrar, 1963.

————. *Sights and Spectacles 1937–1956*. New York: Farrar, 1956.

Nabokov, Vladimir. *Lolita*. 1955. New York: Vintage, 1989.

————. *Pale Fire*. 1962. New York: Vintage, 1989.

————, and Edmund Wilson. *The Nabokov-Wilson Letters*. Edited by Simon Karlinsky. New York: Harper, 1979.

Straus, Roger. Letter to Mary McCarthy. November 15, 1954. Farrar, Straus and Giroux Collection, New York Public Library.

22

Taking Risks

Frances Fitzgerald

Mary McCarthy was a very large force in my life, both as a writer and as a friend for twenty-five years or so. She was important to me in many ways, but here I want to discuss one powerful way in which she had a hold on my imagination. It was in the risks she took.

Some years ago there was a celebration for Mary—she had just given her papers to the Vassar College library—and a number of people, including myself, spoke about her and her work. It was one of the bravest things that I ever did, because of course she was there. In preparation for the speech I went to a bookstore to find her most recent collection of essays, and while I was wandering around the store, it occurred to me that if I were to attempt to find all the books she had written, I would have to look in almost every section of the store—except perhaps in the sections marked Child Care or The Occult. The range of her work—novels, short stories, memoirs, literary criticism, theater criticism, art history, war reportage—is quite astonishing; in recent times in this country, it is surely unmatched. Mary had, I think, a nineteenth-century conception of the intellectual—or simply the educated person. The conception survived in Europe until sometime after World War II, but after Henry Adams it seemed to die out in the United States. In our age of specialization, compartmentalization, and careerism, it is wonderful to think about the kind of risks Mary took in spreading herself across so many domains.

Of course, the risks didn't all pay off, but that is the thing about risks: they don't all pay off, or they are not risks at all.

Mary—quite recklessly by modern standards—went ahead and followed her interests: she indulged her voracious appetites for literature and for life. In fact, I think her work was her life in the sense that it was not different from it, not something compartmentalized and filed away. It was her response to life in all its forms from art to politics to sex. For this reason I think it important that her work be taught in the universities. Possibly she will not be judged one of the greatest novelists or critics of this century, but reading Mary's work is always exhilarating, for it shows what a daring writer can do, and how broad a compass a writer can have given a sense of freedom and a lot of discipline.

Mary, of course, took other kinds of risks as well. She was sharp, full of edges. She attacked all kinds of distinguished people. She attacked people no one would think of attacking now. She attacked John Hersey for his piece on Hiroshima when it appeared in the *New Yorker*. She attacked him for domesticating the atom bomb. She attacked Arthur Miller for his testimony before the House Un-American Activities Committee. She attacked his plays as well. She attacked Eugene O'Neill; she attacked Tennessee Williams; she attacked most of the playwrights of that day. She attacked Simone de Beauvoir, of course, for her book on the United States. Latterly she attacked Lillian Hellman—and that was the riskiest attack of her career.

Some have painted Mary's assault on Lillian as dark and fateful, the start of a great tragedy that ended in both of their deaths. I disagree. Mary thoroughly disliked Lillian Hellman's work and her politics. Nonetheless she attacked Lillian on that fateful television program with a lightness of heart and in the spirit of a fair literary fight. To say, as she did, that everything Lillian wrote was lies, "including the ands and the thes" could hardly be taken literally (Interview with Dick Cavett). When Lillian responded by suing her for libel, she was genuinely surprised. What she did not understand was that Lillian, who was older than she, had taken up suing to create the dramas she could no longer write. Mary's attack was play, and so was Lillian's response. Both women were terrific risk takers: they were thoroughly involved with life, and they were not going to let go of a single second of it. The consequences were horrific for Mary, but I doubt she would have retracted an "and" or a "the" from her remarks on that program.

Mary's attacks were not indiscriminate. She attacked only big people, only people with large reputations. She tended to attack those no one else attacked, and always very precisely, very wittily, and with no cheap shots. People were afraid of her, of course. But they were afraid of her not in the way they are afraid of a bad review in some trendy magazine of the moment. They were afraid because she was so brutally honest. When she attacked, she always let you know where she stood. She left herself open, and in that way she took enormous risks.

Agnostic as she was about most matters, Mary believed in the search for the truth. Perhaps she even believed that the truth was available, for she was a stickler about factual accuracy and the dictionary definition of words. (When I picture her, it is often with a huge dictionary open on her knees.) It was for this reason that she particularly disliked Lillian Hellman's work, for Hellman, the dramatist, tended to alter the facts to fit her dramatic purposes. Mary had a much stricter standard, and thus to my mind better results when it came to nonfiction.

Possibly the most important work she ever did was the attempt to tell the truth about her own life. In this she took far more risks than in attacking others, for she was quite merciless about herself. In the course of her life she did a lot of things she did not approve of, and she wrote about them as frankly as if she were not involved. She concealed nothing—or at least nothing that she knew about—and consequently she told us many new things about the human condition.

One of the first McCarthy works I read was a story that Mary wrote in 1954 called "The Pessary," which became Chapter 3 of *The Group*. (We don't use the word anymore, but a pessary is a diaphragm.) The story was clearly about herself and the man who became her first husband—and it shocked me terribly, though I must have read it almost ten years after it was written. It was about the mechanics of sex and about the dreadful moments that anyone who grew up in the 1950s would have had to go through in dealing with them. She was quite matter-of-fact, quite cold, about the less than idyllic result. The story shocked me because I had to say to myself, I could never do that, I don't have the guts.

In the last book she published during her lifetime, *How I Grew*, Mary went back over this period, the period when she was living in New York after she left Vassar. As it turns out, she slept with a great many men in those days, and often quite recklessly. I must say, I like the idea of her in her late seventies, when she was feeling old and in pain, writing about her sexual adventures half a century before. As usual, she writes about herself in a completely detached fashion.

This was not some literary strategy or conceit, for it was exactly the way she faced her last illness. In this book she is quite nonjudgmental about herself, and one imagines that she might have done the same things all over again, just in the interests of experience.

Where did this come from, this risk taking, this brutal truth telling? Possibly it had something to do with the fact that Mary's mother and father died when she was very young: they died very quickly, almost overnight, and she wasn't told until later. Then she and her brothers had a Dickensian few years in the "care" of her McCarthy grandparents. It was the survival of the fittest, and she decided to survive, but she had to cast off all dreaminess and sentimentality in order to do it. Who knows? Others, including her brothers, have reacted differently to similar circumstances. In any case, Mary never felt sorry for herself. There was no wishful thinking in her life and no hypocrisy.

Happily Mary had another set of grandparents—the Prestons—who were kind to her and who had the means to send her to Vassar and introduce her to worldly pleasures: nice clothes, good food, art, and architecture. While Mary perhaps disappointed them by moving into a world of left-wing intellectuals in New York, she never renounced their "bourgeois" ways. This too, I think, was brave of her. She gave a speech at Vassar some time ago called "Living with Beautiful Things." She was serious about that. She didn't care that she flouted all the bohemian conventions, and all the bluestocking notions that books are the only acceptable accoutrements to life. As I said, there was no hypocrisy about her.

Mary never felt sorry for herself, because she enjoyed life so much. Visiting her house in Maine, you would see how much she enjoyed it from the care she took of it, as well as her garden and her food. Her cooking was really good. Some who went to her house disapproved of the time and attention she gave to food on the grounds that it was a waste of energy to think about something so mundane, so material. But cooking gave her pleasure, and she cooked exactly as she wrote: with rigor, and with the ambition to do something difficult, something adventurous, and to get it exactly right. It would be strange to say that she took risks with her *tartes aux framboises*, but there it is. Mary took wholly unacceptable risks even in preparing dinner parties.

WORKS CITED

McCarthy, Mary. *The Group*. New York: Harcourt, 1963.

———. Interview with Dick Cavett. *The Dick Cavett Show*. PBS. October 18, 1979.

———. *How I Grew*. San Diego: Harcourt, 1987.

———. "Living with Beautiful Things." *Occasional Prose*. San Diego: Harcourt, 1985. 101–26.

23

Memories of Another Catholic Girlhood

Maureen Howard

The academy is not my grove. I have taught for many years, yet I will never be completely comfortable with the idea of the writer as captive academician. Mary McCarthy, while devoted to the Bard campus, never seems to have been easy with the notion either, though she was, from all accounts, both generous to, and hard on, her students. To be hard on students is to be generous to them, to have expectations for them and for their work. But McCarthy's intelligence was independent of academic disciplines, quite fiercely so, and she was fierce about being an intelligent woman. Her mind, as much as her beauty, was the equipment she came with. Comes to us still, take it or leave it.

From my first discovery of her theater reviews in *Partisan Review*, tiptoeing into the almost deserted periodical room of the library at Smith College, to my rereading her provocative Northcliffe Lectures, published as *Ideas and the Novel*, Maureen Therese Kearns has taken Mary Therese McCarthy very seriously. For a woman writer coming of age in the 1950s, to read Mary McCarthy was a jolt in the right direction. That direction is the arrow (a bright, pulsing neon) pointing upstairs. Upstairs is the head bone, gray matter—how neutered that image, yet the mind, the intellect as "upper story" is a metaphor which McCarthy attributes to D. H. Lawrence. His mistrust of the intellect, she writes, "is strange, certainly, in a man who himself lived almost wholly for ideas. The fact that they were his own made the difference, apparently; he had hammered them out for himself" (27). She comments with familiar wit that those ideas were not fresh or new.

But what McCarthy was readily drawn to in Lawrence was not so much the mind/body problem, with the body clearly winning out, as the discovery, a wry discovery: "blood and instinct as superior to brain was a mental construct incapable of proof except on the mental level" (27). (That was written in 1980—before *construct* was worn to death in her students' discourse.) What McCarthy admired in Lawrence—the mind figuring itself on the page, the living act of thought and the purpose of mind to *say*—is what I will always admire in her work. Reading her elegant sentences, I hear her, though I met her only once, and McCarthy's style is hardly conversational. The diction of the essays and in the narrative of *Memories of a Catholic Girlhood*, to me her most perfect work, is formal, though there is often a debater's urgency to the argument and in argument she is often her own most worthy opponent. Her stories have their arguments concerning sexual initiation, the price of vanity— their thesis, if you will. Her arguments have their story—that Flaubert had great need of Charles Bovary who was not, like Emma, *moi* is the story that she tells in the fine essay "On *Madame Bovary*." And she reminds us again, in "The Fact in Fiction," that in our reading we must not constrict an author's voice, but discover the choices, the freedom of tone, and variance in sensibility.

The upper story of mind in the best of McCarthy does not float free of the lower—the passionate or instinctual ground floor—though I think she would not have extended the metaphor, for her work is so ardently reasoned. There is clearly some passion in her reasonable and well-crafted fiction—more in her essays and finest reviews, an eager tone in the argument which betrayed feeling and which made me sit alone in the periodical room of Smith College reading Mary McCarthy. I don't mean to say that in the prehistory of the prefeminist 1950s, her theater criticism empowered me to follow the neon sign to the life of the mind, or that in that unenlightened era I saw that women in the arts could be more than one of the guys, but Mary McCarthy surely offered me a broader view: life after the English major, life after the wedding march. Her criticism was sharp, savvy, urbane. It would be only a matter of a year or so before I felt her to be mostly wrongheaded about the theater, shocked that she didn't "get" *The Iceman* or *Godot* or that she didn't hear the dark note under the bright spill of Wilde's lines, or that Shaw knew when he was into self-parody, for there was—I wanted to argue with her directly—that old Shavian madman who engineered not only the ideas but the heartbreak, the emotions, in *Heartbreak House*. I have never been disappointed in Mary McCarthy for being overly clever when she was young and would hate to look back at the flippant display in my own early reviews. But often, quite often, I did not, do not agree with her.

Though I remember being elated when she took on *Pale Fire*, gave herself to the intricacies of that wacky, lush book, understanding at once the narrative subterfuge of Nabokov's perverse biography ("A Bolt from the Blue"). The intelligent woman who insisted upon the "common sense—the prose of the novel" ("The Fact in Fiction" 267), who singled out the novel from the other arts as being the only form she did not find possible as performance (*Ideas and the Novel* 60), fell for the wonderful performance that is *Pale Fire*. "Wonderful"—is that one of those flutey words—like "splendid"—McCarthy faults in Henry James? I have always found writing novels an act of performance, so let me say it was grand, grand her enthusiasm for *Pale Fire*.

Still, there is a defensive note in her writing that "it matters to me not at all that I do read the politics" in Virginia Woolf's fiction and in Elizabeth Bowen's. She meant, of course, *Realpolitik*, not gender politics, and it is interesting to note how much recent criticism examines the political and historical realities of Woolf's novels. Mary McCarthy's distinction between the novel of sense and that of sensibility would not be mine, nor would her preference for sense. How absorbed she was in this problem, how often she worried it out—that the novel might perhaps be dead without sense, without mission; how confounded she was that Dickens and George Eliot were moved by their own work. "There must be no indulgence, no false note." She read by this strict code.

In the late essays her reading was energetic, as always, and independent of fashion. She was not afflicted with a fashionable mind. I give my students her essay "The Fact in Fiction." As writers of fiction we find it all too easy to drown in our own sensibilities, lose ourselves in the damp cellar of mindless self-expression. McCarthy's demands for the cognitive value in fiction were clear and strong. I think she was conscious of the fact that her own gift was nonfictive. There is about her novels, in the reading, something of the effort of the writing which is not present in the wonderful storytelling of her finely researched works on Florence and Venice.

And then there is *Memories of a Catholic Girlhood*. It is unlike any other autobiography—distinguished, singular. Isn't that what we say when it's real art? The very pace of the writing is superb, the italicized postscripts a brilliant invention. Though, of course, she lied. I knew that she lied when I first read "C'est le Premier Pas Qui Coûte" (102–26). I knew that no Catholic secondary school, even the lofty Mesdames de Sacre Coeur, let kids have a go at theology. The religious education was all catechism, dogma, doctrine plain and simple in Bridgeport as well as in Seattle. But turn the page: "The proofs of God's existence," she confesses, "are drawn from the Catholic Encyclopedia. My own questions are a mixture of memory and conjecture" (124).

Then there is this: "Maybe the strange mixture is why I don't remember very much. Or, as time and much of life has passed, my memory—which for the purpose of this tale has kept me awake sorting out what I am certain of, what maybe I added to what, because I didn't see or know the people—won't supply what I need to know." Those are the words of Lillian Hellman in "*Maybe*," an odd, powerful work written as fiction after the Cavett debacle (Interview with Dick Cavett). I have always read it as a riposte to McCarthy, who had called her a liar. I was a friend of Lillian Hellman's, not a close friend for I keep in my private life to a small domestic circle. Let me say that I hated the fact of their argument; for both of these women that last match with no final round. I have no particular knowledge to exonerate Hellman, yet I will never know what truth Mary McCarthy was after. Their argument was politics of an era *and* it was personal, or it was about Cinderella and her unlovely stepsister, or about the display of honor and dishonor. That is a bit of mythmaking on my part: it was all too real to these women, painfully facing each other down. What I think Mary McCarthy did not miss, but certainly disliked in Lillian Hellman, was performance, the ongoing performance of that flamboyant life.

I was asked to write, not by Lillian, in defense of Hellman, an article that would be carefully placed. I did not lend myself to this: I wrote, however, a novel, *Expensive Habits*, in which the central figure, a woman journalist, sets herself to writing an exposé of the old heroines of the Old Left. She comes upon two elderly women who, with conflicting stories, close her out. There is no truth to get at, beyond what the reporter has guessed. She writes small fictional accounts of these women and of their lover. Even these she destroys. The expensive habit of the title is lying. And it is writing. To me—now I am writing fiction—Mary McCarthy's obsession with Hellman's duplicity, or maybe with her political grandstanding, her "artistic" license, partakes of a mad double plot that might have been written by her beloved Nabokov. She would not like my moving the facts of the case to fiction. Or that I see her as the missionary, the very missionary we Catholic girls laughed at, stern and diligent among the heathens, believing in truth—not about Hellman, or *Partisan Review* politics, or old boyfriends—but the undeniable facts that drew her to the upper story of almost blessed intelligence which made her work valid. As for the secular act of writing, there was in her own performance a sense that writing was to her a touch sacred.

WORKS CITED

Hellman, Lillian. *"Maybe": A Story*. Boston: Little, Brown, 1980.

Howard, Maureen. *Expensive Habits*. New York: Summit Books, 1986. Penguin, 1987.

McCarthy, Mary. "A Bolt from the Blue." Review of *Pale Fire* by Vladimir Nabokov. *The Writing on the Wall and Other Literary Essays*. New York: Harcourt, 1970. 15–34.

———. "The Fact in Fiction." *On the Contrary*. New York: Farrar, 1961. 249–71.

———. *Ideas and the Novel*. New York: Harcourt, 1980.

———. Interview with Dick Cavett. *The Dick Cavett Show*. PBS. October 18, 1979.

———. *Memories of a Catholic Girlhood*. New York: Harcourt, 1957.

———. "On *Madame Bovary*." *The Writing on the Wall and Other Literary Essays*. New York: Harcourt, 1970. 72–94.

———. *On the Contrary*. New York: Farrar, 1961.

———. *The Stones of Florence*. 1959. New York: Harcourt, 1963.

———. *Venice Observed*. 1956. New York: Harvest/Harcourt, 1963.

———. *The Writing on the Wall and Other Literary Essays*. New York: Harcourt, 1970.

Nabokov, Vladimir. *Pale Fire*. 1962. New York: Vintage, 1989.

24

Remembrances
of an Old Friend

Arthur Schlesinger, Jr.

I first met Mary McCarthy over half a century ago. It was at dinner at Harry
Levin's in Cambridge, Massachusetts, in the winter of 1940–1941. Edmund
Wilson was there too. I remember being entranced by Mary, her beauty, her
wit, her charm, and her intellectual passion. I was also filled with indignation
over the fact that someone so young and beautiful should be married to
someone who seemed to me so old, no matter how interesting and significant
a figure Edmund Wilson was. Mary, in fact, was twenty-eight and Edmund
only forty-five; the difference in age was less than the difference in age between
my wife and me today.

That was the beginning of a friendship that grew after the war. I used to see
Mary and Bowden Broadwater in Wellfleet and in Newport. One book, the
first book of my New Deal series, was partly written in Mary McCarthy's barn
next to her Wellfleet house. At one point Mary kindly offered to take a look
at the manuscript. I gave it to her. She read it with care and returned it with
one of the most scathing letters I've ever received. I remember her comment
on the prologue: "Pre-Raphaelite," she said. My problem was that I was writing
the book after the 1952 campaign, in which I had written speeches for Adlai
Stevenson, and I fell too easily into the slackness and lushness of political
oratory. I saw at once how right Mary was, recalled the manuscript from the
publisher, spent weeks reducing the rhetorical content, and greatly improved

the book. It was typical of Mary that she applied her exacting standards to friends as well as to everyone else.

I saw much of her in later years in Washington, Paris, and Castine. I was involved in her effort to found a magazine, and we were political allies—at least some of the time. But I really want to talk about what one is to make of Mary McCarthy today. Clearly she remains a force to be reckoned with. Recent neoconservative attacks by Hilton Kramer, Joseph Epstein, and John Wain show an anxious and unseemly determination to write Mary out of the competition, as if rightist critics still feel threatened by her. Perhaps they should. Had she known them, she would have been much tempted to use them in her fiction.

Could today's culture produce and sustain someone like Mary McCarthy? I hope so, but I think the odds are somewhat against it. I hazard the hypothesis that Mary McCarthy was essentially a child of the 1920s. She inherited and embodied the rebel spirit of that mischievous literary decade, the aesthetic concerns, the satiric bent, the revolt against censorship, prohibition, and other forms of puritanism, the faith in drink and sex and personal freedom, the indifference to politics, the delight in iconoclasm, the contrarian and *contra mundum* reflex that could be easily confused with radicalism, as for a time it was in the case of Mencken. All these were elements in the literary sensibility of the 1920s. Edmund Wilson has a vivid and relevant passage in his 1960s journals: "As a character in one of Chekhov's plays says he's a man of the '80s, so I find that I am a man of the '20s. I still expect something exciting: drinks, animated conversation, gaiety, an uninhibited exchange of ideas" (48). This, I surmise, is one of the reasons he attracted Mary.

We know now that the literary adventurers of the 1920s were also possessed by internal demons, but there seemed to those of us a few years younger a careless gaiety about them that was infinitely attractive: they were free spirits. I was five years younger than Mary, but, like her, I knew literary men and women of the 1920s, and, like her, I was touched, fascinated by the romance of the 1920s, all the more romantic against the grim backdrop of depression America—unemployment, bread lines, a discouraged and demoralized country that saw no reason for *joie de vivre*.

As a child of the 1920s, she could never really take politics very seriously. Remember her wonderful piece "My Confession," and you will see what I mean. Though she had sharp political opinions, and was a reliable liberal Democrat most of the time, she really wasn't all that interested in politics per se. She was more interested in the play of personalities on the political stage, in the drama of politics, politics as a theater of irony, hypocrisy, and betrayal. It was the 1920s sensibility, modified a bit by the so-called crisis of capitalism.

She did have a certain uncharacteristic weakness for metapolitics, visible in her enthusiasm for Hannah Arendt, though I rather supposed that it was a sympathetic personal chemistry that led Mary to take Hannah Arendt's Hegelian-Heideggerian abstractions so seriously. Indeed, after Hannah's death she spent a couple of years arranging and editing her posthumous manuscripts, for which, I might add, she got very little gratitude or acknowledgment from Hannah's heirs. Those two minds, it seemed to me, could hardly have been more different: Mary's so specific, concrete, empirical, sharply observant, stabbing, sparkling, filled with intellectual élan; Hannah's so abstract, pretentious, pedantic, Germanic, opaque, humorless.

Yet Mary adored Hannah, there was no question about it. Once the *Times Literary Supplement* asked various notables to make nominations for the most overrated writer of the century. Isaiah Berlin, the great British historian of ideas and a good friend of Mary's, nominated as the most overrated writer of the century Hannah Arendt. He soon received a postcard from Mary in Paris saying, "She thought the same of you." This did not prevent Isaiah and Mary from continuing to be warm friends.

What would Mary have made of the current cultural preoccupations? She was a feminist by example, not by exhortation. She considered ideological feminism, as she said, "bad for women in its self-pity, shrillness, and greed." Mary had times in her life, above all in her childhood, also in her first two marriages, when she was indeed a victim; but she was too proud to exploit victimization. She abhorred self-pity and she would have revolted at that branch of feminism that cherishes the image, the cult, of the woman as victim. A truly liberated woman, she rejoiced in her femininity. She loved to cook, she cared about her dress, she had beauty, sex. All these things meant a great deal to her and she saw no reason to apologize for them.

As for political correctness on the campus, she already had her say on that in *The Groves of Academe*. With what appalled delight Mary would have contemplated the campus scene today!—where the study of literature has given way to the study of literary theory, where obsessions about racism, sexism, patriarchalism, and so on, the ideology of oppression and victimization, now influence the teaching of literature and, to some degree, of history. The reduction of humane studies to political agendas, the insufferable humorlessness with which this is done, and the self-righteous assault on free inquiry and the Bill of Rights—I think she would have found it all both depressing and hilarious. The unpardonable sin in this new world, it seems, is insensitivity, hurting someone's feelings—so freedom of speech must be curtailed in the interest of protecting people's sensibilities. Of course the essence of the First Amendment, as Justice Holmes reminded us, is not just "free thought for those who agree with us"—what virtue resides in that?—"but freedom for the thought that we hate" (328). And the current belief in, of all places, the university, that the thought we hate must be proscribed lest it offend is a dangerous belief. The idea that hurting someone's feelings is the unpardonable sin puts me on a dangerous road—at the end of which lies Salman Rushdie.

Of course, Mary, as I say, would have found all this both hilarious and abominable. She thoroughly believed in offending people. She believed in provocation as incitement to thought, to reform, to life itself. Her concern for the First Amendment was such that at one point in her life she even seriously considered going to law school. The current academic scene, I am sure, would have both entertained and enraged her.

Diana Trilling, in her recent memoir, writes, "The intellectual culture of this country as Lionel and I knew it in the earlier decades of the century no longer exists" (420). She has in mind the easy discursiveness, the free range of reference, the refusal of received ideas, the always ready wit. That world, God knows, had its constraints, but it seems a relatively free world compared to the morbidly constrained academic world of today.

Mary's world was contiguous to Diana's but it was lighter, livelier, and more fun. Mary may have cast her cold eye, but she was a tremendous life enhancer, with her endless delight in the oddities of living, her endless interest in the way things worked, her endless curiosity about people and ideas and human predicaments, her endless exuberant anger over hypocrisy and mendacity and cruelty. She was a free spirit who conquered her internal demons and increased the intensity and joy of living. I would like to think that the humane and witty and idiosyncratic culture she embodied will withstand current assaults of ideology and dogma.

WORKS CITED

Holmes, Oliver Wendell. "Freedom for the Thought That We Hate." Lerner, Max, ed. *The Mind and Thought of Justice Holmes*. New York: Modern Library, 1943. 325–28.

McCarthy, Mary. "My Confession." *On the Contrary*. New York: Farrar, 1961. 75–104.

Trilling, Diana. *The Beginning of the Journey*. New York: Harcourt, 1993.

Wilson, Edmund. *The Sixties*. Edited by Lewis Dabney. New York: Farrar, 1993.

Bibliography

WORKS BY MARY McCARTHY

"An Academy of Risk." *On the Contrary*. 242–48.

"America the Beautiful: The Humanist in the Bathtub." *On the Contrary*. 6–19.

"The Appalachian Mountain Revolution." *The Hounds of Summer and Other Stories*. 156–192.

"The Art of Fiction." Interview with Elisabeth Niebuhr. 1962. Gelderman, Carol, ed. *Conversations with Mary McCarthy*. 3–29.

"Artists in Uniform." *On the Contrary*. 55–74.

Birds of America. 1971. New York: Harvest/Harcourt, 1992.

"A Bolt from the Blue." Review of *Pale Fire* by Vladimir Nabokov. *The Writing on the Wall and Other Literary Essays*. 15–34.

Cannibals and Missionaries. New York: Harcourt, 1979.

Cast a Cold Eye. 1950. New York: Harvest/Harcourt, 1992.

"Characters in Fiction." *On the Contrary*. 271–92.

A Charmed Life. 1955. New York: Harvest/Harcourt, 1992.

"Class Angles and a Wilder Classic." *Mary McCarthy's Theatre Chronicles 1937–1962*. 21–29.

The Company She Keeps. 1942. New York: Harcourt, 1967.

"A Conversation with Mary McCarthy." 1966. Interview with Edwin Newman. Gelderman, Carol, ed. *Conversations with Mary McCarthy*. 68–87.

Correspondence with Hannah Arendt, 1949–1975. Brightman, Carol, ed. *Between Friends.*

"Cruel and Barbarous Treatment." *The Company She Keeps.* 3–21.

"Elizabethan Revivals." *Mary McCarthy's Theatre Chronicles.* 13–20.

"The Fact in Fiction." *On the Contrary.* 249–70.

"The Friend of the Family." *Cast a Cold Eye.* 43–84.

"Gandhi." *On the Contrary.* 20–23.

"General Macbeth." *Mary McCarthy's Theatre Chronicles 1937–1962.* 235–48. Also collected in *The Writing on the Wall and Other Literary Essays.* 3–14.

"Ghostly Father, I Confess." *The Company She Keeps.* 249–304.

The Group. 1963. New York: Harvest/Harcourt, 1991.

The Groves of Academe. 1952. New York: Harvest/Harcourt, 1992.

"Hanoi." *The Seventeenth Degree.* 170–322.

"The Hounds of Summer." *The Hounds of Summer and Other Stories.* 193–240.

The Hounds of Summer and Other Stories. New York: Bard/Avon, 1981.

How I Grew. San Diego: Harcourt, 1987.

"The Hue and Cry." *The Writing on the Wall and Other Literary Essays.* 54–71.

Ideas and the Novel. New York: Harcourt, 1980.

The "Iliad," or the Poem of Force. By Simone Weil. Translated by Mary McCarthy. *politics* 2 (November 1945): 321–31; *politics* Pamphlet 1 (1945).

Intellectual Memoirs: New York 1936–1938. New York: Harcourt, 1992.

Interview with Dick Cavett. *The Dick Cavett Show.* PBS. October 18, 1979.

Interview with Elisabeth Niebuhr. *Writers at Work.* 2nd series. New York: Viking, 1963. Reprinted in Gelderman, Carol, ed. *Conversations with Mary McCarthy.*

Interview with Jack Paar. *The Jack Paar Show.* NBC Television. November 29, 1963.

"Introduction." *Mary McCarthy's Theatre Chronicles 1937–1962.* vii–xxi.

"Language and Politics." *Occasional Prose.* 83{100.

Letter to Dwight and Nancy Macdonald. July 1948. Dwight Macdonald Papers, Yale University.

"A Letter to the Editor of *politics.*" *On the Contrary.* 3–5.

Letter to Thomas Mallon. March 23, 1973. Mary McCarthy Papers, Vassar College Library.

Letters to Carol Gelderman, 1980–1989. Collection of C. G.

Letters to Roger Straus. October 22, 1954; and November 12, 1954. Farrar, Straus and Giroux Collection, New York Public Library.

"Living with Beautiful Things." *Occasional Prose.* 101–26.

MacDowell Medal acceptance speech (August 26, 1984). Gelderman, Carol, ed. *Conversations with Mary McCarthy.* 250–52.

"The Man in the Brooks Brothers Shirt." *The Company She Keeps.* 81–134.

Mary McCarthy's Theatre Chronicles 1937–1962. New York: Farrar, 1963.

Memories of a Catholic Girlhood. 1957. New York: Harvest/Harcourt, 1981.

"Mlle. Gulliver en Amérique." *On the Contrary.* 24–42.

"My Confession." *On the Contrary.* 75–104.

"No News, or, What Killed the Dog." *On the Contrary.* 32–42.

The Oasis. 1949. New York: Bard/Avon, 1981.

Occasional Prose. San Diego: Harcourt, 1985.

"On *Madame Bovary.*" *The Writing on the Wall and Other Literary Essays.* 72–94.

"On Rereading a Favorite Book." *Occasional Prose.* 179–86.

On the Contrary. New York: Farrar, 1961.

"One Touch of Nature." *The Writing on the Wall and Other Literary Essays.* 189–213.

"Our Woman of Letters." 1987. Interview with Michiko Kakutani. Gelderman, Carol, ed. *Conversations with Mary McCarthy.* 257–67.

"Portrait of the Intellectual as a Yale Man." *The Company She Keeps.* 167–246.

"Preface." Chiaromonte, Nicola. *The Worm of Consciousness.* xiii–xvi.

"Saying Good-bye to Hannah." *Occasional Prose.* 35–42.

"Settling the Colonel's Hash." *On the Contrary.* 225–41.

The Seventeenth Degree. New York: Harcourt, 1974.

Sights and Spectacles 1937–1956. New York: Farrar, 1956.

The Stones of Florence. 1959. New York: Harvest/Harcourt 1963. Illustrated edition Harvest/Harcourt, 1987.

"Tyranny of the Orgasm." Review of *Modern Woman, The Lost Sex* by Ferdinand Lundberg and Marynia Farnham. *The New Leader.* April 5, 1947: 10. *On the Contrary.* 167–73.

"The Vassar Girl." *On the Contrary.* 193–214.

Venice Observed. 1956. New York: Harvest/Harcourt, 1963.

"The *Vita Activa.*" *On the Contrary.* 155–64.

"A World out of Joint." Interview with Miriam Gross. Gelderman, Carol, ed. *Conversations with Mary McCarthy.* 170–78.

The Writing on the Wall and Other Literary Essays. New York: Harcourt, 1970.

"Yonder Peasant, Who Is He?" *Cast a Cold Eye.* 157–82.

OTHER WORKS

Atlas, James. *Delmore Schwartz: The Life of an American.* New York: Farrar, 1977.

Barrett, William. *The Truants: Adventures among the Intellectuals.* New York: Anchor/ Doubleday, 1982.

Blumenthal, Sydney. "The Epic Errors of Robert Caro." *New Republic.* June 4, 1990.

Brightman, Carol. Letters to Mary McCarthy, January 31, 1985, and July 28, 1988. Mary McCarthy Papers, Vassar College Library.

———. "Mary, Still Contrary." *The Nation.* May 19, 1984: 611–18.

———. "Memorandum on my conversation with Mary McCarthy." February 22, 1985. Carol Brightman's personal papers.

———. "Writing Dangerously." *Mirabella.* August 1992: 134–44.

———. *Writing Dangerously: Mary McCarthy and Her World.* New York: Clarkson Potter, 1992. San Diego: Harvest/Harcourt, 1994.

————, ed. *Between Friends: The Correspondence of Hannah Arendt and Mary McCarthy, 1949–1975.* New York: Harcourt, 1995.

Broadwater, Bowden. "Ciao." *Paris Review.* Winter 1961: 41–51.

Brower, Brock. "Mary McCarthyism." *Esquire* 58 (July 1962): 60–65.

Caffi, Andrea. "Violence and Sociability." *politics* 4 (January 1947): 23–28.

Camus, Albert. "Neither Victims nor Executioners." *politics* 4 (July/August 1947): 141–47.

Caro, Robert. *Means of Ascent: The Years of Lyndon Johnson.* New York: Knopf, 1990.

————. *Means of Ascent: The Years of Lyndon Johnson.* New York: Random House, 1991.

Castronovo, David. "Edmund Wilson." *Dictionary of Literary Biography: Modern American Critics, 1920–1966.* Ann Arbor, Mich.: Gale-Bruccoli, 1988. 304–15.

Chiaromonte, Nicola. *The Worm of Consciousness and Other Essays.* New York: Harcourt, 1976.

Cook, Rev. Bruce. "Mary McCarthy: One of Ours?" *Catholic World* 199 (1964): 34–42.

Costa, Richard. *Edmund Wilson: Our Neighbor from Talcottville.* Syracuse, N.Y.: Syracuse University Press, 1980.

Crowley, John. "Mary McCarthy's *The Company She Keeps.*" *The Explicator* 51 (Winter 1993): 111–15.

Dickinson, Emily. *The Complete Poems of Emily Dickinson.* Boston: Little, Brown, 1960. Poem 1129.

Donzelot, Jacques. *The Policing of Families.* With a foreword by Gilles Deleuze. Translated by Robert Hurley. New York: Pantheon Books, 1979.

Dragnet. NBC weekly series: December 16, 1951, to September 6, 1959; January 12, 1967, to September 10, 1970. Terrance, Vincent, ed. *The Complete Encyclopedia of Television Programs 1947–1978.* Volume 1. New York: A. S. Barnes, 1979.

Duffy, Martha. "She Knew What She Wanted." *New York.* November 6, 1989: 87.

Duras, Marguerite. *La Création étoufée.* Quoted in Gayle Greene and Coppelia Kahn, *Making a Difference.* New York: Routledge, 1981.

Dvosin, Andrew J. "Literature in a Political World." Doctoral dissertation. New York University, 1977.

Edel, Leon. *Henry James.* 5 vols. Philadelphia: Lippincott, 1953–1972.

Eliot, T. S. "The Love Song of J. Alfred Prufrock." *Collected Poems 1909–1962.* New York: Harcourt, 1963.

Epstein, Joseph. "Mary McCarthy in Retrospect." *Commentary* 94 (May 1993): 41–47.

Fadiman, Clifton. "Three Novels." Review of *The Company She Keeps* by Mary McCarthy. *The New Yorker.* May 16, 1942: 72–73.

Fanning, Charles. *The Irish Voice in America: Irish-American Fiction from the 1760s to the 1980s*. Lexington: University Press of Kentucky, 1990.

Fitzgerald, Frances. Letter to Carol Southern. October 3, 1991. Carol Brightman's personal papers.

Gates, Henry Louis, Jr. *Loose Canons: Notes on the Culture Wars*. New York: Oxford University Press, 1992.

Gelderman, Carol. *Henry Ford, the Wayward Capitalist*. New York: Dial, 1981.

————. *Mary McCarthy: A Life*. New York: St. Martin's, 1988.

————, ed. *Conversations with Mary McCarthy*. Jackson: University Press of Mississippi, 1991.

Giles, Paul. *American Catholic Arts and Fictions: Culture, Ideology, Aesthetics*. Cambridge: Cambridge University Press, 1992.

Gilmore, David. *Manhood in the Making*. New Haven, Conn.: Yale University Press, 1990.

Gordon, Mary. *The Company of Women*. New York: Random House, 1980.

————. *Final Payments*. New York: Random House, 1978.

————. "Getting Here from There: A Writer's Reflections on a Religious Past." *Good Boys and Dead Girls*. 160–75.

————. *Good Boys and Dead Girls, and Other Essays*. New York: Viking, 1991.

————. "I Can't Stand Your Books: A Writer Goes Home." *Good Boys and Dead Girls*. 160–75.

Gross, Beverly. "Bitch." *Salmagundi* 103 (Summer 1994): 146–56.

Gross, Miriam. "A World out of Joint." Interview with Mary McCarthy. Gelderman, Carol, ed. *Conversations with Mary McCarthy*. 1991. 170–78.

Grumbach, Doris. *The Company She Kept*. New York: Coward, 1967.

————. "The Subject Objected." *New York Times Book Review*. June 11, 1967: 36.

Guerard, Albert. "Some Recent Novels." *Perspectives USA* 1 (Fall 1952): 168–69.

Hamilton, Andrew. "Dinners without Drudgery." *Popular Mechanics*. April 1947: 174+.

Hanscom, Larry. "Contrary Mary: Vassar '33." *Newsweek*. September 2, 1963: 80–83.

Hardwick, Elizabeth. *A View of My Own*. New York: Farrar, 1962.

Hardy, Willene Schaefer. *Mary McCarthy*. New York: Ungar, 1981.

Heilbrun, Carolyn. "A Man's Woman." Review of *Writing Dangerously* by Carol Brightman. *Women's Review of Books* X, 4. January 1993: 17–18.

Hellman, Lillian. *"Maybe": A Story*. Boston: Little, Brown, 1980.

Holmes, Oliver Wendell. "Freedom for the Thought That We Hate." Lerner, Max, ed. *The Mind and Thought of Justice Holmes*. New York: Modern Library, 1943. 325–28.

Howard, Maureen. *Expensive Habits*. New York: Summit Books, 1986. Penguin, 1987.

Howe, Irving. *Politics and the Novel*. 1957. New York: Columbia University Press, 1992.

Jarrell, Randall. *Pictures from an Institution*. 1954. Chicago: University of Chicago Press, 1986.

Jones, James. *The Merry Month of May*. New York: Delacorte, 1971.

Joyce, James. *A Portrait of the Artist as a Young Man*. 1916. New York: Penguin, 1964.

Kakutani, Michiko. "Our Woman of Letters." 1987. Gelderman, Carol, ed. *Conversations with Mary McCarthy*. 257–67.

Kazin, Alfred, *Starting Out in the Thirties*. Boston: Little, Brown, 1965.

Kiernan, Frances. "Group Encounter." *The New Yorker*. June 7, 1993: 56–61.

Kufrin, Joan. *Uncommon Women*. New York: New Century, 1981.

Lottman, Herbert. *Albert Camus: A Biography*. Garden City, N.Y.: Doubleday, 1979.

Lundberg, Ferdinand, and Marynia Farnham. *Modern Woman, the Lost Sex*. New York: Harper, 1947.

Lurie, Alison. "True Confessions." Review of *How I Grew* by Mary McCarthy. *New York Review of Books* 34 (June 11, 1987): 19–20.

Lyall, Sarah. "Book Notes." *New York Times*. August 11, 1993: C-17.

Macdonald, Dwight. "Atrocities of the Mind." *politics* 2 (August 1945): 227.

————. "Comment." *politics* 1 (May 1944): 102.

————. Letter to Nicola Chiaromonte. February 14, 1952. Macdonald Papers, Yale University. Quoted in Carol Gelderman, *Mary McCarthy: A Life*. 170.

Mailer, Norman. "The Case against McCarthy: A Review of *The Group*." *Cannibals and Christians*. New York: Dial, 1966. 133–40.

————. "Some Children of the Goddess." *Cannibals and Christians*. 104–130.

Malcolm, Janet. "Annals of Biography: The Silent Woman." *New Yorker*. August 23 and 30, 1993. 84–159.

Mallon, Thomas. *Aurora 7*. New York: Ticknor, 1991.

McKenzie, Barbara. *Mary McCarthy*. New York: Twayne, 1960.

Muste, John. "The Thirties, the Forties, and the Fifties." *Masterplots II, Nonfiction Series*. Magill, Frank, ed. Englewood Cliffs, N.J.: Salem, 1989. 1500–1506.

Nabokov, Vladimir. *Lolita*. 1955. New York: Vintage, 1989.

————. *Pale Fire*. 1962. New York: Vintage, 1989.

————, and Edmund Wilson. *The Nabokov-Wilson Letters*. Edited by Simon Karlinsky. New York: Harper, 1979.

Newman, Edwin. "A Conversation with Mary McCarthy." WNBC-TV interview, December 4, 1966. Reprinted in Gelderman, Carol, ed., *Conversations with Mary McCarthy*. 68–87.

Niebuhr, Elisabeth. "The Art of Fiction XXVII: Mary McCarthy—an Interview." 1962. Gelderman, Carol, ed. *Conversations with Mary McCarthy*. 3–29.

Phillips, William. "The Esthetic of the Founding Fathers." *Partisan Review* 4.4 (1937–1938): 11–21.

————, and Philip Rahv. "Criticism." *Partisan Review* 2.7 (1935): 16–24.

Podhoretz, Norman. *Making It*. New York: Random House, 1969.

————. "Miss McCarthy and the Leopard's Spots." *Doings and Undoings*. New York: Farrar, 1964.

Rabinowitz, Paula. *Labor and Desire: Women's Revolutionary Fiction in Depression America*. Chapel Hill: University of North Carolina Press, 1991.

Rahv, Philip. *Essays on Literature and Politics, 1932–1972*. Edited by Arabel J. Porter and Andrew J. Dvosin. Boston: Houghton Mifflin, 1978.

————. "10 Propositions and 8 Errors." *Partisan Review* 8 (1941): 499–506.

Rosenberg, Harold. "The Herd of Independent Minds." *Discovering the Present: Three Decades in Art, Culture and Politics*. Chicago: University of Chicago Press, 1973. 15–28.

Schlueter, Paul. "The Dissections of Mary McCarthy." Moore, Harry T., ed. *Contemporary American Novelists*. Carbondale: Southern Illinois University Press, 1964. 61–64.

Seltzer, Mark. *Bodies and Machines*. New York: Routledge, 1992.

Shinn, Thelma. *Radiant Daughters: Fictional American Women*. Westport, Conn.: Greenwood, 1986.

Smith, Logan Pearsall. "Myself." *Afterthoughts*. 1931. *Columbia Dictionary of Quotations*. New York: Columbia University Press, 1993.

Stock, Irving. *Mary McCarthy*. Minneapolis: University of Minnesota Press, 1968.

Straus, Roger. Letter to Mary McCarthy. November 15, 1954. Farrar, Straus and Giroux Collection, New York Public Library.

Strouse, Jean. "Making the Facts Obey." *New York Times Book Review*. May 24, 1992: 1, 16–17.

Trilling, Diana. *The Beginning of the Journey*. New York: Harcourt, 1993.

Trilling, Lionel. Letter to F. W. Dupee. May 23, 1939. F. W. Dupee Collection. Columbia University, New York.

————. "On the Teaching of Modern Literature." *Beyond Culture: Essays on Literature and Learning*. 1965. New York: Harvest/Harcourt, 1979. 3–27.

Wald, Alan M. *The New York Intellectuals: The Rise and Decline of the Anti-Stalinist Left from the 1930s to the 1980s*. Chapel Hill: University of North Carolina Press, 1987.

Weil, Simone. *The "Iliad," or the Poem of Force*. Translated by Mary McCarthy. *politics* 2 (November 1945): 321–31; *politics* Pamphlet 1 (1945).

Wilson, Edmund. *The Sixties*. Edited by Lewis Dabney. New York: Farrar, 1993.

————, and Vladimir Nabokov. *The Nabokov-Wilson Letters*. Edited by Simon Karlinsky. New York: Harper, 1979.

Woolf, Leonard. *Downhill All the Way: An Autobiography of the Years 1919–1939*. London: Hogarth, 1970.

Yeats, William Butler. "Solomon and the Witch." *The Collected Poems of W. B. Yeats*. New York: Macmillan, 1961.

Index

About the Editors and Contributors

THE EDITORS

EVE STWERTKA is Professor Emerita in English at The State University of New York, Farmingdale, where she also held the position of Associate Dean of the School of Arts and Sciences. As an undergraduate at Bard College in the late 1940s, she was a student of Mary McCarthy's and later worked as an editorial assistant on *Partisan Review.* Stwertka writes nonfiction books for children and young adults. She is a trustee of the Mary McCarthy Literary Trust.

MARGO VISCUSI worked for eight years (1969–1977) as secretary to Mary McCarthy in Paris and is now a trustee of the Mary McCarthy Literary Trust. She has been a writer, editor, and director of communications for three major New York foundations and at UNESCO in Paris. Viscusi has held the positions of Director of Publications at Hunter College and Executive Assistant to the President of the New York Public Library. She is a founder and current president of Poets House in New York and a director of the Corporation of Yaddo.

THE CONTRIBUTORS

CAROL BRIGHTMAN's *Writing Dangerously: Mary McCarthy and Her World* won the National Book Critics Circle Award for Biography in 1992. She edited

Between Friends: The Correspondence of Hannah Arendt and Mary McCarthy, 1949–1975.

MARY ANN CAWS, Distinguished Professor of English, French, and Comparative Literature at the City University of New York Graduate School and University Center, wrote *The Poetry of Dada and Surrealism, The Eye in the Text, The Metapoetics of the Passage, Reading Frames in Modern Fiction, The Art of Interference, Women of Bloomsbury,* and *Robert Motherwell: What Art Holds.*

TERRY A. COONEY is Professor of History at the University of Puget Sound in Tacoma, Washington. He is the author of *The Rise of the New York Intellectuals: "Partisan Review" and its Circle* and *Balancing Acts: American Thought and Culture in the 1930's.*

MORRIS DICKSTEIN is Director of the Humanities Center at the Graduate School and University Center, City University of New York, and Professor of English at Queens College. His books include *Gates of Eden: American Culture in the Sixties* and *Double Agent: The Critic and Society.*

STACEY LEE DONOHUE received her Ph.D. in English from the Graduate School and University Center of the City University of New York in 1995. She is currently Assistant Professor of English at Central Oregon Community College.

FRANCES FITZGERALD won the Pulitzer Prize for *Fire in the Lake: The Vietnamese and Americans in Vietnam.* Other books include *America Revised: History Schoolbooks in the Twentieth Century* and *Cities on a Hill: A Journey through Contemporary American Cultures.*

THOMAS FLANAGAN's latest novel is *The End of the Hunt.* An earlier work, *The Year of the French,* won the National Book Critics Circle Award for Fiction. He is the author of *The Irish Novelists, 1800–1850* and is Professor of English at the State University of New York at Stony Brook.

CAROL GELDERMAN is Distinguished Professor of English at the University of New Orleans. She has written biographies of Henry Ford and Louis Auchincloss, and is the author of *Mary McCarthy: A Life.*

BEVERLY GROSS writes on twentieth-century fiction. She teaches in the English Department of Queens College and is a former literary editor of *The Nation.*

AVIS HEWITT's 1993 dissertation explores the uses of feminism in Mary McCarthy's fiction. She teaches American literature at the Northern Arizona University in Flagstaff.

MAUREEN HOWARD is the author of a memoir, *Facts of Life*. She has published several novels of which the most recent are *Expensive Habits* and *Natural History*. She is a Professor in the School of the Arts, Columbia University.

FRANCES KIERNAN, who was a fiction editor at the *New Yorker* for nearly twenty years, is now working on a biography of Mary McCarthy. Her article "Group Encounter," on Mary McCarthy and her Vassar class's sixtieth reunion, appeared in the *New Yorker* in 1993.

PERRI KLASS, Assistant Professor of Pediatrics at Boston University School of Medicine, writes both fiction and nonfiction, including most recently a collection of essays, *Baby Doctor*, and a novel, *Other Women's Children*. Her short stories have won five O. Henry awards.

THOMAS MALLON's novels include *Aurora 7*, *Henry and Clara*, and the forthcoming *Dewey Defeats Truman*. A former English professor at Vassar College, he is also the author of books about diaries and plagiarism.

RHODA NATHAN is Professor of English at Hofstra University and Vice President of the Bernard Shaw Society. Her most recent books are a biography of and a book of critical essays about Katherine Mansfield.

PRISCILLA PERKINS is Assistant Professor of English at Cameron University in Lawton, Oklahoma. Her work focuses on connections among late nineteenth- and early twentieth-century American literature, medicine, technology, and psychology.

KATIE ROIPHE is the author of *The Morning After: Sex, Fear and Feminism on Campus*. She recently received a Ph.D. in English from Princeton University and is working on a new book.

MARGARET SCANLAN is the author of *Traces of Another Time: History and Politics in Postwar British Fiction* and numerous articles on modern fiction. A Professor of English at Indiana University South Bend, she is currently writing a book on terrorism in fiction.

ARTHUR SCHLESINGER, JR., holds the Albert Schweitzer Chair in the Humanities at the Graduate School and University Center, City University of New York. Among his numerous books are *The Age of Jackson*, *A Thousand Days*, *The Cycles of American History*, and *The Disuniting of America*. He has won the Pulitzer Prize for History and for Biography and the National Book Award.

GREGORY D. SUMNER is Assistant Professor in the College of Liberal Arts, University of Detroit Mercy. He holds both a Ph.D. in American History from Indiana University and a J.D. from the University of Michigan Law School and is the author of *Dwight Macdonald and the "politics" Circle: The Challenge of Cosmopolitan Democracy*.

HARVEY TERES teaches American literature at Syracuse University. He is the author of *Renewing the Left: Politics, Imagination, and the New York Intellectuals*.

JILL WACKER is a Ph.D. candidate in American literature at the University of Pennsylvania. She is completing a dissertation titled "Becoming Suitable: Self-Fashioning and the Rag Trade in American Literature, 1865–1925."

ALAN WALD is Professor of English at the University of Michigan and the author of five books on the literary Left in the United States, the most recent of which is *Writing from the Left*.

TIMOTHY F. WAPLES is a doctoral candidate in English at the University of Pennsylvania. His dissertation is titled "A Harrowing State to Maintain: Individualism and Identity in the Cold War Careers of Ralph Ellison, Mary McCarthy, and Frank O'Hara."

ISBN 0-313-29776-2

90000>

EAN

9 780313 297762

HARDCOVER BAR CODE